Chi and Creativity

氣

Elise Dirlam Ching
and Kaleo Ching

Chi and Creativity
Vital Energy and Your Inner Artist

BLUE SNAKE BOOKS
BERKELEY, CALIFORNIA

Published by Blue Snake Books

Blue Snake Books are distributed by
North Atlantic Books
P. O. Box 12327
Berkeley, California 94712

Cover art by Kaleo Ching
Cover design by Suzanne Albertson
Book design by Lyn 'Unihipiliowailelepualu Hilliard
Printed in the United States of America

Blue Snake Books' publications are available through most bookstores. For further information, call 800-733-3000 or visit our websites at www.northatlanticbooks.com or www.bluesnakebooks.com.

PLEASE NOTE: The creators and publishers of this book disclaim any liabilities for loss in connection with following any of the practices, exercises, and advice contained herein. To reduce the chance of injury or any other harm, the reader should consult a professional before undertaking this or any other martial arts, movement, meditative arts, health, or exercise program. The instructions and advice printed in this book are not in any way intended as a substitute for medical, mental, or emotional counseling with a licensed physician or healthcare provider.

LIBRARY OF CONGRESS CATALOGING-IN-PUBLICATION DATA

Ching, Elise Dirlam.
  Chi and creativity : vital energy and your inner artist / Elise Dirlam Ching and Kaleo Ching.
        p. cm.
  Summary: "A guide to realms where the energetic body, physical body, emotional body, and creative spirit meet and dialogue, through practical exercises in chi awareness, self-help acupressure, chi kung movement and meditation, guided imagery, journaling, and art. The adventure is one of self-discovery, integrative health, and personal transformation"--Provided by publisher.
  ISBN-13: 978-1-58394-184-3
  ISBN-10: 1-58394-184-3
  1. Qi gong. 2. Hygiene, Taoist. I. Ching, Kaleo. II. Title.

RA781.8.C477 2007
613.7'148--dc22
                            2007005028

2 3 4 5 6 7 8 9 Versa 14 13 12 11 10 09

To the Divine Spirit in Each of Us

Mahalo

Mahalo nui loa to the Acupressure Institute, California Arts Council and National Endowment for the Arts, Haight Ashbury Free Clinic's Jail Psychiatric Services, John F. Kennedy University, Naropa University-Oakland, New College of California, Oakland Festival at the Lake, San Francisco Jail Health Services, San Francisco Sheriff's Department, University of Creation Spirituality, and Wisdom University; to the caring staff and faculty of these institutions where we have done much of our work; and to the students who have contributed their images and stories that so greatly enhance this book.

To the Acupressure Institute's mentors of Traditional Chinese Medicine, especially founder Michael Reed Gach, Joseph Carter, and Alice Hiatt for their consultation on the acupressure contents of this book, Candace Coar, Sylvia Nachlinger, and Brian O'Dea.

To Michael Grady, chair of the Arts and Consciousness Program at John F. Kennedy University, and Matthew Fox, founder of Creation Spirituality, for their support.

To Gilles Marin, wizard of Taoist healing arts, founder and director of the Chi Nei Tsang Institute, and teacher of Chi Kung, for sharing with us his deep wisdom, friendship, and spirit of *aloha*.

To our many other teachers of Tai Chi and Chi Kung, especially Jeff Bolt, Mantak Chia, Mary Christianson, Cynthia Eaton, Bruce Kumar Frantzis, Bernard Langan, Ou Wen Wei, T. Y. Pang, Peter Ralston, Don Russell, Lenzie Williams, and John Zhang.

To our teachers of hatha yoga, especially Rodney Yee. To our teachers of meditation, especially Zen master Jeff Kitzes.

To Lanakila Brandt, Dane Kaohelani Silva, and Maka'ala Yates for their sharing of *aloha, lomilomi,* and Hawaiian healing arts and culture.

To Randal Churchill, Marleen Mulder, and the late Ormond McGill of the Hypnotherapy Training Institute for sharing their wisdom of subconscious realms.

To Elise's professors of English at Ball State University and of Transpersonal Psychology at John F. Kennedy University. To Kaleo's professors of art at the University of Hawaii, the University of New Mexico, and the Tamarind Institute of Lithography.

To Sharon Dirlam, sister, and her husband, John McCafferty, advisors; Marlene DeNardo, Aileen Donovan, and Andy and Mary Franklin, our prayer family.

To North Atlantic Books/Blue Snake Books and everyone there who makes the sharing of this book possible and the producing of it a delight, especially publishers Richard Grossinger and Lindy Hough, associate publisher Mark Ouimet, project editor Hisae Matsuda, art director Paula Morrison, cover designer Suzanne Albertson, and copy editor Adrienne Armstrong.

A very special mahalo to Pili (Lyn 'Unihipiliowailelepualu Hilliard) for his abundant *aloha,* his mastery in designing this book, and his contributions to this book's Hawaiian language entries.

To our ancestors, our families, and the spirits of our parents, James and Nancy Ching and Art and Edith Dirlam. To the people of Hawai'i and their spirit of *aloha.* To our guides and guardians from the spirit world. To the winged and four-legged creatures, especially our Australian shepherd companion, Teekkona.

Contents

Illustrations

photographs unless noted are by Kaleo Ching

photographs of Kaleo's masks and paintings are by Lee Fatheree

*photograph of authors and photographs of Kaleo unless noted are by
Pili (Lyn 'Unihipiliowailelepualu Hilliard)*

additional photographs are by Elise Dirlam Ching and Charlie Lucke

Tables & Diagrams

Preface

Dimensions of *Chi and Creativity*

- **Chi awareness** cultivates your understanding and command of Chi, your vital life force, a bioelectric current of energy. It begins with awakening Chi, then directing the Chi flowing in and around your body through Chi hand techniques, Chi awareness explorations, meditation techniques, and a simple Chi Kung movement form. You will learn to feel Chi flowing through your Chi palms, organs, meridians, and circuits in your body. You will learn to access the Chi in the universe around you and within you and to channel it in creativity.

- **Guided imagery** is a form of hypnosis, a way of accessing and dialoguing with the memories, realms, and processes of your subconscious during deep relaxation. It helps you to integrate your discoveries with Chi with your ongoing journey through life.

- **Journaling** gives words to your discoveries and helps guide you further on your journey. Its voice may transform into collage, drawing, or painting, into myth, story, poem, or song, as you follow your inner path.

- **Creativity** in art (or whatever creative channel you love) uses techniques learned by your conscious mind to give voice, form, and movement to your inner discoveries. It is the language of the subconscious, of deep inner mystery and wisdom, of the realm of dreams.

Foundations of *Chi and Creativity*

"Transformative!" "Joyful!" "Inspirational!" These are the words our students use to describe our holistic process combining Chi and creativity. This book is our way of sharing with you this magical journey.

In our many years of teaching together, we have witnessed how Chi and creativity open a portal into another dimension. The body, mind, emotions, and spirit awaken to the new adventure. Through Chi awareness, they explore. Through guided imagery, they dialogue. Through journaling, they speak. Through creative expression, they join to embody the inner discoveries along the path to greater balance and integration.

Kindness, permission, and freedom are important for the process—a climate where there is no judgment, just the inspired joy of exploration and discovery.

Chi and Creativity draws on lessons and understanding acquired over our many years of practice and study with Chi through Tai Chi, Chi Kung, Traditional Chinese Medicine, and massage and with creativity through art and writing. We have studied many systems with many teachers and practiced thousands of hours on our own. *Chi and Creativity* is a synthesis of our experience.

We hope you are inspired by our book to teach, inspire, and help others in their process toward personal empowerment. Ultimately we hope that this will affect not only you, but your family, your community, and the world.

Because this book is an interactive effort between us (Elise and Kaleo), autobiographical sections and personal narratives are labeled with our names. All other parts reflect our collaborative voice.

The stories included about students and clients are basically true. Sometimes names and details have been changed to protect privacy. Sometimes two or more stories have been blended into one.

For this book we are using "Chi" (also known as "Qi") and "Chi Kung" (also known as "Qigong" and "Chi Gung" and meaning "work with Chi") because of the familiarity of these romanizations of the Chinese words.

 This icon indicates an experiential exploration in Chi and creativity.

How to Use *Chi and Creativity*

- *Explore from beginning to end.* The explorations often build on what has come before, so you may find it helpful to work through them in order. You may find that some you wish to explore through all the layers and depths of their possibilities. Others you may want to explore more lightly, then perhaps return to them at a later time. They are meant to be tools for your use, to be adapted to your personality, pacing, and level of experience. We have found through our own studies of Chi over the years that awareness builds in layers, but each layer may be cultivated, deepened, and expanded over time. There are layers within layers, mysteries within mysteries, awaiting your discovery.

- *Be creative.* All our Chi awareness, guided imagery, writing, and art explorations are meant to encourage you. We offer them to you as form, as structure, but please remember that *this is your journey.* We encourage you to try them and to adapt them as you travel on your magical journey in creative, personal ways.

- *Respect your needs and be a kind guide to yourself.* Honor the wisdom and messages from your body/mind/spirit. You as participants empower yourselves by making discoveries and decisions in what these processes and practices mean to you. Be sensitive to your sense of comfort and responsible for your level of participation. Ultimately, you are your own guide, and your body, psyche, and spirit are your own most constant teachers.

- *Let* Chi and Creativity *be a loyal companion.* May our book be a companion for your inner journey, a friend with whom your relationship grows over weeks, months, years.

Who Can Benefit from *Chi and Creativity*

- *Chi and Creativity* can be used by spiritual seekers.

  Meditators and those who practice contemplative prayer sense the presence of the divine in the Chi flowing in their bodies, in others, and in the universe. They learn to cultivate Chi for greater focus, concentration, and stamina in their practice. For example, Tan Tien breathing applied to meditation cleanses the body by bringing more nutrients to all the organs and cells and increasing their efficiency. Meditation combined with Chi awareness guides the practitioner to be still, listen, and observe the dynamic universe within: its cells, joints, tissues all breathing and thriving within a fluid body and its rhythms of Chi. Chi Kung movement can help relieve joint stiffness from long periods of sitting.

- It can be used by those interested in vital energy.

  They learn to harvest universal energy, store and build their vital energy, strengthen their immune systems, harmonize emotions, manage stress, and cultivate overall wellness.

  Healers learn to strengthen their own Chi for working more effectively with clients. They learn to ground, protect, cleanse, and replenish their Chi through Chi breathing, meditation, and Chi Kung movement. They learn to feel and dialogue with the Chi flowing in and around their clients' bodies to enhance their understanding and effectiveness as practitioners.

  Tai Chi, Chi Kung, and martial arts practitioners learn to deepen their understanding and connectedness with Chi.

- It can be used by those who enjoy creativity.

  Whether through writing, making art, cooking, gardening, sewing, dancing, acting, or singing, explorations with Chi and creativity add fuel to creative fires.

Artists add more tools to their creative tool chest. They learn to use their hands as channels of Chi, their senses to feel Chi, the five elements for alchemical transformation as they make art. They learn about moving paint onto canvas or coaxing clay into sculpture from the wisdom and integration of the three Tan Tiens that govern the Chi of the body, spirit, and mind.

Writers free the stuck Chi which blocks creative expression to bring forth the words of dreams, of emotions in the heart, of memories tucked in the tissues of the body.

Performers learn to connect with the energies of heaven, environment, and earth for support and inspiration and to move from the core and the wisdom of the Chi body.

- **It can be used by those interested in the realms of the subconscious.**

Hypnotherapists learn to expand their methods of induction and exploration of subconscious realms and to guide the client in combining the discoveries through hypnosis with creative expression.

Sojourners in the world of dreams or shamanic journeying learn new sensitivities to perceptions and information they receive on their travels.

Psychotherapists may use it as a resource of supplemental techniques for working with clients and as a framework for understanding clients. For example, a client's behavior might be influenced by the dominance of the fire element in his personality. Or work with a client might deepen through introducing guided imagery, art, and journaling into the therapeutic process of self-discovery and healing.

- **It can be used by adventurers on the inner or outer journey.**

Chi flows in us and around us, interconnecting everything. The five elements also permeate our daily life. Metal is in our breath and in the stuff of stars. Water is in our bodies and in the rivers, lakes, oceans, and rain. Wood is in the sinews of our bodies, in the trees around us, in the homes where we live. Fire warms our blood and our days. Earth feeds our inner bodies and supports us from below.

Universal Spirit Meditation

Go to a serene place in nature and assume a meditative posture familiar to you. As your eyes gently close, let your mind receive the comfort of your haven. Feel the temperature around you. Let your feet spread over the soft welcoming earth beneath you. Let your spirit enter into the spaciousness of your inner being.

Breathe softly, deeply. Do you smell a fragrance, hear a sound, see a color?

Inhaling, allow your breath to enter your nostrils and glide up into your mind's eye. Listen to the sound, the vibration, of your mind. Listen as your breath opens like a blossoming lotus, spreading, expanding, then pressing gently into the inner lining of your cranium and releasing. *Ask the Universal Spirit for clarity and vision on your journey, and let go.*

Let go, and the breath falls like gentle rain, the rain of Hawai'i, *ka ua li'ili'i*. Breath glides into your throat and descends into the spaciousness of your heart. What are the colors and sounds of gentle rain as it falls in your chest? Breath expands, pressing gently into the cavern walls of your inner ribs, then softly releases. *Ask the Universal Spirit for understanding and compassion on your journey, and let go.*

Let go, and the breath falls like gentle rain, *ka ua li'ili'i*, through your body. What is the sound of rain falling into the ocean in your pelvis? What are the temperatures and textures as it descends deep within? Can you feel the embryo of creativity in the cavern of your pelvis? Hear its breathing? Can you feel your breath as it travels like a wave across the spacious ocean—a wave spreading and pressing gently into the muscular walls of your pelvis—and then releasing, with kindness? *Ask the Universal Spirit for abundance and creativity on your journey, and let go.*

Breath falls like gentle rain through your legs, washing and cleansing, descending into Gaia, the mother. Can you feel her kindness and love? Pause now and enjoy her embrace.

As you inhale, your breath ascends. What is Gaia's fragrance ascending lightly through your body and into the heavens? Exhaling, allow this fragrance to descend from the heavens and condense into gentle rain. What is the sensation of gentle heavenly rain entering your body, cleansing and purifying, then flowing into the basin of your pelvis?

Your breath is soft as you inhale. Gratitude travels into every cell in your body. Breathe gently, then release the blessings of your mind, heart, and body into the world.

Introduction

Midwife says
anticipation always ends.
Just be vigilant as the dragonfly
who uses mouth and legs
to clean her eyes.
Your time too has come
to push into the light.

Every cell of your being is pushing its way into the light. Listen. Your muse beckons you to come out and play. How does she stir in you? Do you lose all sense of time as you spread paint on fresh canvas or sing through your flute or let the beat of drums intoxicate you in dance? Do your hands thrill at the magic of listening and sculpting in massage, as they dialogue with the sacred rhythms of the body? Or do they tingle with recognition at learning a new skill that feels somehow familiar, as you channel ancient wisdom?

Feel every cell of your being basking in vital energy. How do you experience Chi? Do you feel its current warming your heart or prickling beneath your skin? Do you see it glimmering around a friend's body? Do you sense the Chi in the charged atmosphere of a room where sacred ritual is being shared? Do you rejuvenate in the nurturing Chi of nature? Do you receive or transmit Chi in healing energy work or massage?

With wonder and curiosity, creativity looks at the world—not so much what we do as how. Chi awareness is as simple as a tingling in your fingertips, as deep as the sea of the subconscious, as vast as the limits of the universe. Chi awareness and creativity can impact all aspects of our lives—everything from cooking, horseback riding, or gardening to building relationships, raising children, or choosing our life's work.

For example, some of our students who own horses have discovered that their communication with their animals deepens with their Chi awareness. The horses respond to their riders' more confident focus, balance, and posture. Chi awareness can also be applied to other animals, as well as plants. A dog feels its person's energy and intention communicated through the leash that connects them. Gardeners tell us that Chi awareness applied to plants makes them grow healthier and more vibrant.

Creativity through art can attune you to nuances of an animal's or a plant's structure, moods, and needs that you may never have perceived before. What markings on your drawing make the sounds of a horse galloping through the meadow? What vibrant lines convey the long stretch of its body? What is the color of its wild joy? Or how do you shape the subtleties of an orchid's petals, stamen, and pistil? What patterns does soft rain make as it trickles into the flower's cup?

The Chi of horse and rider or of artist and drawing joins in the dance of creativity. Chi and creativity meet in the realm of the senses to join the inner and outer worlds. Whether we are moving or meditating, writing or drawing, we are stirring a deep cauldron of fragrances and tones, of textures and symbols, just waiting to release their secrets. Our discoveries in Chi awareness and creative self-expression surface from the complex and honest depths of the soul to link the universe within and the universe beyond.

As you explore Chi and Creativity, *feel all levels of your being responding:*

- **Energy**

  Your internal organs, meridians, and vessels—the processors, channels, and repositories of energy—come into greater balance, so that the physical, emotional, mental, spiritual, and creative Chi may flow.

- Body

  All the systems of your body experience greater wellness, balance, alignment, and harmony.

- Mind

  Emotional layers and subconscious depths of your inner world open to exploration, then reveal and express themselves through the language of guided imagery, writing, and art.

- Spirit

  An ethereal thread of Chi links you to the heavens and the earth. Feel wonder at the universal source of wisdom and power within and without. Feel its creative presence in your cells and tissues, in the oceans, plants, and stars. Feel its channels of Chi and its creative inspiration in all that you perceive and all that you undertake.

Ultimately this journey in Chi and creativity is about relationship: to self—body, mind, and spirit—and to others. We as living creatures are not so much entities as processes governed by patterns. We are not our bodies. If you look at a picture of yourself as a baby, do you recognize yourself? What about your body is the same now as then, and what has changed? Nor are we our minds. Thoughts come and go; emotions come and go; likes and dislikes come and go. We have forgotten most of what we once knew. So much that we consider to belong to us is not really ours at all, for everything is in flux. If not even our bodies or minds are ours, how can we say our houses are ours, our pets are ours, our children are ours, the earth is ours?

We are custodians with the intelligence to care for what we touch or to destroy it. We are interactions of the five elements of metal, water, wood, fire, and earth, and each of our actions affects all around us. Through becoming aware of ourselves as vessels and channels of Chi—a force that connects us to all that is within, around, and beyond—we become more aware of and attuned to our interconnectedness with all that exists. We become better custodians of the bodies that carry us, the minds that guide us, the earth that supports us, and the universe that includes us.

As you work through the experiences in this book, keep this question with you: *What are you learning about your life's journey—your relationship with other sentient beings, with the living earth, with your community, your culture, your work in the world, your place in the universe?*

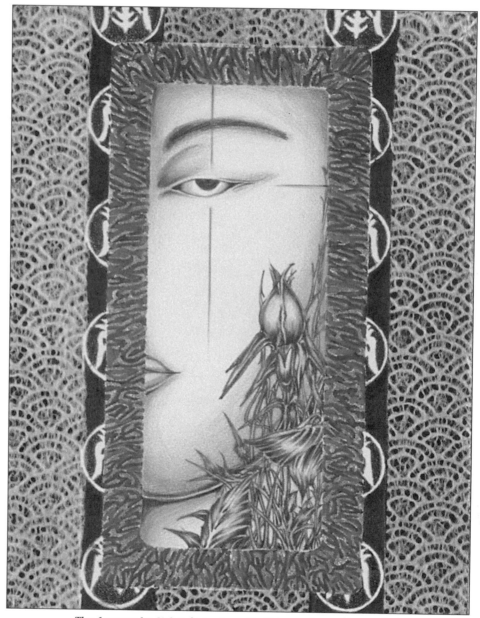

The Journey by Kaleo (mixed media lithograph, 28″h x 20″w)

Chi Awareness

Chi awareness has the potential to transform how you understand and perceive your entire life. Once you begin to experience your body as a vessel of Chi, the universe as a source of Chi, and your life as an interaction of Chi, your consciousness expands to incorporate this essential dimension. The human body is a detailed, organized network of intelligent systems working to warn, defend, heal, and guide you toward wholeness and harmony. The body/mind/spirit is a microcosm in the macrocosm of the universe. Chi awareness helps to bring energetic healing and wholeness to the microcosm, harmonizing it with the Chi of the macrocosm. To cultivate Chi awareness, we explore its principles (*see* Chapter II, "Chi Awareness Principles" on page 23) and practices based on ancient Taoist wisdom of working, playing, living, and being with Chi.

Awakening Chi

Explorations in sensing and channeling energy through Chi hand techniques bring us in touch with the presence of Chi in and around our bodies and permeating our lives (*see* Chapter III, "Exploring Chi" on page 51, and Chapter IV, "Exploring Chi and Creativity" on page 79).

Five Element Alchemy

The alchemy of the five elements of metal, water, wood, fire, and earth according to Traditional Chinese Medicine is a holistic philosophy, a healing art, and a practice in Chi awareness. It is also a potent catalyst for creativity, as you approach and learn from your creative self-expression in a new way through the kaleidoscopic lens of the five elements (*see* Chapter V, "Five Element Alchemy: Foundations" on page 105, Chapter VI, "Five Element Alchemy: Practice" on page 113, and Chapter VII, "Five Element Alchemy: Integration" on page 155).

Acupressure

Acupressure is Chi awareness and gentle healing touch of self or other applied to acupuncture/acupressure points (acu-points) that lie near the surface of the skin along the energetic meridians of your body. It comes from awareness of the patterns of Chi flowing in the body developed over the 5,000 year history of Traditional Chinese Medicine. In this book we offer basic acupressure points that are easy to locate, but profound and effective, with descriptions of acu-point functions that focus on their general uses and applications to creativity (*See* "Acupressure Points" on page 113 for specific guidelines).

An acupressure point can be a portal to the subconscious world and a vehicle for sensing and channeling the Chi flowing through you into creativity. For example, as you lie in meditation and breathe gently and fully into your lungs, each breath resonates through your heart and opens and closes your heart center, Conception Vessel 17. As you relax, you find yourself entering into the vortex of this acu-point. As you surrender, you find yourself going deeper. You may travel to a place and time when you felt the intimacy of shared love, or the awe of life, or the joy of creativity. Rich images stored in the energetic field and tissues of the heart may surface to infuse your creative expression and bridge body and psyche, past and present, inner and outer reality.

Meditation

Meditation is the inner dimension of spiritual practice, done lying, sitting, or standing, with focus on a chosen object for meditation, such as breath, mantra, or divine image. It may encompass contemplative prayer, which addresses a higher spiritual source. It leads us to a quiet and centered relationship with the interior wilderness, where we can attune to the flow of Chi or sink into guided imagery.

- ### Lying Meditation

  Lying meditation is an excellent preparation for guided imagery, for going into the subconscious, for inner journeys to the places akin to the dream world. Lying meditation is restorative. It is deeply relaxing. It uses an opening posture, with the back of your body fully supported by the earth, the front of your body fully open to the heavens. It allows for the maximum degree of surrender. It allows you to begin to develop breath and Chi awareness in a very relaxed way (*see* "Lying Meditation: Exploring Tan Tien Breathing" on page 47 for guidelines).

- Sitting Meditation

Sitting meditation can also be used for guided imagery. If done with proper alignment and props, it allows for maximum ease combined with wakefulness. To practice simple sitting meditation, sit erect near the edge of a chair or a cushion, and maintain the natural concave curve in your lumbar spine. If on a cushion, have your hips higher than your knees; if on a chair, have your feet planted evenly on the ground hips' width apart; use folded blankets for support under hips, knees, or feet as needed. Rest your hands in your lap or on your knees. Lengthen the back of your neck so that your eyes look at the ground in front of you in a soft gaze or let them gently close (*see* "Sitting Meditation with Zhan Zhuang Awareness" on page 192 for more detailed guidelines).

- Standing Meditation: Zhan Zhuang

Zhan Zhuang means to stand like a stake, a staff, or a tree. It develops body strength. It allows you most powerfully to feel the current of Chi flowing between heaven and earth through your body. It helps you to adjust ingrained imbalances in your posture (*see* "Zhan Zhuang Meditation" on page 187).

Chi Circuits

The primordial pathways of the Micro- and Macrocosmic Orbits take us deep into the history of our Chi bodies. Activating them connects us powerfully with the Chi of our origins and of the heavens, earth, and environment and helps balance the seven chakras, or "wheels of energy," in our bodies (*see* Chapter IX, "Chi Circuits and Chakras" on page 221).

Chi Kung Movement

Chi Kung, meaning "work with Chi," is an ancient Chinese system for systematically accessing, moving, and channeling energy in the body for optimal health, wholeness, and longevity. It follows similar principles and philosophy to Tai Chi, but it is a healing art, whereas Tai Chi is also a martial art. Moving Chi Kung helps us to stretch and strengthen our bodies and minds and to bring Chi awareness into action, in order to move through daily life with more groundedness, readiness, and integration. This process requires taking risks, gently extending your limits. You learn to "walk like a cat": to move with awareness and balance; to land on your feet; to be sometimes assertive and strong, sometimes flexible and receptive, sometimes withdrawing and quiet.

When practicing Chi Kung movement, you become aware of the structure of the form, the flow of Chi, and the integration of body and psyche. Your body becomes grounded and open, your mind free and supple. Body and mind are one.

Chi Kung movement can be very precise or very loose. It can be reverent and sacred; it can be playful and creative. It is a way of being in your body that encompasses walking down the street, hiking in the mountains, dancing, gardening, doing bodywork, or enacting sacred ritual. It permeates your daily life!

In this book we offer the opening sequence of a Chi Kung form called Tiger's Breath (*see* Chapter X, "Tiger's Breath Chi Kung" on page 259). It is a simple, easy-to-learn set that cultivates strength and flexibility and cleanses and nourishes the body, mind, and spirit. When you first do Tiger's Breath Chi Kung, your conscious mind is active as it memorizes the steps. After a while, when the form sinks into the subconscious realm of your body's memory, you experience it as moving meditation. It is a ritual, a mantra of movement, which prepares you for journeys into creative expression.

Guided Imagery

Kaleo's Journal: One Who Never Dreams

Carla: Nothing happened! I never see anything. No colors, no shapes. Nobody came to visit. It's always like this for me in guided imagery. I don't even dream at night!

Kaleo: Well, that happens sometimes. By the way, did you happen to feel anything?

Carla: Well, I kind of felt this cloudiness around me.

Kaleo: Let's go back to that cloudiness. Close your eyes and look within. How would you describe the color of this cloudiness?

Carla: Well . . . actually, it kind of feels like a blueness.

Kaleo: Reach out and touch this blueness. How does it feel?

Carla: It's foggy. Cool. A mist that surrounds me.

Kaleo: Do you feel safe and ready to explore this blue?

Carla: Okay.

Kaleo: Just keep your eyes closed and breathe naturally. Feel your breath entering your nostrils and gliding softly up your nasal passages. Notice how the sockets of your eyes fill with your breath. As you exhale, feel your eyes sink and relax. On the next inhalation, invite your breath into the vault of your cranium, where it embraces your brain. As you exhale, feel your brain relaxing, getting heavier, its weight sinking comfortably into the cranial basin. Go deeper into rest. As you breathe naturally, each wave of breath brings comfort and serenity to your brain. Each wave brings calm.

Breathing normally, notice how your breath is like a cool blue mist. Smell its fragrance. How refreshing! Feel how this cool mist expands and fills your cranium. Feel the slight tingling sensation in your dream center in the back of your head below the ridge of your occiput. Notice how this sensation spreads to the center of your brain and to the front of your head right behind your third eye. How pleasant you feel. Just breathe normally and enjoy the sensation of the mist. What is the texture of its blueness?

The magic of this, Carla, is that it's so natural, so easy. Enjoy and feel yourself letting go. Notice the blue mist traveling down your brainstem and spinal cord to bring release and relaxation to your entire spine. Feel the weight of your body sinking into the supportive table beneath you. You feel so safe that you just go deeper and deeper into your body. You reach a place of quiet wonder.

Now, reach out and touch the blueness around you. What does it feel like? What is its temperature? Its texture? Look at it. How deep is it? Understand that it holds wisdom for you. You may want to move through it and discover what's on the other side. Or it may call you back to a certain place and time in your life that are important for you. It's totally up to you. There's a timing, a rhythm, in the universe that we follow. The blueness beckons. Listen to your own timing and rhythm as you explore. It's totally up to you. . . .

Guided imagery is a magical journey into subconscious realms to access hidden wisdom, images, and messages. It is like dreamwork. Everyone has images waiting to surface from the subconscious, just as everyone has dreams. You only need to give them an outlet and work with them in order to bring their meanings into your life. Not everyone, however, has an easy time evoking images, just as not everyone has an easy time recalling dreams. If you find yourself having difficulty, spend extra time with the guided imagery explorations in this book. Also, perhaps your preferred perceptual mode is not visual, but auditory or kinesthetic. For example, is your ancestral spirit speaking, chanting, or dancing when you encounter it in the realm of the subconscious; and what are the sounds, temperatures, and textures of your inner landscape? You are unique and will experience guided imagery in your own unique way.

You may read over a guided imagery exploration in this book until you feel familiar with its contents, or you can have someone read it smoothly and soothingly to you, or you can make a recording of it yourself and play it back. Find a comfortable meditative position, sitting or lying. Use your breath and Chi as guides. Allow your breath to be nurturing and relaxing. Allow it to help your Chi to flow smoothly. Awareness of flow of Chi will enhance your experience of guided imagery, for the mind and the Chi have an intimate rapport.

In your inner landscape, find a safe and serene place. If you encounter terrain that seems too difficult at any time in your journey, you can always return to this safe haven (See "Your Personal Place in Nature and Circle of Chi" on page 83). Go at your own pace, one that is comfortable for you. Remember that guided imagery provides a structure, a path. Then listen to your own inner voice, your own knowing. You are empowered to step off the path, come back to the path, take a side trip, and create your own journey whenever you desire.

If you meet spirit guides, ancestral spirits, or totem animals on your journeys, ask if they have your best interests at heart. If not, you may send them away. Remember, you extend the invitation. It is your journey, and you are in charge. You determine who you allow into your inner world.

When you emerge from your journeys, keep in touch with the images and guides you encounter. Invite them with you in your waking and dreaming life. Honor their presence with attention and care.

Your subconscious is the largest part of your mind, so bringing its images and messages up to consciousness can get you in touch with a vast source of inner wisdom. The subconscious mind regulates life processes such as breathing, heartbeat, digestion, hormonal flows, Chi flows, sleeping, and dreaming. It stores personal and ancestral memories in the body's tissues. Each one of your trillions of cells has DNA (deoxyribonucleic acid), genetic material, in its nucleus. We believe your DNA contains biological blueprints of your ancestors with messages and wisdom from your entire ancestral line. Thus past and present meet. Through journeys into the subconscious, your ancestors share their wisdom with you, as they have shared life itself. You are your ancestors!

Ancestral Totem: Raven

Journaling

Writing in your journal can be like meeting a good friend for coffee. As you share the stirrings of your soul, this companion, your journal, listens patiently, receiving your words and the emotions behind them, then reflecting them back to you.

Keep your journal in your own unique way. Some people use tattered and doodled spiral notebooks; others use elegant designer diaries. We have seen a journal scribbled on torn café napkins, smeared with lipstick and coffee stains, but ultimately bound into a timeless treasure. Some people use multi-colored pens and pencils, others pastels and collage, others black only. Some write in total privacy. Others love the stimulation of a crowded café. Whatever you choose, start by asking your journal why you picked this place, this writing instrument, this receptacle for recording. Spelling, punctuation, and grammar are not important here. What matters is that you come from your body, mind, and spirit!

Feel free to keep your journal private, so that you can be as honest and thorough as possible. Explore, create, experiment, take risks—whatever feels right. Give voice to whatever wants to surface. *Do not deny your voice!* As with stuck Chi in your body, it is important to move stuck Chi in your psyche.

For several years Kaleo taught part-time for the Haight Ashbury Free Clinic's Jail Psychiatric Services, leading inmates in Chi Kung movement, meditation, journaling, and art. Through meditation and guided imagery, he invited participants to enter into a safe inner place. In order for them to feel really safe, he promised they could choose either to keep whatever journaling or drawing they made or to tear it into minute pieces before returning from the sanctuary of the classroom to their cells. Many responded by liberating their buried inner feelings into a scrawl of journaling or the images of collage. These often inspired creative self-portraits through maskmaking.

Try to write in your journal regularly. Record anything—hopes, struggles, ideas, sketches, letters to friends, things to do, secret desires, private prayers, intuitions. Keep it, along with pen and flashlight, by your bed and upon waking record your dreams. Bring your journal with you each time you practice

Chi awareness or creativity. Record your expanding awareness of Chi—its sensations and patterns of flow in your body and in the heavens, the earth, and the environment. Record how Chi flows through you in creative expression.

Journaling is an experiment, and the questions included herein are catalysts. Use them as far as they inspire you, but most important is your relationship to the words and images flowing through you. The pen or pencil is an extension of your body, a Chi sword gliding over, spiraling into, or piercing the spaciousness of the pages in your journal. The words themselves have energy, sounds, lines, shapes, and patterns. They may make the patter of gentle rain. They may stab like sharp needles. They may soothe like easy waves. They have a rhythm, like a heartbeat. Sometimes they hide shyly and sometimes they leap out at you. Notice ones that beckon you, and circle, color, or connect them. Then notice the patterns that appear and the lessons they reveal from your inner being.

Use alchemical processes on your journal entry to transform it and the emotions it carries: Cut it to pieces; baptize it in a river; burn it to release its smoke and create with its ashes; bury it in your garden and then harvest it. Transform your journal into a dance of words and colors, of images and textures, of Chi and creativity.

Creativity

Creativity conjures mystery, fascination, intimidation, envy, longing, liberation. Creativity is about the relationship of the self to the Self—of the embodied ego, who moves through the daily world earning a paycheck, pushing a grocery cart, grooming the dog, or mulching the garden, to the higher Self, that person in harmony with spirit. Creative self-expression is a tool for the process of what C. G. Jung calls individuation.

Creativity from your body, mind, and spirit gives form to abstraction, voice to the inner dialogue. It is a vehicle for greater self-knowledge.

Creativity gives you the opportunity to release fear ("I might make a mistake!") and embrace self-discovery ("Anything is possible and the journey is mine!").

Creativity is about the wonder of discovery. Sometimes the adventure leads us into darkness, sometimes into luminosity. Creativity is the balance of opposites: the integration of structure and freedom, body and psyche, dragon and tiger.

Creativity expresses the relationship between positive and negative forces and experiences in one's life. Through warm yellows and reds and cool blues and greens, between settings of night and noon, in themes of sadness and joy, polarities do their metaphorical dance. In one word or color, you might express a mood of exhilaration, a place and time of light, where darkness has shrunken to the black eye of Yin in the white body of Yang; in another you might express harmony and balance, like the complete circle with Yin tail in mouth of Yang, Yang in Yin.

Creativity is a goddess who must be nurtured, seduced, respected, appeased. She is like a bird. In the Tai Chi movement "grasp sparrow's tail," the metaphorical sparrow lands on your outstretched hand but cannot be grabbed and captured, for she will feel your intention and the contraction in your arm muscles and will be disturbed into flight. To embrace her you must keep your arm still and, instead, shift the weight of your body onto your back leg to bring her close to you. Then the bird, as the muse, will perch quietly and alertly, ready for your relationship to unfold.

Creativity is the language of dreams, the little known, the unknown, the subconscious. Its vocabulary consists of word, movement, color, space, line, shape, density, and energy, which can take you to the heights or depths of your soul at a pace safe for you. It is a language by which your ancestors, your sacred source, and your inner artist send you messages.

The following principles derive from long hours of our experience teaching, creating, practicing. They are based on the premise that creativity nurtures understanding, healing, and compassion for self and others.

Principles of Creativity

- ### Study the Lessons

Inspiration has a hard time expressing itself without some training. To write creatively, it is helpful to learn writing techniques; to make art, it is helpful to learn about art materials and techniques; but these processes can happen joyfully together. It helps to read writers and study artists whom you like, identify techniques, styles, subject matter, then try the craft yourself. You want to have a variety of tools in your tool box, a variety of spices in your kitchen. The same principles apply to massage, martial, verbal, or performing arts.

- ### Let Go of the Lessons

The shadow side of the craft of creativity is the trap of conformity. Writers and artists do and should learn from each other, even imitate each other as practice. But creative principles as dogma can produce a generic form of creativity, recognizable and ultimately boring. Creating originally and well means honoring the wisdom trained and honed within.

Letting go of the rules and advice does not mean throwing them out but transcending them; using them but not being controlled by them; developing the trust in yourself that comes from caring practice. Letting go can be both frightening and freeing. At some point fear recedes and faith in self becomes firm. This is the point where creative process and personal growth commune. The work of art leads its creator deeper on the inner journey. Whose opinion matters when the final authority lies deep within?

- ### Self and Others

Who is your audience? Is your creative process for yourself only, or do you intend to share it with others? Ultimately creating for yourself is something to be shared, if only indirectly through your increasing insight. Ultimately creating for others is personal, as the subject matter, symbols, metaphors, forms, themes, and images come from personal observation and experience, even when disguised behind third person voice or hidden in abstract expressionism.

- ### Yin and Yang of Creativity

Complementary and interdependent opposites, Yin and Yang dance through creativity. Yin is the receptive, inward looking, intuitive dimension of creativity, while Yang is the active, outward expressing, manifesting dimension. The relationship of creative inspiration, which is predominantly a right brain process (Yin), to craftsmanship, which is more of a left brain function (Yang), can take on adversarial tones very quickly. This battle may manifest in creative blocks. It may show in such attitudes as "I'm not creative—this drawing is lousy" or "How can I edit this when it comes from my heart?" How can a drawing be lousy if it is an embodiment of your truth; how can the work of the heart be prepared for sharing? The beauty of art is that it is your soul revealed; the challenge is that it is a form of communication. The key to this relationship between right and left brain processes is separation of Yin and Yang, understanding them, working with them, and bringing them back into dialogue in a cohesive whole.

The right brain process often seems more exciting—exploring new wild crevices of imagination, discovering, receiving wafts of inspiration, giving them voice or form, putting them together. The left brain task perhaps feels more tedious, yet it commands respect and helps you to decide what to change, to keep, and to omit.

Creativity is a cycle of Yin and Yang. Try separating inspiration and reworking by an incubation period. Many times a lapse of a few days, between the flash of creativity and reworking the creation, helps hone the piece more smoothly. Or try getting up and moving in Chi Kung to shift your awareness and bring fresh perspective. When Chi flows smoothly through the Yin and Yang meridians of your body, it can also flow more smoothly through the Yin and Yang of creative expression.

Try sharing your piece with a friend. You will discover the Yin and Yang of subjectivity and objectivity. Not only will the observer see flaws you missed, but share new epiphanies about your creative piece. But remember, as you keep open and take in new lessons and awarenesses, the work of art is yours, and you are its ultimate creator and guardian; moreover, the real work of art is the process of growth within yourself and between yourself and others.

- **Yin and Yang of Emotions**

Many, perhaps all, of the spiritual paths of the world emphasize compassion for self and others. One of the steps of the Buddhist Eightfold Path is right conduct. Applied to creativity, this means being mindful of the effects of creative process on self and others. Sometimes creativity brings up joy and celebration. Sometimes it brings up pain and rage. How can you portray the light and dark, the illumination and despair, the heights and depths, of your experience with honesty and compassion?

- **Honor Your Sources**

What are your origins—of body, mind, emotions, spirit? What are your creative sources? Who came before you? Who taught you? Who fed your spirit? How can your creative process honor the complex layers of its origins, of your origins?

- **Creativity as Prayer**

When you portray something creatively, it becomes part of your spiritual family. Nurture the company of inner guides. Keep the spirits present and the relationship of body-life and spirit-life active. Poems and stories and works of art are allies from the spirit world, friends from a wider reality.

- **Take Risks**

Creativity is about relationship: of self to subject matter, writer or artist to audience, self to materials, parts of self to whole. Like any relationship, it is dynamic. It involves taking risks—of one's own choosing and pace, with self-responsibility. In creativity, like Chi Kung, you move ever more deeply, expanding, growing, then assimilating the wisdom into your body.

Transformation becomes deeper with time, practice, and commitment. It is like a relationship with a mountain peak, requiring new ways of seeing, listening, walking, breathing, adapting to sun, wind, storm, the moods of the mountain. The risk is internal, for one is climbing the inner mountain, but the experience is just as challenging, just as rewarding. Creativity demands openness to change. Not only will you as creator change words into poem or paint and canvas into art. You will be changed by them.

CLIMBING CASTLE PEAK
by Elise

Scratching up an old melted mountain
bending to wind like low twisted whitebark pine
heads tucked like mountain hemlocks
hair flattened against faces like dead needles
you and I persist

So many to follow:
flesh scoured down to dirt caked bone
small mystery trails in three inch dust
crumbly porous rocks rising and falling
a skinny path, a scary place to squat
no room for error, only exhilaration
wood turned stone from millenniums of seasons
stars hidden in a blue cape waiting for us to lose our way
to show themselves remote, numerous, laughing

You stop to scratch in dirt your own private glyphs
choose a bone for your pack, a stone for your pocket
a smell of coyote mint for curious nose
stop to drink stout tea
eat bread crusted by nine thousand foot wind
pluck burs from a paw sore dusty dog
roll ritual tobacco
crouch in a grotto of stone

For the moment we give ourselves to climbing
red brown old cooled andesite neck of rock

With you here I am safe to feel myself slipping
along my just dead mother's bones
that close I feel here to home

Creativity Through Art

In this book we include creative explorations mainly using art. But you may explore the connection between Chi and creativity in any form you prefer for creative expression. When working and playing with discoveries and images through art, the techniques you use can be as simple or as sophisticated as you like. If you have little art experience, you might like to begin with a large sketch journal, colored pens or pencils, magazines, scissors, and glue for collaging. If you are experienced in art, you can work in your favorite medium.

We have found that an abundance of art supplies is like a feast. Its colors, textures, shapes, and images arouse your muse and inspire creative freedom. Remember: The media you use are not just pencils, pastels, or tinted acrylic medium; they are channels of Chi. Each color has its own Chi, its own personality, resonance, emotion, memory. The high floating song of bright yellow, the pulsing, throbbing of crimson red, the deep-sea mystery of phthalo blue—each is an extension of your own flowing Chi.

You may also add herbs and spices, with their aromas, colors, textures, and qualities, to your art. Mix them with acrylic media and apply them to your drawing or collage. Or combine them and bundle them in a medicine pouch to add to your sculpture. Use them in art as symbols for the nourishment and healing you are seeking for your body, mind, and spirit.

See "Materials, Herbs, and Spices for Art" on page 301 for a selected list of art supplies, including herbs for use in art.

Integrating Chi Awareness and Creativity

Chi awareness guides you into subsurface levels of reality, where your muse awaits. It opens the way to conversing, embracing, and dancing with your muse and cajoling her to express her deep creative powers. As you journey deep into the core of your body during Tan Tien breathing, you may find yourself exploring the cavern of your muse, then creating art from her lair. As you descend through the portal of an acu-point, you may find sensations and images, which then spill into the colors and textures of collage.

The holistic process of Chi awareness and creativity can transform old memories to facilitate healing. Emotional wounds and blockages lie within the strata of muscles and tissues, while muscle spasms from physical injury impact emotions. As physical and emotional blockages begin to dissolve under the influence of healing attention, blockages to creativity can also dissolve.

Throughout our many years of teaching and practice, we witness constantly that people who practice Chi awareness have increased focus, stamina, and alertness. Their practice inevitably becomes personal and intimate, cultivating awareness of the layers of the subconscious body and mind.

Warrior-Healer: Gilles

Realize that the explorations in Chi and creativity offered in this book are open invitations for you to enter their realms in your own personal way. Life is full of Chi. Life throbs with creative potential. Invite yourself on a journey of discovery according to your own interests and inclinations, your own desires and needs. The universe shares with you its Chi, creativity, and cumulative wisdom. The ancients, your ancestors of blood, landscape, and spirit, share with you their Chi, creativity, and cumulative wisdom. Their spirit lives on through you. What forms of Chi, creativity, and personal wisdom do you wish to share? What is your legacy to leave for those who follow you?

Chi Awareness Principles

II

Benefits of Chi Awareness

Chi awareness practices benefit you in the following ways:

- **Organ-Meridian System**

  They balance the Chi flowing through your organ-meridian system and build stamina and Wei Chi (protective Chi); thus more energy becomes available for you to use in healing self and others and in creative self-expression. Physical, emotional, mental, and spiritual stress or trauma can cause blockages in organs and meridians. When the Chi gets stagnant and putrid, the organs cannot function properly. This can cause even more blockages and disease. Chi stagnation feels like a house where all the windows are closed, the rugs are dirty, and clutter abounds. Opening the organ-meridian systems feels like opening the windows, cleaning and purging the house, and letting in fresh air and sunshine.

- **Five Elements**

  They balance the five elements to bring greater harmony to your body, mind, and spirit. The six pairs of Yin and Yang organs and their twelve meridians are associated with the five elements of Traditional Chinese Medicine: Metal governs the lungs and large intestine; water governs the kidneys and bladder; wood governs the liver and gall bladder; fire governs the heart and small intestine, plus the pericardium and triple warmer; earth governs the spleen and stomach.

- Eight Extraordinary Vessels

They access your deep inner body to harmonize its reservoirs of Chi, the Eight Extraordinary Vessels, which include four pairs: the Yang and Yin Bridge Vessels; the Yang and Yin Regulator Vessels; the Belt and the Penetrating Vessels; and the Governing and the Conception Vessels. The Governing and Conception Vessels are the only ones of the Extraordinary Vessels that have acu-points of their own. The others utilize points from the twelve organ meridians. Although their spheres of influence overlap and interconnect, in general the Bridge and Regulator Vessels affect the sides, legs, and arms through the coronal and sagittal planes; the Belt Vessel affects the circumference of the body through the transverse plane; the Penetrating Vessel affects the axis in the core of the body; and the Governing Vessel and Conception Vessel affect, respectively, the back and front of the head and torso through the median plane. The Governing and Conception Vessels form the pathway for activating the Microcosmic Orbit.

- Musculoskeletal System

Chi awareness practices move your muscles, connective tissues, and bones as one integrated unit, nourishing the bone marrow, which produces red and white blood cells, lubricating the muscles and joints, and enhancing the circulation of blood, hormones, and lymph. They increase flexibility and align and strengthen your body from inside to outside. They teach you body mechanics to prevent injury to joints, connective tissues, and muscles. The spiraling, wrapping, and unraveling of muscles and fascia along bones store Chi and calcium in bones and build bone density. The gentle movement of your musculoskeletal system soothes, relaxes, and heals trauma.

- Lymphatic System

They activate and move your lymph, which filters and removes toxins and metabolic waste products from your body and strengthens your immune system. Without musculoskeletal movement, lymph, having no pump of its own, stagnates.

- Cardiovascular System

They stimulate your cardiovascular system, so that your heart does not have to work so hard in pumping. They enhance circulation of blood (where Chi goes, blood follows) and support its function of carrying oxygen and nutrients to the cells and cleansing the vital organs of your body.

- Respiratory System

They cultivate full breathing and full use of your lungs. They strengthen your lungs and their function of inhaling and transforming Chi for use by your body. They strengthen your respiratory and pelvic diaphragms, which massage, cleanse, and nourish your internal organs.

- Digestive System

They gently massage your digestive system. They relieve Chi stagnation and excessive heat, cold, or damp and open space in the abdominal cavity, so that the digestive organs are less cramped, more content, and freer to function at their full potential. They calm your nerves and help your digestive tract to function free of the stress that can lead to digestive ailments, such as gastric ulcers and bowel irregularities.

- Endocrine System

They stimulate and tone the hormonal glands of your body, maximizing their efficiency and harmonizing their functions.

- Craniosacral Rhythm

Chi awareness practices gently pump your cranium's sphenoid and pelvis' sacrum bones, stimulating the rhythmic flow of cerebrospinal fluid, which nourishes and protects your brain and spinal cord. Advanced Chi Kung practitioners often "listen" to the craniosacral rhythm and move to its subtle pulsations through the entire body. Not only your body's brain and nervous system, but also your cardiovascular, respiratory, endocrine, digestive, and musculoskeletal systems all respond and breathe to this rhythm.

- Mind

  They teach your mind to direct the Chi to flow in harmony in your body. They tonify and balance Yin and Yang, right and left brain, intuitive and analytical processes. They cultivate focus, concentration, clarity, and insight.

- Emotions

  They cause the meridians of Chi to begin to release and heal emotional spasms in the musculature and fascia of your body. They activate circuits of Chi to balance your chakras and related emotions. They harmonize the emotions of the five elements. Your body is like a superb computer with an incredible memory, where everything that has happened to you in your life is stored. As emotional stress dissolves, negativity releases, and Chi flows more smoothly, it is easier to cultivate a more positive attitude toward life, so that more Chi is free for creative endeavors.

- Creativity

  They stimulate acu-points, often releasing powerful memories and emotions longing for voice and creative outlet. They open such Chi circuits as the Micro- and Macrocosmic Orbits, which affect deeply the core of your body, and may trigger images, sounds, colors, and textures and arouse your muse. They add an energetic component to creative endeavors. Whether you are painting on canvas, whipping a dessert, building a cabinet, or cultivating your garden, when you sow your ideas and scan their creations with Chi awareness, you reach a deeper level of mastery.

- Spirit

  They cultivate mindfulness, perseverance, groundedness, and centeredness. They gently nourish understanding and compassion for self and others. They can help you to connect with your inner guides. They bring awareness of ancestral sources and ancient wisdom, in the microcosm of the inner world on a cellular level in the DNA, and in the macrocosm of the universe on an energetic level, for we are all energy, all interrelated in spirit.

Chi Kung at Halemaʻumaʻu Crater: Elise

Elise and Kaleo's Journal: Moving Meditation

Ē Ke Akua, ē kumu mai ola. Ē nā kūpuna. Kan, li, chen, tui, kun, ken, sun, chi'en . . . . We invoke the Divine, the ancestors, and the eight natural forces of water, fire, thunder and lightning, lake and rain, earth, mountain, wind, heaven.

The mantra resonates within us as we move in Chi Kung before the island dawn. All liquids, the waves of the ocean, the moisture in the heavens, the fluids in our bodies, flow to the rhythms of earth, moon, and sun. Chi is all, every cell, every molecular structure, every photon throughout the universe. Textures and colors bathe us in this early morning vigil of stars.

Soft winds blow. The first glow of sun awakens the earth beneath our feet. We feel the flesh, bones, and Chi of the ancestors in the 'āina. Power rises into our toes, feet, lower legs. Our feet sink and legs press, weight of flesh dropping into earth. Power ascends from deep in earth's core and rises into our legs, our bodies. We pulse with the heartbeat of the ancestors. Of the earth herself.

Our hands and arms glide over the currents of the island breezes, and our bodies move through their silken temperatures absorbing the Chi, light, and sounds of this ancient place.

Our muscles glide over, wrap around bones, tug at sinews. Bones turn, shift, drop within their facets and sockets. Sacrums pump, dancing with the sphenoid bones and cranial sutures. Internal organs roll, push, pump, as electrical charges surge, all in harmony in the universe within, in harmony with the universe without. The way it's been for millions of years.

Chi Kung celebrates the wonders, mysteries, and powers through the joy of dancing prayer.

Practice Guidelines for Chi Awareness

Cultivating Chi awareness helps you to understand and nurture yourself as an energetic being in relationship to the great network of Chi that surrounds, infuses, and intertwines us.

Chi is moving energy. Energy is natural, inherent, and essential. However, moving energy without proper intention and caution can be counterproductive. Chi has been likened to electricity. Like electricity, it is beneficial. Proper flow and balance of Chi are essential to harmony of body/mind/spirit. However, misdirected flow can result in disharmony, like improperly wired electricity.

NOTE: If you have a known injury or weakness, consult a medical practitioner before embarking on the journey of Chi awareness, Chi Kung, and related practices. Although much can be learned from books and other media, we recommend that you complement your personal study with classes from a qualified teacher.

The following are some guidelines for practices in Chi awareness:

- *Keep a Chi journal.* Monitor your evolution in Chi awareness. Record self-observations and discoveries. Sketch ideas for Chi applied to creative self-expression.

- *Select a pleasing environment.* Go to a place that is comfortable, quiet, sheltered from the wind and harsh elements. Outside is lovely if weather permits. Realize that Chi accumulates in your place of practice. Notice how the presence of the elements affects you. Standing on earth in shoes with soles of natural fiber can help you connect more strongly with earth's abundant Chi. How do you respond to your feet grounding on earth in standing meditation? To the clarity of air (metal)? To moving in Chi Kung by the river? To the embrace of trees? To the warm sun on your skin? If possible, you might want to practice in the presence of an element in your being that needs strengthening.

- *Practice regularly and with moderation and common sense.* Try to practice at about the same time each day, if possible. Morning is best, but any time is better than no time. Ten minutes six days a week is better than one hour once a week. If you are just beginning practices in Chi awareness, limit them to one hour a day unless under the guidance of a qualified teacher. Start with five to ten minutes of standing meditation and build up your practice slowly. Be a responsible, competent, and caring guide for yourself. Adjust explorations for your own body, personality, and current state of mind and health. Follow your own inner wisdom.

- *Begin with intention and practice with mindfulness.* You might begin with an invocation to the Taoist ancestors, whose 5,000 years of evolving wisdom support practices with Chi. Stand in meditation, grounded and centered on the earth. Find your quiet, calm center. Take several long, slow breaths. As your belly expands, feel your energy gathering and centering in your pelvis. As your breath travels into your chest, allow it to bring stillness and peace to your heart. As your awareness travels to your mind, allow it to bring focus balanced with relaxation. Feel your feet and your perineum at the base of your torso soft and open to the Chi of earth. Feel the crown of your head soft and open to heavenly Chi. Practice with presence, focus, inner calm, self-observation, self-acceptance, and mindfulness in action through your experiences with Chi.

- *Let your body be hydrated, your belly light.* Keep hydrated during your practice. Water lubricates the body, feeds and fills the cells, dissolves and flushes toxins, and conducts Chi. Have a belly that is not too full for practice. You might want to eat a light healthy snack, so your blood sugar does not drop too low, but not a full meal. This will allow you to: breathe and move more freely (food takes up space); have more Chi available (digestion requires Chi); and feel more energetic and alert (digestion may bring on sluggishness).

- *Stay centered and open, and "hang loose."* Maintain awareness of your body as a vessel of Chi, connected through Chi to earth, heaven, and the environment. Keep in mind to "hang loose." Your body should feel easy and fluid. If you feel pain or tension, back off until you feel a flow and ease. Your practices with Chi should lead to increased bodily flexibility and strength, but not to pain. This means being mindful of balance, alignment, and ease of breath. Eventually you will open up more this way.

- *Enjoy!* Make time for structured practice (the techniques and forms you are learning) and for creative exploration (for example, walking meditation, laughing Chi Kung, free-flowing Chi Kung, dancing Chi Kung). You are more likely to engage a practice if it is interesting and pleasurable as well as effective. As much as you take your practice seriously, make it also fun!

- *Monitor your physical, energetic, and emotional responses.* Most people who engage in Chi awareness practices notice enhanced energy and emotional harmony. However, if you notice unusual fatigue, reduce the intensity and duration of your practice. At times, as the Chi moves through your body, you may find yourself belching, passing gas, perspiring, trembling, laughing, becoming tearful, restless, nauseous, or dizzy, so sit down or take a break if you need to! If you notice anxiety, depression, insomnia, or any other detrimental emotional symptoms, stop your practice and seek qualified guidance.

- *Give waste Chi to the earth.* Remember that Gaia, the earth mother, supports us. During your practice, when you feel physical, energetic, or emotional tension or toxicity releasing, give it to the earth. She is a giant composter, transforming and recycling discarded Chi. Much of our natural garbage and waste products are energy resources for the earth. As she turns our watermelon rinds, wilted lettuce, and coffee grounds into food for our gardens, she can also alchemically transform negative energy into Chi that supports, embraces, and nurtures us.

- *End with Chi closure and gratitude.* When you finish your practice, gather the Chi in your pelvic Tan Tien for safe storage. You can do this by placing your right hand over your left over your navel (men) or your left hand over your right over your navel (women). Then ask yourself: What are you grateful for today? Your health? Your commitment to your practice? The Chi the universe has shared with you? You could sing your own song of gratitude, chant your mantra, whisper a personal prayer.

Spirit Boat by Kaleo and Elise (Elise's lower leg sculpture, 4'h x 2'w x 6"d)

Knowing Your Body

Elise's Journal: Body and Spirit

Because of shattering my left thigh bone in a motorcycle accident over twenty years ago, my left leg is filled with metal and my left knee only flexes 75 percent. The orthopedist cautioned me against vigorous exercise and warned me arthritis was inevitable. If full lotus posture is a requirement for Nirvana, I'll never make it, and I'll never do Kung Fu like Jackie Chan.

Instead, Chi Kung, Tai Chi, and hatha yoga have challenged me to work from a deeper level of awareness with the idiosyncrasies of my body. When my knee becomes inflamed, I have come to understand better how to nurture and heal it, at the same time strengthening it. Competition is Yang, urging me to challenge my limitations. But if I allow it to dominate, the injury speaks up and insists that I slow down, ease up, reevaluate. Vulnerability is Yin, a quiet but stern teacher. The dance of Yang and Yin balance entices me to find my body's own inner rhythms of healing.

Chi Kung is an internal energy practice gifted us from the ancestors. The ancient ones have left a legacy that comes to life in our practice. Its rewards come from an inner awareness that opens doors to creative exploration. When I relate to my body as a vessel of ancestral messages and a vehicle of spirit, my entire relationship to myself begins to change.

Chi Awareness: Surrendering to Gaia

Go to a place in nature that feels safe for you. It might be a meadow of wildflowers or a grassy spot in a park or in your backyard. Smell the fragrances coming from mother earth. Feel the warmth of father sun. You may even be able to feel the energy of the earth rising and also pulling at your body. Lie prone and press your belly into the earth. Receive her Chi. What does earth's Chi feel like? How does it support you from below?

Smell the fragrance of the earth and all its hidden nuances. Can you hear the ants, bugs, worms, and rodents crawling through the earth? Sense their diligence, their perseverance, their responsibility on this earth. Feel the wealth of nutrients in the soil. Feel the presence of the ancestors. Feel the grass, shrubs, flowers as they grow. Their roots dig deep and their bodies reach for the sun. Understand their place in the cycle of life. Realize one day you will return to the earth mother. Thank her for your body and its composition. Thank her for the energy, the life.

Turn over and lie supine. How does it feel to have your belly open to the sun? Inhale and feel heaven's Chi entering you on your breath, as earth supports you from below. Look at the sky's expansiveness, the clouds, the birds in flight. Visualize your body sinking into the ground, as your spirit ascends into the skies.

Understand that nature has its own strengths and weaknesses. It has times of peace and times of fury, times of joy and times of trauma. It has injuries and illnesses and ways of healing.

Your body is nature. It has strengths and weaknesses. Gaia, the earth mother, accepts you as you are. Can you accept your body as it is?

Elise in Puna, Hawai'i

Journaling: Your Body's Journey

What are your body's strengths? Its weaknesses? What is its history of injuries and illnesses? Of healing? Have there been times when your body image went through a major crisis? What did you learn from this and how did your relationship to your body change?

Consider your body's weaknesses, injuries, sources of physical or psychic pain and your body's strengths, joys, healing journey. What do you need to do next for healing and self-acceptance?

Principles of Chi Awareness

Developing Discipline, Focus, Coordination

Chi awareness cultivates focus and concentration and connectedness between your body and mind. Your motor skills and coordination improve. The communication between your brain and nervous system and your musculoskeletal system will be more fluid and your body will respond more effectively to the messages. You will become more coordinated, balanced, flexible, grounded, and strong. Be aware of how Chi awareness integrates and embraces your entire being.

Focus is Chi channeled with intention. Look for it dazzling in a *Waterlilies* painting by Monet. Or soaring in Mozart's *Magic Flute*. Taste it in a succulent dish by Sam Choy. Watch its insightful wit in *Crimes and Misdemeanors* by Woody Allen.

Relaxing

All Chi awareness practice begins with relaxation. The process is as important as the result, and the process begins with sinking into your innermost being to a space of calmness, free of tension. When you are under stress, your body contracts and becomes acidic with hormones designed for fight or flight (sympathetic mode). When your mind and body relax (parasympathetic mode), healing hormones flood your body.

Relaxation promotes physical release, mental equanimity, and the free flow of Chi. Relaxation is the starting point. It means quieting the dominant Yang and opening to the receptive Yin. It means letting go of the need to be in control and surrendering to inner stillness. Through observing and surrendering, you have the ability to do creative problem solving. You are able to feel, listen to, and flow to the winds and whims of your creativity.

You may begin Chi awareness practice with sitting or standing meditation (*see* Chapter VIII, "Chi and Meditation" on page 187 for detailed guidelines), with relaxation of the entire body from crown of head to base of feet, including relaxation of the mind, releasing tension, expectations, distractions, and mental attachments that interfere with practice. Relaxation into the inner being also allows you to let go of the stresses, disappointments, losses, and pressures of daily living and to fill the inner void with the breath of inspiration. It allows you to release the emotional toxins of stress that damage the physical, mental, and psychic dimensions of your body. It encourages your body to breathe and heal itself. Ultimately, relaxation becomes the threshold between the physical and spiritual dimensions of your being.

Awareness of the Inner Body

Your entire body is a living, breathing organism. Your nose, mouth, and skin breathe. At a more subtle level, your muscles, bones, organs, eyes, ears, crown, perineum, axillae, palms of hands, and soles of feet also breathe. You breathe as the pores of your skin open and close, respiratory diaphragm descends and ascends, joints extend and flex, muscles and fascia spiral and wrap, and inner organs expand and contract.

Chi awareness practices harvest and store Chi from the universe in your body, as cells receive energy from the meridians, oxygen and nourishment from the blood, purification from the lymph, and signals from the brain to live and function. As your skull lifts and your pelvis sinks, the spine lengthens and extends and the intervertebral disks relax and breathe. Your organs also lift and expand with Chi and blood. You will notice how this expansion has a positive effect on your posture, attitude, immune system, and energy.

You become aware that Chi affects your inner well-being, physically, mentally, and emotionally. As your Chi radiates, whether positive or negative, strong or vulnerable, it influences your relationships to people and the world. Chi is magnetic. People sense your Chi and respond to it.

As you work with Chi, you enter the inner realms of your body from the seven directions: your crown, perineum, front, back, left and right sides, and core. You feel the ethereal thread—the axis that runs from the heavens through the center of your body into the earth—expanding and contracting, drawing the breath into your very core. As you enter the expansive universe within, you enter the Yin and the Yang of ancient wisdom: birth and death, grief and hope, loss and inspiration, failure and success. You explore the wisdom, power, and creativity within yourself.

As you express your creativity through a painting or a poem, enter into the inner world of its body. Feel its texture, its structural intelligence, its flesh and bones, its wisdom and power. Feel its breath. Touch its aura of Chi.

Grounding

Your body has an axis, which we refer to as the ethereal thread of Chi, just like the earth herself. Your axis aligns you with heaven and earth. As you sit, stand, or move with Chi awareness, feel aligned and balanced around this axis. Feel how your body sways around it, in attunement with the rhythms of your inner body, the breath of the heavens, the pull of the earth. Allow yourself to feel connected and rooted to the Chi of the earth through your feet and perineum, the center of the base of your torso. Feel the vast support of the earth beneath you and receive her gravitational and energetic grounding, her strength. Feel your deep connectedness to Gaia, your earth mother.

Coming from the Center

On your axis is the nucleus of your energetic being. This center, called the pelvic Tan Tien, is situated inside the body two finger widths below the navel at the level of the sacrum. It is hypothetically vast, having the potential of extending far beyond your body's mass. You also have an emotional/spiritual center, the Tan Tien of the heart, and a mental center, the Tan Tien of the mind. Chi awareness guides you to integrate the Tan Tiens of the pelvis, heart, and mind. It guides you to center yourself with the outer realms of heaven, environment, and earth.

In Chi awareness flow of Chi and movement of the body originate in and return to the pelvic Tan Tien. Coming from this center exercises and nourishes the internal organs in and near the abdominal area: the lungs, kidneys, liver, heart, and spleen, as well as organs of digestion, elimination, and reproduction. Chi flows and spirals into and around the organs and moves through the Spleen and Stomach, Liver and Gall Bladder, and Kidney and Bladder meridians, which run through the mid torso. The action moves lymph, which flushes toxins and supports the immune system. The movement of the abdomen facilitates the circulation of the blood, with its fresh oxygen and nutrients, in the organs and throughout the body.

Be aware of how coming from your center influences your journey through life. Look at a great painting or listen to a great musical piece. You can feel its center, its energetic core, its Tan Tien. Watch a great athlete, dancer, or healer. It feels like there is an umbilical cord connecting the artist and the rhythms, lines, and shapes of the work. The creation originates in the artist's core. Have you ever sat in an audience in the presence of a great performer, director, or teacher? You can feel the centeredness that comes from wisdom and experience and how it holds the audience. The entire room breathes as one.

When you create, whether artist, bodyworker, or dancer, coming from center increases your energy and accesses a deeper source within your being.

Bridging

The sacrum bridges to the brain and skull via the vertebral column and spinal cord. As the sacrum moves the vertebral column, it affects the skull and brain and vice versa. The brain and spinal cord are covered with a fascial layer called the dura mater, which bridges the cranium and the sacrum. Within this tube flows the cerebrospinal fluid, which protects and nurtures the brain and spinal cord. In stillness, with practice, you will feel the craniosacral rhythm as cerebrospinal fluid flows, its silent movement radiating throughout your body.

Your brain and nervous system form a bridging network that spreads throughout your whole body. Signals travel from brain to spinal cord to peripheral nervous system and back to brain, brain sending out messages (Yang) and receiving responses (Yin). Your hand is an extension of your brain. It is your brain.

Bridging occurs among the systems of your body, between the directions of your body (front and back, right and left, top and bottom), and between the Yin and Yang meridians of your body. Bridging occurs between the Microcosmic and Macrocosmic Orbits, self and universe, inner world and outer world, artist and creation.

Spiraling

In Chi Kung movement the body spirals. This spiraling is physical (wrapping of fascia, muscles, tendons, and ligaments around bones) and energetic. It can be felt in gross movements, like the internal rotation of the large front thigh muscles (quadriceps) around the femur bone, or in subtle movements, like the spiraling vortex of energy in the heart of your palm (Pericardium 8).

The concept of spiraling also helps to deepen your understanding of Chi Kung as a practice of relationship. Movements in Chi Kung are respectively receptive, spiraling inward, and active, spiraling outward. These movements are always in relationship, one not superior to the other, but interdependent. Spiraling is circular and dynamic, like a coil or a spring, moving round and round and up and down, thus moving in and around the body, connecting it to the ground beneath the feet and the sky above the crown of the head. You move into harmony with the spiraling forces of heaven and earth.

This awareness also affects creativity. Creation is not a linear process, but a spiraling one, circling round and round, higher toward the divine sources of creative inspiration, deeper toward the treasures in the recesses of your subconscious. As you paint, you do not create a picture from beginning to end, but spiral in, spiral out, to the center, to the edges, swinging from deep forest green to crystalline white to throbbing crimson. You layer in, layer out, and as you unveil and reconceal layers, you become better acquainted with the layers within yourself and the layers of the universe beyond.

Balancing Yin and Yang

Spiraling is inherent in the balance of Yin and Yang, a concept fundamental to Chi awareness. Yin and Yang form a familiar symbol of separate parts balanced in a harmonious whole: like an image of two fish, one white, one black, each with the other's tail in its mouth and with the other's image in its eye. Examples illustrating Yin and Yang encompass the spectrum of experience: vulnerability and strength (physical), right and left brain (mental), female and male (emotional), empty and full (energetic), earth and heaven (spiritual).

All is a balance of Yin and Yang. When the abdomen expands, the body is Yang; when it contracts, the body is Yin. As the weight shifts from foot to foot, Yin and Yang oscillate, the weighted leg being Yang, the weightless leg being Yin. The weighted Yang leg fills with Chi, blood, and oxygen, while the weightless Yin leg relaxes. As the Yang outer body spirals one way in motion, the Yin inner body spirals in the opposite way, keeping the body grounded and centered. As the Chi flows up a Yin meridian, it meets and interacts with its Yang partner (for example, the Chi flows up the Yin Kidney meridian and down the Yang Bladder meridian). Being aware of the inner microcosm of the physical and energetic body (Yin) helps you find balance with the macrocosm of the universe (Yang).

The Yin/Yang principle dissolves the tension of opposites. Dark is not bad and light good. Strength is not an asset without vulnerability. Rather, the opposites meet in an eternal dance.

As you move into creativity, be aware of the balance of Yin and Yang, between idea and manifestation, right brain and left brain processes, dark and light, incubation and production, stillness and action.

Microcosm/Macrocosm

Your meridians of Chi spiral with your muscles, fascia, connective tissue, and bones. Your body pulses with the flow of Chi, nerve impulses, blood, lymph, and cerebrospinal fluid. Chi flows through the body in rhythm with the energy beyond the body—in other living beings, in the environment, in the earth, in the heavens. The microcosm (Yin) of the inner body moves into harmony with macrocosm (Yang) of the outside world. The Chi flowing through you and connecting all is the breath of the universe. As you engage the Micro- and Macrocosmic Orbits, you experience that you, the microcosm, and the universe, the macrocosm, are one. You are the stars. You are creation.

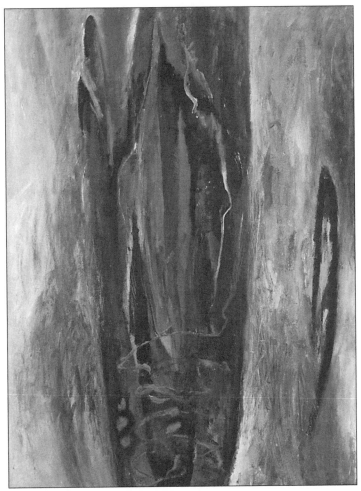

Spiraling Microcosm/Macrocosm by Kaleo (acrylic painting, 38″h x 30″w)

Chi and the Internal Alchemy of the Five Elements

The five elements are alchemically aligned with the internal organs and their energy meridians laced with acu-points: metal with lungs and large intestine; water with kidneys and bladder; wood with liver and gall bladder; fire with heart and small intestine plus pericardium and triple warmer; earth with spleen and stomach. Chi awareness practices help to bring health and harmony to the organs and meridians.

Always the emphasis is on balance. Emotional imbalance in the element of metal might result in grief or hopelessness. Imbalance in the water element might cause fear or adrenaline addiction. Imbalance in the wood element might cause anger or stagnation. Imbalance in the fire element might cause emptiness or hysteria. Imbalance in the earth element might bring worry or apathy.

The five elements weave together your being and the forces of the physical world. For instance, you come to look at a 3,000 year old bristlecone pine in a new way based on the connection of wood to your inner body, seeing not only the tree's quiet, passive, rooted strength, but feeling the ancient spirit of its power in the movement of your body's tissues.

The alchemy of the five elements affects not only your body, Chi, and psyche, but also creativity. Five element alchemy holds much wisdom, mystery, and opportunity for discovery. It cultivates an awareness that can permeate every dimension of your life with deeper meaning and understanding. Allow your relationship to the alchemy of the five elements to deepen naturally as you engage Chi awareness and creativity.

Creativity

Practices in cultivating Chi bridge the Tan Tiens of the mind, the heart, and the pelvis, connecting you more intimately with your creative spirit. They guide you into deeper inner awareness and understanding of your emotions, your ancestral wisdom, and your spiritual sources. When your body and meridians are open, when the Chi flows smoothly, when the emotions are unblocked, when the mind focuses its intention, and when the spirit is free, creativity flourishes.

Principles of Chi Breathing

Chi breathing is full, deep, relaxed breathing. It is breath massaging your inner body. It is a marriage of Chi and breath. Most people take very shallow breaths, filling only the top part of their lungs. Chi breathing, on the other hand, reaches deep into the torso. Those with a meditation practice often already know how to breathe into the lower abdomen.

If you are not familiar with the abdominal and Tan Tien breathing techniques, at first they may feel challenging and awkward. But if you continue to practice, before long, they should feel easy, natural, and beneficial. Reverse breathing is a more specialized technique, which you may find useful and powerful, but is not essential to the explorations in this book.

Abdominal Breathing

In abdominal breathing your soft belly expands on the inhalation and contracts on the exhalation. On the inhalation the respiratory diaphragm descends and caresses the adrenals; the abdominal cavity and its organs open with the breath; and the abdomen expands. You breathe gently and deeply into the abdomen, filling the lower, then middle, then upper lobes of your lungs, thus using their full capacity. In abdominal breathing the inhalation is Yang (more active) and the exhalation is Yin (more passive). Abdominal breathing is easy and natural and can be done at any time. It helps you sink easily into a relaxed state of mind for meditation or for journeys in guided imagery to subconscious realms.

Tan Tien Breathing

Tan Tien breathing follows the same principles and rhythm as abdominal breathing but brings the breath into the floor, sides, and back of your pelvic bowl and lower torso, as well as abdomen and ribcage. On the inhalation your entire girth and pelvic basin expand. On the exhalation they contract.

Tan Tien breathing has many benefits. It efficiently oxygenates the body and draws in fresh Chi from the air. It brings fresh Chi, blood, and movement to the lower abdomen. It massages your internal organs and entire digestive tract.

It builds energy by massaging the kidneys, adrenals, and Ming Men (Governing Vessel 4/Gate of Life). It helps alleviate hormonal imbalances and menstrual dysfunctions, such as cramping, abdominal bloating, and hot flashes.

Tan Tien breathing is easy and natural deep breathing and can be done at any time. It maximally promotes the flow of Chi in and around your vital organs. It connects you with your physical core. Sometimes, with proper direction, it can connect you with your emotional core. It can trigger the release of emotions hidden between membranes or tucked in secret folds in your body's depths.

Reverse Breathing

In reverse breathing your abdomen and pelvic basin contract from all sides, as the respiratory diaphragm descends, bringing air into the lungs, and the urogenital diaphragm ascends, massaging the abdominal organs. On the exhalation, your abdomen expands into all sides, as the respiratory diaphragm ascends and the urogenital diaphragm descends. Reverse breathing is Chi-stimulating deep breathing. In reverse breathing the inhalation is Yin and the exhalation is Yang. This is an important principle in martial arts applications, for the exhalation is utilized with offensive moves, whereas the inhalation is the time when the martial artist is most vulnerable. Reverse breathing is useful for Yang movements in Chi Kung, bodywork, or martial arts, but can potentially drain Chi if practiced extensively. Use reverse breathing with prudence and moderation.

Chi Breathing and Creativity

How does breathing affect creativity? If you find yourself stuck during creative process, you may pause, go into your inner body, and listen. Then engage Chi breathing and find your creative Chi beginning to surge again. Chi breathing connects you with a fuller range of your breath than ordinary breathing does, and thus with a fuller range of your inner creative resources. As you enter deep relaxation and inner body awareness facilitated by abdominal or Tan Tien breathing, you also enter more easily the domain of subconscious awareness, where hidden images, sensations, and emotions lie waiting for your attention.

Kaleo's Journal: Brothers

Kaleo: Satyajit, when did you stop writing?

Satyajit: Since childhood, I've always loved to read and write. I loved writing poems and stories but stopped about six years ago, when my brother, Subhankar, died. I was born in a house in India with a mud floor and tin roof. Now I'm a physician and own a Victorian in San Francisco. But I feel apathetic and listless. I don't understand. I'm only forty-five and have had a thorough medical evaluation. Nothing is wrong. But I feel depressed, fatigued, totally unmotivated.

Kaleo: I'm holding acu-points on your Lung meridian that will help alleviate your feelings of depression. Just breathe. Breathe and sink. Let go. Feel the Chi circulating through your lungs, traveling through your body. Feel your abdomen soft and expanding on the inhalation. Breathe way down deep, into your belly. Your subconscious guides your breathing. It knows exactly what to do. Allow it to take you on a journey. It knows exactly where to go. All you have to do is trust. Now tell me, where are you?

Satyajit: I'm in my mother's home in India with Subhankar, my brother. We are eating at the table. Always, there's that silence. That silence and that coldness. Subhankar sputters: "This family will be the death of me, the death of me." I don't know what's happening. I'm usually the gentle scholar, but I lose control. I smash my plate on the floor. My mother's curry and rice splatter. Subhankar glares at me with a mixture of alarm, curiosity, and suspicion. I scream: "I've come so many miles from California to visit, and this is all you can say! I had it rough too! I was only five years old and you gave me away. I grew up with strangers. Do you know how traumatic that was? Sure, papa died, and at twenty years old you had to support mama and all six kids. It's been hard for you. But all you do is work. You never married, you just work, come home, go to your room, and shut the door behind you. Mama's in the house, and you shut the door! In a couple of days, I'm going back to San Francisco. Talk to me!"

(Satyajit's eyes open and he weeps:) Subhankar never said anything. That's the last time I saw him. He died three months later of a heart attack.

Kaleo: Close your eyes, Satyajit, and let's go back to India. Breathe slowly, deeply. It's easy. You already know the way. Return to that table in your mama's kitchen. There you are with Subhankar. What would you like to say to him? Now is the time.

Satyajit: "Your cold silence cut deeply into me. Now I feel so guilty. I understand you did what you had to do. You had to send me away when I was a child. Thank you for raising the family and helping mama. Thank you for helping me out through school. I worked very hard to earn my degrees. I hope you're proud of me."

Kaleo: What gift have you brought for your brother?

Satyajit: "Subhankar, I have a gift for you. This book. Yes, that's your name in gold printed on the leather cover. It's a book about you. It's your story. I've written your story!" Subhankar looks surprised. That old suspicion is still there. But now there is gratitude. He takes the book. He's holding it in his hands. He mutters, "Thank you." You know, I can feel the cold silence lift. It leaves the kitchen table.

Kaleo: Open the window, Satyajit. Let the cold and the silence out. When you're ready, say good-bye to Subhankar. You're ready to return now.

Satyajit: (After Satyajit returns to this reality, he looks at Kaleo and says) I know now what I need to do. After Subhankar died of a heart attack, I stopped writing. Now I will write his story. Perhaps through writing I can retrieve the part of me that died with him and bring a part of him back as well.

Lying Meditation: Exploring Tan Tien Breathing

Find a warm, comfortable place with a smooth firm surface to lie in meditation. Remove shoes and eyeglasses. Lie on your back. If you feel any tension in your lower back, place a pillow under your knees so that they stay gently flexed. It is important to be comfortable!

Lengthen the back of your neck so that the ridge in the back of your skull (occiput) slides away from your upper (cervical) spine. Use a small pillow or rolled towel as desired to keep your neck neutral.

Now lift one shoulder at a time and slide each shoulder blade down your back toward your waist so that it flattens against the floor. Then allow your arms to rest on the floor, slightly out from your sides, with palms facing upward. Or if it feels more comfortable, you may flex your elbows and fold your hands over your belly.

Feel your entire body comfortable, aligned, and relaxed. Feel the earth beneath your back supporting you. Feel the heavens above filling your body with fresh Chi as you breathe. Feel your breath entering, exiting, each breath long, slow, deep. Your breath is relaxed, your body relaxed, your mind relaxed.

Let your belly be soft. Feel your soft belly rising with the inhalation. Feel your respiratory diaphragm descend, drawing the breath into the bottom, then middle, then top of your lungs. Then feel your belly gently, naturally falling as the exhalation leaves the top, then middle, then bottom of your lungs. This is abdominal breathing.

After a few long relaxed abdominal breaths, bring your attention to your entire pelvis and lower torso—floor, front, sides, and back. As you inhale, let your entire waist area expand. Feel the breath pushing into the floor of your pelvis as your belly rises, your sides expand, and your lower back presses into the ground in a gentle, easy way. Feel the breath entering the bottom, then middle, then top of your lungs. Then let your entire waist area and pelvic basin release and relax, as the exhalation leaves the top, then middle, then bottom of your lungs. You are engaged in Tan Tien breathing.

Breathe this way for a few leisurely breaths. Feel how Tan Tien breathing massages your internal organs. Feel how it uses all the corners of your lungs. Feel how it makes maximum room for fresh Chi to enter with the air into your lungs, to course through your entire body and feed all your cells. Feel how it releases old breath and Chi on the exhalation.

On the inhalation feel how the breath from your open lungs embraces your heart. On the exhalation feel your heart, too, opening, ready to receive. An awareness comes to your heart. What emotion, image, or sensation appears? On the inhalation your heart embraces this awareness; then on the exhalation your heart lets it go. And then you rest.

Journaling: Tan Tien Breathing

Write about your experience of Tan Tien breathing in your journal. As you first lay down in meditation, what was your breathing like? How did it change as you began abdominal breathing? How did it change during Tan Tien breathing?

What awareness came to your heart? How did your heart respond?

Whenever it occurs to you, in an easy, natural way without strain, try bringing Tan Tien breathing into your daily life. Notice your responses and keep track of them in your journal.

Creativity and Principles of Chi Awareness

Art: Principles of Chi Awareness Collage

 Have before you a large sheet of white paper, glue, scissors, and a pile of photo-rich magazines. As you scan the magazines, choose images that most signify your relationship to each of the following qualities:

- Focus (calm, aware, intention clear)

- Relaxation (surrendering and letting go from inner to outer body)

- Groundedness (rooted, Chi connecting deep into the earth)

- Centeredness (awareness of and connectedness to your pelvic Tan Tien)

- Yin and Yang balance (balance of opposites)

- Creativity (sources of creative inspiration in your mind, heart, pelvic Tan Tiens)

- Chi breathing (full, relaxed, easy flow of Chi, protecting and nurturing all parts of your body)

Make a collage of these images, adding new images, words, or sketches to support and connect them as you feel moved.

Journaling: Principles of Chi Awareness Collage

 When you have finished, look at your collage. Write your responses to it in your journal. What does it mirror back to you about your relationship to the principles of Chi awareness? What qualities are already strong in your awareness? What qualities does it ask you to strengthen? How can the principles of Chi awareness support your creative process?

Expanding Chi Awareness: Carolyn

III
Exploring Chi

Chi Interactions: Environments, People, Activities

Everything is Chi. Chi fields, vibrations, and waves are everywhere. The chortling from our dog, Teekkona, as we massage her is the sound of Chi. The warmth in her body created by massage is the flow of Chi. The adoration in her eyes is the look of Chi.

The action and interaction of massage generate and direct Chi. The healing connection between giver and receiver transmits Chi. The healing energy in the room is cumulative Chi.

We all have Chi. We all use Chi. We all share Chi.

Everyone has a Chi field or vibrational energy or aura. It reflects the diet, life style, experiences, attitude, and openness or guardedness of the person. It reflects the person's culture, age, generation, gender. People's Chi fields may vibrate with depression or inspiration, with fear or determination, with anger or motivation, with disconnectedness or joy, with worry or centeredness. Some may reflect deficiency—a need to be filled, nurtured, indulged. Some may reflect excess—hyperactivity, intense emotion, dominance. Some may reflect abundance—love to give, faith to share.

Each activity also has its own Chi. You may notice how some activities infuse you with greater Chi, whereas some require you to replenish expended Chi. Activities also affect the Chi of a place. Notice how the Chi builds in your place of meditation or in your art studio, accumulating over time.

Each environment has its own field of Chi. Some environments sap your energy, while others enhance it.

Make it a practice to be aware of who, what, and where make your Chi feel weaker or stronger.

Elise and Kaleo's Journal: Cumulative Chi

We're doing our Chi Kung, playing with the slanted rays of the sun filtered through the bay laurel branches of our favorite haven of trees. Sounds of the stream flowing over downed trees and bulky boulders mingle with the sounds of our breath. For the past thirteen years, we've come here with Teekkona, our Australian shepherd. The first time we brought her, she was a ball of soft fluffy puppy fur, romping, rolling in the leaves. Now her muzzle glints with silver and her trot is a bit stiff, but her eyes are bright with Shen as she lies on her belly in the soft leaves and cool earth. She loves watching us and feeling our Chi as we gently interact with the sun, trees, and soil.

Every time we practice in this place, Chi builds. The accumulation of Chi in the form of wisdom, creativity, and caring is also why a bodyworker likes to practice in a special room, an artist likes a personal studio space, a writer likes a private den. The Chi of this place feeds us. Stagnant Chi releases from our bodies, as we wash flesh and bones with our Chi palms. We release old Chi to the earth for alchemical transformation. The earth is wise and nurturing; she knows how to convert our waste to fresh fertile creative Chi.

Chi Awareness: Environmental Chi

Go to a place in nature where you know the Chi fills you with positive, nurturing, healing energy. Find a comfortable, inviting niche in this setting, where you will not be disturbed. Sit or lie in meditation. Close your eyes and feel how the darkness comforts you. The embrace of this place encourages your trust. As you trust, you relax, and healing hormones flood your being. Your outer and inner environments infuse you with nourishing Chi. Enjoy the air and Chi of the environment entering your body on the inhalation. Feel your breath exiting and mingling with the environment on the exhalation. Feel this place sharing with you its fresh healthy Chi and absorbing and recycling your exhaled waste Chi. Feel your relationship reciprocal, mutually supportive. Feel its rhythm, your rhythm. When your experience feels complete, let the inhalation arouse your body and open your eyelids. Now exhale a blessing of thanks into this environment.

Journaling: Environmental Chi

 What environment did you choose to go to for its supportive, healing Chi? Realize that this may be a place for you to go to inspire and enrich your practices with Chi, to write in your journal, to do art in nature.

What environments in your daily life support your body, mind, and spirit and inspire your creativity? What environments feel negative or unhealthy for you? What can you do to change the environment you live in so that it is more positive and supportive? What can you do to enhance your creative space so that it welcomes and encourages your muse?

Chi Awareness: Interpersonal Chi

Working with a partner, stand about ten feet away from each other. As your partner stands in relaxed meditation, observe the Chi reflected in his or her demeanor, posture, expression.

Feel the Chi exuding from your partner. Is it guarding and creating boundaries? Or does it push confidently forward? Or does it feel soft and satiny, inviting you in?

Now walk slowly toward your partner until you feel you are touching his or her Chi field and stop. Feel the vibration of this aura as you touch it with the aura of your body. Gently push into it, rub against it, even bounce on it. There will be a time when you feel that you adhere to each other, when both of your auras are one, as if a large Chi field encapsulates both of you. Understand how connected you are. In this state, go deeper, and feel your hearts connecting. Then notice what Chi, emotions, and images surface within you.

When you feel ready, with your partner still standing in meditation, very slowly take small steps backward away from your partner. Notice the elasticity of the Chi stretching as the distance between you increases. How far do you go before the connection breaks?

How does the separation affect your heart, emotions, Chi, and physical body?

Now trade places with your partner and repeat this exercise.

Journaling: Interpersonal Chi

Describe the sensations, feelings, shifts in your body and emotions as you communicated through Chi awareness with a partner. How did your partner's Chi affect you? When you were up close, which part of your body felt touched? Heart, head, gut? What images or emotions emerged? How did you feel when you separated?

Who in your life strengthens your Chi and who weakens it? How would you describe the Chi fields of people who support you and your creativity? What colors, emotions, or elements do you notice? And because Chi is an interactive web, how do you empower and support them as well?

Chi Awareness: Chi of Creative Activities

What you routinely do in a place creates Chi. Go to the rooms in your home. Notice the Chi of your bedroom, work space, kitchen. What activities take place in each of these rooms? With whom do you share them? How would you describe the Chi of each place? What room or corner of a room in your home brings you the most joy? The most comfort? The most stimulation?

Go to the room that most stimulates your creative juices. For example, if you love to cook, go to your kitchen. Notice its Chi. Is creativity spurred by carefully organized spices, dishes, utensils, cookbooks? Or does the muse of the kitchen thrive on a chaos of herbs, spices, bowls, spoons, jars of dried fruits, tins of nuts, scraps of recipes tucked and scattered everywhere? Notice your kitchen's smells, their layers: teas, coffees, herbs, spices, baked desserts, stir-fried greens. The smells are signals that arouse the slumbering muse. A kitchen, like an art studio or a martial arts dojo, can be a place of purposeful discipline or wild play.

Friends, family, ancestors inspire you to create. Your kitchen has not only the cumulative Chi of your creative culinary endeavors, but also the Chi of those with whom you have shared your special dishes and the Chi of those who have influenced your cooking. Perhaps you use your grandmother's own Chinese wok blackened by decades of oils and spices, or your family's secret Cajun recipe passed down through generations, or your favorite Auntie Tita's *haupia* (pudding) recipe, or the pan in which you helped your little brother bake his first cupcakes, or the knife your father used to carve the holiday turkey. Their touch is there. Your touch is there. Memories live in this space. They embrace you when you enter. The love you have put into each dish you have created lives in the corners, the contents, the smells of this place.

Journaling and Art: Chi of Creative Activities

As you sit in the room of cumulative creative Chi, write in your journal or create a collage-drawing. Describe or depict the Chi field of this place. What are your sensations, emotions, bodily shifts when you enter your space of creative activity? What are the fragrances, colors, textures, sounds? What artifacts, mementos, well-used tools are there?

In this atmosphere of creativity, whether in your kitchen, before your ancestral altar, at your writer's desk, or in your artist's studio, how can you strengthen the field of creative Chi surrounding you? Do you need to remove something to unblock the flow of Chi? Or add something to nourish creativity?

Where in your body does your muse reside? What artifacts and tools does she store there? What cumulative creative Chi thrives in this space? When you and your muse enter the realm of creativity in action, do you share a feeling of friendship, of conflict, of challenge?

What activities in your life enhance your energy, your creativity, your relationship with your muse? What activities drain them?

Exploring Chi Through Your Senses

Your Chi is always interacting with that of people, places, and activities. You can enhance your awareness of this interactive web through cultivating your sensory awareness of Chi. The following explorations will guide you more astutely to feel, see, hear, and understand Chi.

Kaleo Teaching Chi Kung Students, Puna, Hawai'i

Feeling Chi

 Stand naturally in your favorite place for doing meditation. Are you in nature, in your studio, or before your altar? Staying relaxed, flex your elbows and extend your forearms in front of you at waist level, palms facing down toward the earth. Let your armpits (axillae) be open and your shoulders relaxed.

Inhale and feel the pores of your skin along your hands and arms softly open-ing. You will feel like a gentle breeze is entering your pores. Exhale and feel the pores softly closing. Inhale and feel the muscles and tissues of your hands tin-gling as Chi spreads through the interconnective tissue. Feel the joints of your fingers, hands, and forearms opening as Chi sinks deeply all the way into the marrow of your bones. Exhale and feel the density of Chi nestling and accumu-lating in your arms and hands.

One with All

Notice how the Chi exudes from your body. Some people more easily feel a tex-ture expanding, while others see a color, hear a sound, or intuit a presence. Notice how, as the Chi expands, it embraces everything around you. Feel your interconnectedness with your environment. You are one with all.

Seeing Chi

It is best to practice this exploration against a solid background in dim light. Bring your palms before you about one foot in front of your chest. Turn your fingers inward to point toward each other. Bring your hands close to each other so that the fingertips are about three to six inches apart. Feel the tingling Chi spiraling out of the fingertips of both hands. Feel how the Chi bounces. It separates the hands and makes it difficult to close the space between them. Have you ever tried to adhere two magnets together? If you bring opposite poles together, they connect quickly, but if you try to bring the same poles together, they resist. Trying to penetrate the Chi separating your two hands feels like trying to connect same poles. Feel the strength of the resistance.

Now point the two index fingers toward one another. Feel the Chi between them. How long does the energy from your index fingers extend?

Now look with soft focus, your eyes melting in their sockets, so that your vision loses its awareness of sharp edges. Notice how your visual field expands. Look not at your index fingers, but what surrounds them. What does the Chi field around and between your index fingers look like? Notice its shape, density, color. Observe: *Can you see what you feel?*

Let your index fingers' tips bounce their Chi between them. Notice what happens to the vibrational field as they bounce. See the rays of Chi. See them dancing. Now feel them dancing: *Can you feel what you see?*

Now, observe a person standing in front of a solid background. Soften your eyes and look for a glow around the body. Notice how, as the person moves, the glow follows. Next, try to see the Chi between two people as they interact. Notice how their different Chi auras reflect their different personalities, moods, and elements. Observe where their auras of energy touch.

Now, observe a powerful work of art, for example *Starry Night* by Van Gogh. Notice its glow of Chi. Or go to a concert. Observe the Chi field around the musicians as they play. Or go into your garden just before sunrise, and watch the flowers as the shadows give way to rays of sunlight. See the petals awaken, Chi quivering and opening before your eyes.

Awakening

Listening to Chi

 Bring your palms before you about one foot in front of your chest. Turn your fingers to point toward each other and make a circle of Chi. Bring your hands close to each other so that the fingertips are just a few inches apart, their membranes of Chi touching. Feel the circuit of Chi flowing in the hoop of your arms and torso. Now, gently wiggle your fingers, hands, and wrists. Notice what the Chi of your hands feels like as the skin glides over the fascia beneath. Now listen with your inner ear. What is the sound of skin gliding? What sounds do the ligaments and tendons of your hands make rubbing over bones as you wiggle your fingers? What is the sound of bones pivoting on each other as you rotate your wrists?

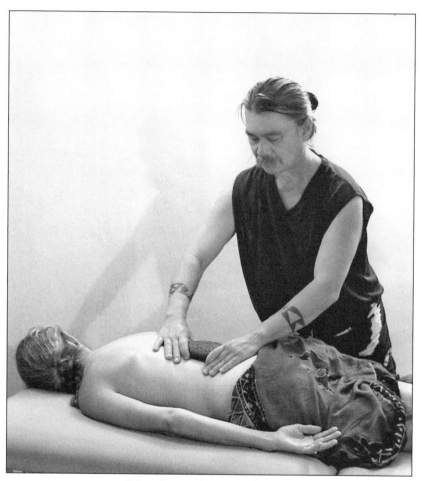

Listening with *Pōhaku* (Stone)

Keeping your Chi hoop in front of you, close your eyes. Turn your auditory awareness more deeply inward. Let whatever sounds are outside guide you deeper into your inner world. Become aware of the sound of your heart beating. Listen to your breath coming in, going out. Be alert to other more irregular sounds, like digestive system gurgles or connective tissue pops. What is your body saying to you? Then listen to the Chi of your hands. What is the sound of Chi traveling between your fingertips and along the hoop of your arms?

Chi Hand Techniques

Your hands are highly intelligent. Whether you are a cook fashioning delicious meals, a Feng Shui master instilling balance and harmony in a home, or an artist applying paint to canvas, significant wisdom and intuition reside in your hands. Chi hand techniques are used on the human body during healing energy work or massage. When working with the body, the practitioner connects with the client on many levels. For instance, work on the sternum bone affects fascia, muscles, bones, and acu-points, as well as the mental, emotional, and spiritual qualities related to the heart chakra.

Chi hand techniques also help to deepen the explorations in this book of creative self-expression through art. If you add an intense red to a pleasant blue, you change the vibrational field of your art piece. If you change the shape or density of a form, you transform the piece physically, energetically, emotionally. As a bodyworker scans the human Chi body to listen and understand, so does the artist's act of scanning the colors and textures of a painting-in-progress impact the piece. The relationship between artist and artwork, as between healer and client, deepens.

When you apply Chi hand techniques, usually you may find that your dominant hand is more effective at transmitting Chi (Yang), whereas your non-dominant hand is more sensitive to receiving (scanning) Chi (Yin). Try both and notice the response.

Remember, when you use your Chi hand techniques to release old waste Chi, give it to the earth. She will compost it for recycling.

- Awakening Your Chi Palms

  Stand naturally and shake your hands vigorously a few times. Then, as your shoulders relax and your shoulder blades sink, flex your elbows and extend your forearms in front of your torso, palms facing each other. Your armpits are open. What do you feel between your palms? You may feel Chi as coolness, warmth, tingling, buoyancy, density, or vibration. Notice the shape of the Chi between your palms. It feels like an orb of Chi. Understand that the Chi radiating from your fingers and palms is fed by the rivers of energy in your body that end or start there: Lung meridian/thumb;

Large Intestine meridian/index finger; Pericardium meridian/middle finger; Triple Warmer meridian/ring finger; Heart and Small Intestine meridians/pinky finger.

Chi Ball: awaken, squeeze, stretch, pump, wave, vibrate

- **Squeezing and Stretching Your Chi Ball**

  Hold your Chi ball. Feel the density of Chi between your palms. Bring your palms closer to each other until you feel the Chi compacting into a ball. Understand that the sensation of Chi you feel between your palms is the Chi of your body and mind at this moment. Notice what happens when you press or pump your hands together and squeeze the ball. Notice what happens as you pull your palms away and stretch the ball. How elastic is your ball of Chi?

- **Chi Pump**

  Open your Chi palms by gently spreading open the bones of your hands. Feel a wave moving from the heart of each palm and spreading out. Then pump the Chi through the centers of your palms.

- **Chi Wave**

  Hold your Chi ball. Leave your non-dominant hand relaxed and still; then slowly and gently wave your dominant hand. Focus your attention on the space between your hands. Feel the waves of energy transmitting from your dominant hand, traveling through the space, and caressing the palm of your other hand.

- Chi Vibrator

Hold your Chi ball. With your non-dominant hand relaxed and still, quickly and energetically vibrate your dominant hand. Focus your attention on the space between your hands. Feel the pulses of energy traveling through the space and vibrating the palm of your receptive hand. Notice this palm beginning to pulse.

- Spinning Your Chi Ball

Hold your Chi ball between your palms. Feel its temperature and texture. Now rotate your hands to spin the ball of Chi, while keeping your palms facing each other, so that you do not drop it. Engage your arms, shoulders, shoulder blades, legs, hips, and hip joints in spiraling this Chi ball. Notice how the spiraling of your shoulder and hip joints generates Chi and builds, nurtures, and spins your Chi ball.

Spinning the Chi Ball

- Chi Nourisher

Place your Chi palms on the aura in front of your heart and lungs and touch this energetic membrane. Feel the Chi from the heavens and the earth filling your body, then flowing through your palms into your heart and lungs. You can also apply your Chi nourisher (one or both palms) more vigorously as a pump to enliven and stimulate Chi where it is weak or sluggish. Or apply it gently and firmly to calm hyperactive areas of Chi.

Chi Nourisher

- Chi Brush

Leave your non-dominant hand and arm relaxed at your side and slightly in front of you, palm facing up. Bring the Chi palm of your dominant hand in toward your other shoulder, until you feel its aura. Feel the skin of this energy body. If you move your Chi palm slightly, you will feel this membrane following. It is like loose skin. Now with your dominant palm, brush gently down the Chi membrane along the inside of your other shoulder and inner arm. Notice the Chi moving down your arm as you cleanse your shoulder, arm, and hand. It feels like you are "smudging" with Chi. Drag the Chi out the ends of the fingers to finish the cleansing. Give this Chi to the earth. Repeat brushing with Chi a few times on the same arm. Then compare your arms. Notice the differences in their temperatures, colors, and vibrations. Brushing with Chi helps relieve any tightness, tension, or congestion in your receptive arm.

Chi Brush

· Chi Trowel

Align the fingers of your hand to create a trowel. Use it to dig around and under to dislodge or uproot stuck Chi.

Chi Trowel

- Tiger's Mouth

Use the intersection of the thumb and index finger at Large Intestine 4 (metal) to activate the jaw of the tiger's mouth for cutting out what is no longer needed.

Tiger's Mouth (Metal)

- Chi Sword

Your index and middle fingers, where run the Large Intestine (metal) and Pericardium (fire) meridians, form the blade of your Chi sword. Relax and curl in your thumb, ring, and pinky fingers; then point your index and middle fingers at your other palm. Feel metal and fire energy beams piercing the membrane of your other palm.

- Chi Quill

Direct the energy beams of your Chi sword into your other palm. Use it as a Chi quill to draw a circle, then a triangle, then inscribe a personal symbol on your palm. Feel its imprint on your palm.

- Chi Drill

Point your Chi sword fingers at your other shoulder's hollow. Feed the energy beam into this cave; then spiral in and down clockwise. Feel the Chi drilling down your arm, through your forearm, and into your palm. Now use your sword fingers to drill out and away counterclockwise from the center of this palm. Notice the color and temperature change in your palm as your Chi drill draws the energy out of your arm.

Chi Sword, Quill, Drill

- Chi Knife

Cut with fire using the energy of the Heart and Small Intestine meridians, which run along your pinky finger and the edge of your forearm. Bring together and extend your thumb and fingers so that your hand and forearm become a knife with your pinky side its cutting edge. Use the fire energy of this knife-edge to slice open or scrape the energetic aura of your forearm. The Chi knife is a handy tool for massage therapists, energy workers, or people feeling a heaviness around them to cut away any unwanted Chi that clings or sticks.

Chi Knife (Fire)

- **Chi Blaster**

  Scoop and gather Chi in your dominant hand. Flick your hand open to blast vigorously through and break up an area of very stuck, congested, clogged Chi. Use doubled hands for a double blast of Chi.

- **Kneading Chi**

  Use your Chi palms to knead, squeeze, and manipulate tension, blockage, or cramping.

- **Chi Rake**

  Spread your fingers gently and use the fingertips/pads to rake energy.

- **Chi Rain**

  Use your fingerpads to wash and soothe an area of irritation or hyperactivity. Tap softly like gentle Chi rain falling on the area.

- Chi Suction

    Your fingerpads can create suction. Place your fingerpads on the Chi aura (about three to six inches) above the center of your other palm. With your fingerpads, suction, lift, and drag the membrane and feel its elasticity. How far does it follow your fingers?

- Chi Siphon

    Point your Chi fingers at the moon, sun, ocean, or your favorite tree. As you inhale, feel your fingers siphoning nature's Chi into your flesh, bones, marrow, and joints. Feel the restorative effects of nature's Chi in your body. When you hug someone you love, feel how you share Chi.

Chi Awareness: Scanning with Your Chi Palms

Your Chi palms are highly intelligent. They see, hear, feel, intuit, and understand. For Chi scanning, your non-dominant hand is often more sensitive, but you may also try scanning with both hands, noticing the differences in awareness each hand perceives.

Go to a wall in a room. Use the Chi palm of your non-dominant hand. Let your hand be relaxed with fingers open and gently extended. Place it a few inches in front of the wallboard. Close your eyes and receive the impressions of temperature, density, and texture of the wall into your palm. Allow these impressions to imprint. Now shake your Chi palm to clear it, and place it a few inches in front of a framed picture on the wall. Close your eyes and scan the picture with your palm. What does the surface of the glass feel like? Can you feel the frame's composition of metal or wood? With your eyes still closed, continue scanning the framed picture with your Chi palm until you feel a noticeable shift in your palm. Most likely you have scanned past the picture and are back on the wall of the room. Notice the difference between the wall and the picture. With your eyes still closed, scan with your Chi palm down the wall until you feel a bend. This is where the wall meets the floor. Now scan the floor with your Chi palm. Do you feel the temperature and texture of carpet or wood or linoleum? Notice the variations in temperatures, textures, and densities among floor, wall, and framed picture.

Now place fabric on the floor: perhaps a white shirt, black pants, and red blanket. Close your eyes and scan each of these with the Chi palm of your nondominant hand. Notice how the different colors and fabrics emit different energies. Do you feel your palm being sucked in, pushed away, levitating?

Practice Chi scanning in nature. Scan a bush, the earth, a tree, a river. Each has a different texture, temperature, density. Each has its own personality.

Practice Chi scanning on yourself. With your Chi palm, scan the bones of your other arm. As you scan across your forearm, feel where space becomes flesh and where flesh covers bone. Scan up and down your arm and notice the differences among the long thick bone of your upper arm (humerus), the two thinner bones of your forearm (ulna and radius), and the smaller bones of your hands.

Use Chi scanning any time when you want to feel something's Chi. In time you will be able to feel textures, temperatures, densities, and even colors and emotions in the body. In time you will be able to feel these in a sculpture, a drawing, a dish you cook, a person you meet. If you wish to influence the flow of Chi, combine Chi scanning with other Chi hand techniques on your creative piece.

An Adventure in Chi

The following explorations introduce you to the Chi of your inner world. They invite you to explore the Chi of people, places, and activities and to influence them with Chi hand techniques within the comfort, safety, and privacy of your own subconscious terrain. They are a preparation for bringing your discoveries with Chi into your adventures in the outer world.

Guided Imagery: Your Inner Garden

 Find a comfortable, inviting place, where you will not be disturbed. Sit or lie in meditation. Close your eyes and feel how comforting the dark is. As your belly rises on the inhalation and falls on the exhalation, breathe naturally and fully into your lungs. Feel your breath leaving and relaxing your body on the exhalation.

Your outer and inner environments surround and infuse you with comfort, safety, and healing Chi. Each breath brings more relaxation, more trust, more surrender.

Soft air enters your nostrils and wends its way through your body. Each breath brings in nurturing air and Chi from the environment. You begin to be aware of fragrances of vegetation riding the soothing currents of pleasantly warm air. You find yourself at the entrance of a beautiful garden.

Look at the wonderful field of energy surrounding this garden. Feel how its Chi nourishes you. Reach out and touch this Chi. What is its texture like? Push into it gently. Feel its response to your touch. Feel how it invites you in.

Now enter into this wondrous garden and explore. Spend a few moments in this place. What plants do you smell? What do you see and hear? Touch the plants and feel their textures. Feel how energizing and refreshing it is to be here. Feel the calm and peace this garden offers.

Then return to waking awareness of your body and its senses. Gently open your eyes and return to the environment around you, supporting you.

Journaling: Your Inner Garden

Describe in words, collage images, or sketches in your journal your experience of the Chi of your inner garden. Where was it? What was it like to inhale its fragrances, hear its sounds, feel its textures? What was it like to be invited into your inner garden, to sense and touch its Chi, and to fully enjoy it?

Guided Imagery: Your Inner Mountain

Again, in your comfortable, inviting place, sit or lie in meditation with your eyes closed. As your belly rises on the inhalation and falls on the exhalation, breathe naturally all the way down into the bottom of your lungs. Notice how each breath brings more relaxation, more trust, more surrender.

Soft air enters your nostrils and wends its way through your body. It leads you back to your delightful inner garden once again.

Wander and explore. You discover a path that calls you, laden with soft plant matter. Is it dry leaves, pine needles, flower petals? The path feels so soft that your feet seem to melt in it, yet the ground beneath is firm and supports your walking forward. As you continue along this path, you find yourself spiraling around and up a mountain. As you climb higher, the soft humus gives way to areas of sharp stones, and you have to be more careful. Your breath is becoming more labored and you can feel the sweat on your skin. The vegetation is also changing, becoming drier, sparser, and pricklier. Boulders and hardy low-hugging shrubs have replaced the garden.

As you continue on the path, you notice storm clouds gathering. The air feels electric. It becomes more of a struggle to move through the chill, thinning, charged air. You feel your body and mind shifting to adjust to the changes.

Spend a few moments in this mountain milieu. Then quickly, easily, return to waking awareness of your body's senses. Gently open your eyes and return to the environment around you, supporting you.

Journaling: Your Inner Mountain

Describe in words, collage images, or sketches in your journal what it felt like to leave the garden and climb the mountain. How was it to leave comfort and nurturance and ascend into challenge and privation? Describe the changes you felt without and within: the sharp stones, the charged air, your labored breathing, the attunement of your senses.

Guided Imagery: The Ominous Abode

Again, in your comfortable, inviting place, sit or lie in meditation. As your belly rises on the inhalation and falls on the exhalation, breathe naturally all the way down into the bottom of your lungs. Let your breath bring you into relaxation. You know the way back. It does not take you long to find your way up the mountain path. The air is thin and electric. The sky has darkened with clouds.

You come across a building and recognize it. This structure is somewhere in your memory. It feels forbidding, maybe even dangerous. What is this place? How is it built? What is its emotion?

You may call on a friend, mentor, or guide to accompany you. Who is it? As this being appears at your side, notice how his or her strengths support you. Notice how your Chi becomes stronger and more confident and how your combined Chi wraps a protective shield around you both.

Reach out and touch the building's Chi field. Notice its temperature and density. Push gently and feel it inviting you to enter. Knowing that your friend is with you and that you may leave at any time, go ahead and enter the forbidding structure. Once inside, what do you see? Feel? How do you react? What do your instincts reveal? What emotions surface?

Suddenly, great shafts of lightning split the air just outside the structure. You see their light. Their sound and force reverberate in the space around and within your body. Fear surges through you. How does your heart respond? How does the rhythm of your breathing change? How does your nervous system react? What is your sensation of the Chi inside your body and around it?

Spend a few moments in this foreboding place. Then quickly, easily, leave. Return to waking awareness of your body's senses. Gently open your eyes and return to the environment around you, supporting you.

Journaling: The Ominous Abode

Describe in your journal through words, collage images, or sketches your friend. Who came? What was it like to be in this being's supportive presence? How did your Chi change?

What was the Chi of the building like when you entered it? What was the Chi of the storm like? How did the dark Chi of the building and the bright Chi of the lightning and their contrast affect you?

Guided Imagery: The Chi of Friendship

Again, in your comfortable, inviting place, sit or lie in meditation. As your belly rises on the inhalation and falls on the exhalation, breathe naturally all the way down into the bottom of your lungs. Let your breath bring you into relaxation. You know the way back. It does not take you long to find your way up the mountain path and with your friend back inside that ominous building.

The atmosphere is oppressive. But you find your shared Chi fills you with will and strength. You use your Chi hand techniques to help yourselves. Perhaps you use the Chi nourisher to pump up your energy and courage. Then you choose the Chi knife to cut through the thick air. Or your Chi drill to tunnel your way out.

You and your friend quickly exit the building and leave its field of ominous Chi. You shake and vibrate your body and feel the grip of fear loosening its hold. The shaking disperses the negative Chi from your body. You brush each other off with the Chi brush. Then you feed fresh Chi to each other with the Chi nourisher. As you turn your back on the forbidding structure, you feel a door closing.

How does it feel to return to the path descending the mountain? Walk down the rocky path with your friend until you feel it shift to soft humus. Your beautiful garden welcomes you back into its embrace. The climate here is clear, bright, and warm.

Inside your body you feel the inner climate and temperature, the hormones and rhythms, changing in response. Feel safety and warmth filling and surrounding your entire being.

You and your friend enjoy the comfort of this place and of your friendship and celebrate by sharing a meal from your garden's harvest. Together you enjoy the nurturance of abundant healthy food Chi.

When you have finished, say good-bye to your friend, as you exit the garden and gently return to waking awareness of your body's senses. Gently open your eyes and return to the environment around you, supporting you.

Journaling: The Chi of Friendship

Describe in your journal through words, collage images, or sketches your experience of combining and using Chi with your friend. What kind of Chi tools did you use to combat the negative Chi of the building? How was it to shake the negative Chi loose from your body? To close the door to negativity behind you? Then to enjoy the nurturing Chi of the meal and the friendship afterward?

Chi Hand Techniques and Creativity

Creativity—painting, gardening, doing massage, dancing, moving with Chi, or whatever form you choose—is an adventure, Chi awareness is a map, and Chi hand techniques are skills for the trail. Your Chi palms are extensions of your heart as they scan and listen. They are channels of your heart's truth as they summon, guide, transmit, and create with Chi.

Preparing: Opening the Portals with Chi Suction

When you are preparing to make art or engage other forms of creative self-expression, use your Chi suction for opening the portals to creativity. For example, perhaps your heart feels closed and disconnected. Use your Chi palms and scan your chest. Find the pulsing beam of energy from your heart chakra. Feel for its portal. What is its circumference? Place your fingerpads on its edges and use Chi suction to pull open the portal. You may feel a little vulnerable, but that is okay. You are on the threshold of creative discovery.

When you are finished with your creative process, you can close the portal by bringing your Chi palm in front of it and creating a seal with your intention. You should find that the door opens and closes more readily now.

Realize you may use your Chi suction to pull open the energy of other chakras to help free the flow of Chi where it is stuck.

Creating

In creative processes there is a circuit of Chi between artist and canvas, masseuse and body, Chi Kung practitioner and environment, chef and meal, gardener and earth.

Creativity manifests in the first stroke in massage or the first dab of paint on fresh canvas. Eventually, muscles of the body or textures on canvas soften and elongate luxuriously. Currents of blood, liquid, and Chi flow. Dark caverns illuminate. Inner winds blow. The whole body—whether a person, a painting, a meal, the earth—breathes.

Body moving in Chi Kung, body being massaged, canvas being painted, garden being planted, meal being prepared are all subconscious fields with layers of colors, textures, sounds, fascia, and fluids. They are vast, deep, expectant, anticipating the creative journey.

Your hands are tools of Chi for creative exploration.

Your Chi palms are satellites for receiving, interpreting, and transmitting Chi. They pump colors, carve muscles, nourish a heart. They blast through and break up stuck, congested areas of Chi. They hold and spiral the Chi ball. They brush away old waste Chi from your body, painting, or plant. They knead and squeeze Chi where it is tight and stilted from over-thinking. They cleanse and energize your drinking water and meal while dining.

Your fingers are rakes of Chi, exploring the deep cavity of the belly in massage, spreading paint on canvas, digging into the earth, washing fresh lettuce. They suction, drag, or pull Chi in body or art. Your fingerpads open the Tan Tiens of your mind, heart, and body or wash with gentle rain of color or texture on canvas or body. Your aligned fingers dig out the weeds of distraction.

The end of your hand is a blade that separates energy, scrapes textures on canvas, cleanses and strokes the thick muscles in massage, slices through the air in Chi Kung movement.

Your index and middle finger form a sword or drill, which spirals Chi into the body. As a quill, they inscribe messages or tattoos on skin or canvas.

Your thumb and index finger form the tiger's mouth, which gently pinches a tendon in the body, rips paper for collage, twists the wrapper in making fresh spring rolls, severs unwanted ties.

Whether your media are paints or clay, massage oil, herbs or plants, or the Chi moving through your body in Chi Kung, let the Chi of your hands mingle with the Chi of your media.

Scanning Chi of Creativity: Alina

Understanding

At different times during your creative process, use your Chi palms for scanning—for hearing, seeing, and sensing your work more deeply. In your garden cradle a plant in the Chi of your palms and listen to its messages. In your studio scan your painting to unveil archetypal symbols. As you move in Chi Kung in your special place, scan nature's currents of Chi. As you massage, open to messages from the layers of the body.

As you scan, notice shifts in temperatures, densities, shapes. Be aware of inner images that form, sounds that echo, emotions that tremble within you. Notice the landscape of creativity with its hills and valleys of energy. Feel its air currents pushing or pulling your hand. Find areas of imbalance repulsing you or areas of vitality inviting you to enter. *As you communicate, let go of the urge to analyze what you are doing and discovering. Surrender to the wisdom of your senses, instincts, and intuition, and spiritual guides.*

Exploring Chi and Creativity IV

Sacred Time and Space

Kaleo's Journal: Door to Creativity

The day begins in nature with the ancient practice of Chi Kung. In Tan Tien breathing I am the fragrance of jasmine, the breath of dense bamboo, the medley of birds. As I stand in Zhan Zhuang meditation, my feet sink softly into Gaia, mother earth.

In my bodywork room, fresh sheets cover my massage table. The air tingles with the fragrance of indoor plants. The singing of the mockingbird playfully echos in the room as the light of the sun streams through the partially open blinds. Under my feet, the bamboo floor feels flexible. Israel Kamakawiwo'ole softens the air with *nā mele o Hawai'i* (the songs of Hawai'i). Images of my ancestors, teachers, and guides peer down from the wall. Icons of Pele, Buddha, Christ, and Mary, along with a Tibetan singing bowl and bottles of massage oil, sit quietly on a table in one corner. In another corner a mound of *pōhaku wela* (hot stones) steeps in hot water, awaiting my hands. Then I hear my client knocking. Ritual opens to shared time and space.

Your exploration with Chi and creative process is sacred. It is your time and place to go within, into your inner body, into the lair of the muse. The muse is the keeper of your dreams and longings, your questions and hunches. She is the midwife ready to assist you in their delivery as painting or poem, as hula or massage, when their gestation reaches readiness. She is the guardian of your joy of fulfillment as your soul's progeny emerge through creativity.

Whether you begin at your desk in a quiet corner of your home or in a spacious studio filled with art materials, whether you engage Chi and creativity eight hours every day or only late at night when everyone else around you is asleep, your process thrives in another dimension. Before you begin, how do you create sacred time and space?

Journaling: Your Ritual

In your journal describe your ritual for creating sacred time and space. Do you set up your easel with a fresh canvas and choose painting media? Do you light incense or sage? Do you brew a fresh cup of coffee at dawn, pour it into your favorite mug, and take it to your writer's desk, where you reread your words that have been incubating on the page all night, ready for a fresh flourish to hone them?

Invite your own images of ritual to emerge. Do you go to a corner in your home or a setting in nature? Do you begin by making tea, offering a prayer, lighting a candle? Do you stretch or bow or move in Chi Kung? Do you sink in guided imagery to summon your muse? You may want to sketch your ritual in your journal.

Chi and Creativity Altar

One way to create sacred space is to make an altar. An altar can be a small portable box to carry with you or it can span an entire wall. Your altar can transform a whole room in your home. It can make the secular sacred and invite your spirit guides to inspire you in the realms of Chi and creativity.

Elise's Journal: Chi and Creativity Altar

In 1988 when Kaleo and I met, our first date was to Tai Chi class. We knew that we had much in common, as we sat knee-to-knee observing the fiery Sifu and his adept students in synchronous movement. Now sunny days find us in the park practicing Chi Kung, accompanied by our Australian shepherd Teekkona, who lies in the shadows, guarding our earthy sanctuary from intruding bugs, bunnies, birds, and, of course, other dogs.

The rain drives us inward. I go to my altar, inspired by a Taoist model laid out like the landscape of the mystical inner body. Quan Yin presides. Next come two candles, Yin for the feminine moon, Yang for the masculine sun. Then the triad: a bowl of ashes from the heavens, a bowl of soil from the earth, and a bowl of brown rice, their creation. Next come five cups, white for metal/lungs, blue for water/kidneys, green for wood/liver, red for fire/heart, yellow for earth/spleen. In each is a healing herb from our garden: rosemary for transforming grief into remembrance; thyme for courage; bamboo for growth; oregano for joy; lavender for tranquility. At the end of the altar are incense burner and matches.

Quan Yin is the crown of the altar; candles are eyes; ashes, earth, and rice are the heart, offerings from the compassionate universe; five cups and herbs make the torso with the organs of the altar; incense is the pelvic Tan Tien; fire is the sacrum and tail.

Indoor Chi Kung has its advantage, as my collage journal and art supplies await nearby. I light incense and candles and thank the ancestors who share their ancient wisdom and the spirits of my parents, who continue to inspire me from the other side. I thank *Ke Akua* for all-pervasive spirit and the mystery of the stillness deep within.

Art and Journaling: Your Chi and Creativity Altar

Describe in your journal how you will construct your altar. How will it inspire you? Will it be the top of a small table or a shelf on the wall of your studio? Will a work of your own art adorn your altar? Some of our maskmaking students create altars from their masks using candles, photos, mementos, even a beloved dog's ashes, or a son's umbilical cord.

Chi and Creativity Altar: Mary

What is important for you to include as part of your altar? Will there be pictures of a presiding deity, your teachers, or guides? Of your creative inspirations: Miyamoto Musashi, Maya Angelou, Israel Kamakawiwoʻole, Frida Kahlo? Will you light candles and burn incense? Will there be gifts from the earth and the heavens?

Now gather materials, invoke your muse, and create your altar.

When your altar feels complete, use your Chi palm to scan it. Listen, feel, observe the Chi of your altar, its shifts as your palm moves, its messages.

Your Personal Place in Nature and Circle of Chi

Let your subconscious mind take you on a journey to your personal place in the natural world, to strengthen your awareness of Chi. You may discover a place you have visited before in waking awareness, or one from your dreams, or one from your imagination. Whatever this place is, become familiar with it during this guided imagery. Then bring it into your body when you practice Chi awareness. Notice how your Chi awareness and earth awareness enhance each other.

On your journey you will discover a circle of personal power and protection, a place in your inner being to strengthen your sense of boundaries, of what in your inner and outer experience you want to let in and what you want to keep out. You may find yourself invoking it frequently in waking awareness.

Guided Imagery: Your Personal Place in Nature and Circle of Chi

Find a comfortable secluded place and sit or lie in meditation. Breathe naturally and fully, inhalation filling your lungs as your belly rises, exhalation emptying your lungs as your belly falls.

Feel the weight of your body sinking into the supportive surface beneath you. Each breath takes you deeper in, deeper down, until you find yourself before an opening in the earth. Easily and confidently, you enter the opening. You find it leads through a cave. You travel through the dimness of the cave, noticing its dankness. Listen to its echos mingling with the echos of your breathing and footsteps. Keep following its walls, until you see a shaft of light in the distance. Move toward the light. It is the portal to your own personal place in nature.

Cross through the portal. Where are you? Have you been here before? With all your senses alert, explore this landscape. What do you see around you? What colors, shapes, movements? What sounds enter your ears from near and far? Do you hear the sounds of winds quarreling in the trees, of water gurgling from a mountain spring, of animal rustlings? What smells come to you on the breeze, stirring remote memories or elusive emotions? Do you smell the scorch of flowing lava, or ginger in the tropical rainforest, or a mother wolf giving birth to pups? What tastes enter your lips on the currents of air to titillate your tongue and arouse saliva?

You feel alive as you explore this natural world. Notice a special power spot that calls to you. It may call you on the wind or through the song of birds. It may summon you to a circle of trees, a clearing in the meadow, a grotto of stone, an ancient majestic waterfall. What makes this spot special? Look at its circle of Chi.

Into the Banyan Portal

Enter this circle and notice how you feel within it. Feel its Chi embracing you. Let your body lean into the Chi. Reach out with your Chi palm and touch the Chi surrounding you. What is its temperature? Its texture? What is the feel of the air over your skin, of the earth beneath your feet? The Chi enters your body as you breathe. It comes in through your nose, eyes, ears, the pores of your skin, the soles of your feet, the crown of your head. This is the Chi of your own power circle. Nothing may enter without your permission. Enjoy its support, its protection.

When you are ready, move outside your circle and back through the landscape to the portal, bringing with you the sensations and discoveries of this place and the awareness that you can return at any time.

Pass back through the portal, through the cave, through the earth opening, and into waking consciousness.

Journaling and Art: Your Personal Place in Nature and Circle of Chi

 In your journal describe your place in nature. What sensory experiences were strongest for you? Describe your circle of Chi and its location. What was it like to feel its power and protection?

Now draw or collage your natural place and your power circle. How do you portray the colors, textures, sounds, smells, and tastes? How do you manifest the Chi within your circle? What Chi hand tools do you use as you create?

Guided Imagery: Boundaries and Your Circle of Chi

Sit or lie in meditation. Breathe naturally and fully, inhalation filling your lungs as your belly rises, exhalation emptying your lungs as your belly falls. Relax and breathe deeply. Each breath invites you deeper within. Now, travel back to that path in nature, through the earth opening, through the cave. Notice the portal at the cave's end. Has it changed? Move through the portal and into your personal place in the natural world. Continue on your way until you return to your circle of Chi and enter it. What is the color of the circle? Feel its Chi surrounding and protecting you. No one may enter this circle without your permission.

Listen. Something is stirring outside your circle. Someone has come to visit, someone unexpected, with negativity toward you. Look at this person's aura. What color, shape, or density does the negativity take? Your circle remains closed, and you firmly tell this presence that it is not welcome and to leave. Notice how your protective circle changes in response to your voice. Notice how you feel as this person leaves.

Now invite someone special to the edge of your circle. This person is a mentor, someone who guides, inspires, and supports your creative endeavors. Who is it? Someone you know? Or someone from history or books who has inspired you? Welcome this person to come forward.

He or she now stands at the edge of your circle. What do you notice about this person's aura, demeanor, appearance? How does he or she offer you support? If it feels right, invite this person inside your circle. Notice what happens when he or she enters. How does your sharing of the space affect the Chi inside the circle? How does it change you within?

When your interaction feels complete, how will you summon this person in the future? For now, the person leaves, moving out beyond the circle and fading into the distance.

Now, leave the circle and return through the portal and back through the cave and the earth opening. Notice your breath. Has it changed? Let your breath bring you back, until you find yourself in the present time and place.

Circle of Chi: Dawn

Journaling: Boundaries and Circle of Chi

Describe in your journal through words, images, or sketches: What person with negativity toward you first came to your circle? Describe this person's aura. How was it to have the protective circle separating you and to send this person away?

Who was the mentor you invited to your circle? What sort of emotional response did you have to his or her presence? What sort of energetic response? What inspiration do you feel inside you now from your connection? How can this person support you in your journey of creative self-discovery?

What aspects of yourself support your life's creative process? And what hinder it? How can this person help you dislodge blocks so your creative Chi flows more freely? How can you nurture your relationship and keep this person's presence strong in your daily life?

Sources of Chi

You have felt the Chi within you and around you and explored its relationship to your creative endeavors.

Acupuncture and acupressure also access the Chi in our bodies for healing, connecting with it at points near the surface of the skin along the twelve organ meridians. Through needles or touch they help to unblock stuck Chi, to drain Chi where there is excess, to tonify Chi where there is deficiency.

Chi also resides in the Eight Extraordinary Vessels in the body, which act as reservoirs that store and release Chi for the rivers of meridians. They help to keep the meridians balanced, not overflowing, not empty. The Extraordinary Vessels are especially influenced by Chi Kung, as their influence is interior, and the exercises in Chi Kung movement can reach deeply into the inner body.

But where does Chi come from?

There are four basic sources of Chi from which our bodies draw: inherited Chi from the ancestors; Chi from what we ingest (food, water, herbs); Chi from the air we breathe; and Chi from our surroundings—heaven, earth, and environment.

Chi awareness practices preserve and utilize inherited Chi. They encourage us to maintain healthy dietary practices that nourish rather than deplete our Chi. They guide us to use our breath to maximize our benefit from the air we breathe. And they help us strengthen the connection between our personal Chi and the Chi that flows to us from the heaven, the earth, and the environment.

Journaling: Sources of Chi

Describe in your journal through words, images, or sketches your relationship to Chi through the following questions.

- **Inherited Chi**

  How is your basic health, your constitution as you entered this world? What are your inherited vulnerabilities and strengths? What legacy of creativity have you inherited? Are your ancestors builders, priestesses, scholars? Are they healers, warriors, teachers? What creative energies seem to be natural and ancient in you?

- **Food Chi**

  How is your diet? How does it hinder or nurture your health? How is your attitude toward food and drink? Is it balanced? Chi awareness is about moderation. Obsessive strictness in relationship to food can be as harmful as overindulgence. How might you shift your attitude to create greater health in your diet?

  What is your diet of creativity? Is it balanced with the rest of your life? Do you manifest your creativity in raising children, nurturing your partnership, caring for your body, mind, and spirit?

  What is it like to do creative process in your kitchen, with all its creative expression through cooking and its memories of shared conversation and meals?

- **Air Chi**

  How are your lungs and your breathing? Do you fully use your lungs' capacity? Do you breathe into the top, bottom, front, and back of your lungs? How is the air you breathe? Do you live in an environment with plenty of fresh air and green vegetation, free of dust, mold, and toxins? Or is the air full of pollutants, which exhaust you physically and mentally?

What is it like to sit and write in your journal in a café filled with the aromas of just brewed coffee and freshly baked cinnamon-apple muffins? Do you feel the creative Chi of movements, sounds, smells? Does it inspire you to create?

- **Chi from the Environment, Earth, and Heaven**

How do you spend time in nature? What landscape is most inviting to you? What are the flora and fauna of this place? What is its Chi like?

We feel the Chi of the earth every second of our lives through gravity. Where on this planet is your connection most powerful? What is this feeling of connectedness like? How do you feel if deprived of this connection? How do you foster this connection when you are away?

What is your perception of the universe beyond the earth? How do you relate to the moon, the sun, the other planets in our solar system, and the stars, the galaxy, the cosmos beyond? What phase of the moon most draws you into its presence? What time of day do you most enjoy the light of the sun? Do you feel a special connection to a planet, a star, or a constellation of stars? We are made of the stuff of stars, and they continue to share with us through the web of Chi.

The universe throbs with tremendous creative and healing energies. Chi breathing reminds us to breathe into our lungs, skin, muscles, and bones to absorb universal Chi. It knows where to go and what to do within our beings to heal, support, and inspire us.

For creative inspiration through guided imagery, do you travel into the depths of the ocean to explore the hidden currents of the subconscious? Or do you fly to the realm of the stars to visit with ancestors and spirit guides? Or do you venture into a cave deep within the belly of the earth to discover her secrets?

Chi Awareness to Stimulate Creativity

Often Chi gets stuck by lack of physical, emotional, psychological, and creative movement. Chi awareness exercises, self-massage, or receiving massage from a practitioner can release energetic blocks to creativity. This inner journey with Chi leads you into regions where emotion, intuition, light, shadow, and inner figures lie in wait.

Kaleo's Journal: Releasing Grief, Freeing Creativity

Tim enters my bodywork room. He moves awkwardly and stiffly. He seems to be very uncomfortable in his body. What's going on with him? What emotions lie stuck within the fascial layers? His neck and shoulders are armored. To protect his heart? Chest and throat muscles appear congested and contracted, pulling his head forward. Shielding him from the pain of intimacy? He wears whitish-gray, and his skin color is pale, the color of the lung element. Is he grieving?

His breath is shallow and short. A high-pitched, nasal voice originates from the top of his throat. What emotions squeeze his vocal cords? His eyes and forehead seem strained. Is he holding back tears? He complains of terrible headaches behind his eyes from temple to temple.

He smiles wanly: He is fifty years old and has a long history of heavy alcohol and drug abuse but has been sober for the past two years. Grandfather and father were alcoholics. Father was a strict disciplinarian and psychologically abusive. As a child Tim suffered ridicule and beatings if he was emotionally expressive and not strong "like a real man." Perfection was a standard. Now, intimacy is very difficult for him. His wife and he both feel misunderstood and distant from each other. A deep chasm of resentment is opening between them.

Gary was Tim's psychotherapist. He was vivacious, sensitive, caring, and intelligent. Three months ago he died tragically in a car accident. Tim is terrified of dealing with the loss of and grief for Gary, his mentor.

Tim lies on my bodywork table. My Chi palms scan his body, then gently brush, vibrate, shake, knife through, and spiral into his Chi body. Light massage opens his neck, shoulders, and ribcage. The message he receives is to trust.

As I hold my Chi palm on his sternum (CV17) to connect with his heart, Tim sighs and his chest relaxes. I whisper, "*Ē Ke Akua. E hoʻokuʻu ʻoe i ka mana. E hoʻola hou i kēia kāne. Ē aloha ē, aloha ē, aloha ē*": I invoke the Divine and feel its presence fill the room.

I whisper: "Tim, feel your breath. Let it be soft. Let it bring you comfort. Feel its texture, its humidity. Notice how it hugs the floor of your nostrils and flows into the passage of your septum then glides into your mind's eye. Notice how it brings soothing comfort to your mind, allowing your brain to relax. Let your brain rest. Now feel your breath flowing into the sockets of your eyes. Feel your eyeballs floating weightless on the sea of your breath. And as you exhale, the tension releases as your eyeballs sink comfortably into their sockets. With each breath, you find yourself going deeper and deeper in.

"Observe how your neck, chest, and shoulder muscles hang heavily. Feel their weight tugging at your bones. Now, feel your breath flowing gently into your ribcage. Notice how it presses into the inner lining of your sternum and ribs. Exhale, release, and let your heart relax. Feel its weight sinking deeper into your body, its weight sinking into the supportive table beneath you. Deeper you sink into a state of stillness. Rest, let your heart rest. Now listen to your heart."

From deep within, Tim hears: "Tim, it's me, Gary. I'm here at your side. You know our friendship is always strong. What would you like to say to me? Tell me how you feel."

Tim gasps. His body quivers. He groans. Tears flow. Deep in the privacy of his inner world, he converses with Gary.

Tim's whole body begins to shake uncontrollably, then releases and softens. What he lets go of feels ancient.

Gary continues: "We did a lot of work together, you and I. You know, you've come a long way since we began four years ago. All the work we've done is within you. I'm a part of you in mind, body, and spirit. We can still talk to each other. You know what you need to do now for healing. The answer is within. It always has been."

Tim weeps tears—liquid Chi. He sighs and groans—sounds of Chi. His body quivers—physical Chi.

When the session is done, Tim's neck, shoulders, and chest are relaxed and open. His heart is free to express itself.

I explain: "Chi awareness, massage, and hypnotherapy can help you release energetic blocks. They inspire creativity. They guide you within to access voices, colors, and forms. You do not need to create; the source does."

I encourage Tim to anchor this experience, to bridge the subconscious with the conscious, to bring it into his daily life through journaling and making an altar. He can continue the relationship with Gary through the language of creativity. I encourage him to share his experiences with his wife and to take walks in nature together to nurture and ground the relationship in the element of earth.

Later, Tim does a series of collages with words and images for Gary about their relationship in the past and in the present. He feels Gary still with him, one of his spirit guides.

Guided Imagery: Chi Awareness to Stimulate Creativity

Lie in a comfortable supine position. Place your Chi palms on your navel. Breathe naturally. Feel your lungs receive your breath as your belly rises; feel them release your breath as your belly falls. Relax and breathe deeply, each breath a wave inviting you deeper and deeper within.

Feel your breath aligned with the breath of earth. Feel the rhythms of your body aligned with the rhythms of nature. In this sanctuary of support and nurturing, feel the womb of Chi surrounding you. Each breath invites you deeper into relaxation and you find yourself floating in a ball of Chi. Notice how the ball changes shape. Notice the substance that embraces you. It is a liquid so ancient, so enduring, so soothing. In comfort and safety, feel the texture and density of the liquid Chi around you. Notice its color. Hear the sounds of its rhythms.

Deeper and deeper you go, until you feel your vital organs moving with your breath. Quietly, bring your attention to your mind, and feel how it gently moves with the flow of your breath. Breath enters into the cranium, and you feel its protective shell surrounding your brain. Feel how the shell breathes, gently expanding and contracting, sutures opening and closing. Feel your brain and spinal cord swaying with breath. Notice the light entering through the third eye and bathing your mind. Feel the embrace of this light.

Then travel down to your heart, and feel your emotions being soothed by the waves of your breath. As the inhalation enters, feel your lungs expanding and massaging your heart. Feel them expanding to press gently into the inner lining of your ribs. Feel the breath bathing and soothing your heart. Feel the embrace of the breath.

Then ride your respiratory diaphragm as it descends on the inhalation, spreading its touch over your internal organs and traveling down to your pelvis. Feel how the depths of your pelvic Tan Tien undulate with the flow of your breath. Feel the rivers of meridians flowing in Yin and Yang balance, their Chi entering your core, filling your core, stored in this sea of Chi deep in your center. Feel the embrace of Chi. Then rest.

Art: Chi Awareness and Your Inner Body

Preparation: Fertile Ground

In our classes we offer a wide variety of supplies, for we have found that an abundance of textures, colors, shapes, and smells inspires creativity (*see* "Materials, Herbs, and Spices for Art" on page 301). So gather your own feast of art supplies. Include a large sheet of white paper and mixed media drawing and/or sculpting materials. What do you choose?

Smudge, dust, and grind the white of the paper with graphite, vine and compressed charcoal, Conté crayons, and chalk pastels. Mold the forms of body and mind with clay. Draw glyphs, paint transparent sheaths, splash or stroke your personal calligraphy with inks. Layer the depths of the ocean or the strata of the earth with acrylic paints. Blend emotions, space, and time with oil pastels and oil bars. Don gloves; add massage oil to the oil bars; then smear, push, shove, and stroke the skin of white paper. Sow this field of white with sand, dirt, and seeds mixed with acrylic medium. Arouse the senses with curry powder, cinnamon, tea leaves, pumpkin, garlic, ginger.

Use healing herbs to work metaphorically. Listen for what your body wants and needs: mullein to clear grief from the lungs; hops to stimulate appetites and desires; oregano for joy; garlic for protection and immunity; horehound to free the voice; comfrey to soothe skin, bones, or spirit; rosemary to enhance memory and ensure fidelity; aloe vera to heal physical or emotional burns or bites; ginger to warm and invigorate; Hawaiian sea salt to purge toxins; flax to clear creative and emotional constipation; lavender for tranquility and purity.

Or, if you are going to sculpt, you might use clay, sticks, earth, bones, jute, hemp, gauze, wire, mesh, raffia, ashes, wigs, skins, scales, newspaper, rags, leather, woven fabric.

Art-making with Chi

Now with your Chi palms, allow your hands to reach for colors and textures in the art supplies. Do not deny yourself. Listen to the intuitive intelligence of your Chi palms. How do your chosen materials feel in your hands? What are their textures, their aromas, their sounds as you prepare to work and play with them?

Art-making: Tomoko

On a large sheet of paper, draw a shape representing your body. Within and around this shape, express your discoveries of the Chi. How thick is the membrane of the Chi aura surrounding you? What are the temperature and density of the liquid in this aura? How do you depict your belly expanding and contracting with Chi and breath? What are the colors and textures of your breath exploring your cranium, massaging your heart and emotions, sinking into the depths of your pelvis?

How do you employ your Chi hand techniques? Scratch, scrape, gather, smooth with your Chi palm. Pump the reds, vibrate the yellows, paw the greens, wave the blues. Spiral with your Chi quill into the caverns. Pull and stretch the sinews of your drawing. Suction stuck areas to extract blockages. Feed wan areas with your Chi nourisher.

Use the art materials and tools at your disposal to assist your Chi palms in their work. Draw, paint, and build with clay, sticks, earth, bones. Sew with hemps, jute, wire. Sculpt with plaster gauze, mesh, raffia.

Use your body to massage with muscle, rip with teeth, caress with skin. Dance on your drawing with your bare feet. Knead the colors and textures with your forearm. Inscribe your own personal glyphs with colored pencil. Heal with lavender, calendula, sage. Get down close and sniff the herbs with your nose.

Observe. How do your emotions shift as your drawing transforms? How do the layers of colors and textures mirror the layers within?

Step back. This drawing is your body. Listen. What is its sound? Inhale and let its sound fill you. Exhale and release the sound. Let its voice take you deeper into your inner journey.

Then rest.

Art-scanning with Chi

When you are ready, look again at your creative piece. Notice how it breathes like your body. Its skin may be thin, sensitive, and vulnerable, or thick and scarred like old armor, or spacious, open, and inviting. It may reveal inner contusions or exude joy and vigor. It may want to wrap your body tightly for protection. It may reveal ambiguity, rapture, loneliness, or deep void. It peels away layers to inner mysteries. Explore it. Let it guide you into your personal mythology.

When you are ready, rub your Chi palms together, then extend them over your drawing and do Chi scanning. Feel the vibrations and textures of thick oil-smeared curves, thin hesitant lines, and nebulous shapes. Feel the temperatures and emotions of aggressive colors, pregnant contours, and curious symbols. Follow the tracks skipping across the skin of your drawing. Just feel and listen.

Art-scanning: LaVonna

Then reach out with your Chi palm and touch your piece. This is your fascia; this is your body. Where does your hand want to go? Wherever it lands, palpate the textures. Press in with your fingertips, then with your fingerpads, then with your palm. Feel how your drawing responds to your touch. Listen. What emotions surface from deep within you?

Then rest.

Art–becoming with Chi

As you stand before your drawing, feel its vital energy. Feel its breath flowing and ebbing. Match the rhythm of your breath with its breath. Listen to the sound of the inhalation cresting, the exhalation receding. Its breath is your breath. Its body is your body.

Become its flesh. Pursue the network of throbbing arteries, delicate capillaries, receding veins. Look for fresh red oxygen-rich blood or bluish blood. Hear the pulse. Is it timid, frenetic, thready, bounding? Look into the heart and its chambers. You may find symbols carved into the walls. What do they reveal?

Enter the matrix of nerves. Feel the impulses firing beneath the surface. How deep do they take you? Are they tense or relaxed, quick or leisurely, expansive or focal? What messages are received and transmitted? Study this map of your nervous system. Where does it lead you?

Ride the rivers of meridians. Feel the Chi spiraling under, around, and through shapes, lines, space. Enter streams and whirl in eddies of energy. Ride them deeper. What currents of the subconscious churn beneath the surface? Drop through a vortex and explore.

Stretch with the fascia, muscles, and interconnective tissues. What memories stir within the layers of flesh? What do the muscular shapes, shining tendons, and sinuous ligaments reveal? Deep inside, where are there wounds and scar tissue? Where are there healing and regeneration?

Descend into the gut with its sacs and long writhing tubes. Listen to its sounds as it ingests, absorbs, and eliminates. Move beyond its blockages of matter and emotions. Feel its determination.

Peer into one of the trillions of cells of your drawing. Track the blueprints of your DNA. Open to the messages from your ancestors. What are their lessons? What do they whisper to you?

Travel into the genitalia. Find where sperm and egg meet. Find the ovum turned embryo, the blood turned placenta, in the womb of your creativity. Look for messages on the pelvic walls, in the underwater caverns of your muse.

Now rest.

Art-becoming: Jessica

Creativity and Ancestral Wisdom

Ancestral sources are creative potential. The environment you move through emerges from ancestral sources: the fires that build mountains, the seeds that birth trees, the animals that first emerged from the seas to populate the land and prepare the way for our ancestors of blood.

Ancestral Origins: Caroline

The ancestors understood the energy pathways through the body. They used the power of energy to overcome or heal, to destroy or create. They used art as a medium of healing and ritual. Your ancestors may be related to you by blood, culture, land, or spirit. Allow your connections to the ancient ones, who shared breath, bones, and body wisdom, to join you as Chi flowing through you in movement and art.

Moving Chi: Ancestral Dance

 Go somewhere you feel safe and comfortable and stand naturally. Feel the climate around you. Is it the warmth of your favorite room? Is it a fresh tradewind carrying fragrances of flowers? Or is it a cozy fog mixed with sunlight?

Feel the heavens above you and the earth below you. The bodies of the ancestors create earth. They lie beneath us and support us.

Close your eyes. As your eyelids meet, surrender to the descent into darkness.

Breathe softly. Invite your breath to fill your belly and caress your pelvic Tan Tien. Feel the inhalation filling the cave of your pelvis. Notice the humidity within. Then feel your breath ascending and filling your lower, then middle, then upper lungs. Notice their dry warm climate. Feel your breath gently pressing into the top of your ribcage, then releasing.

Inhale and feel your pelvic vessel expand. Feel your breath circling the space that guards the womb. Feel it spiraling through your reproductive system and around your kidneys.

Find yourself entering the timeless domain of creation and mystery, of birth and death. Listen to the sounds of creative potential. Then invite the wisdom of the ancestors to move you. Feel your pelvic Tan Tien stirring, your sacrum gently swinging. Feel the sockets of your pelvis gently rotating on the heads of your thigh bones. Feel your pubic bone opening and closing as the passageway of birth.

Your body undulates like the flames of the ancestral fire. Your sacrum sends waves of Chi up your spine and into your inner cranium. Feel the bones in your skull breathing with the rhythm of the waves. Your organs float in warm liquid Chi spreading through your body, infusing all your cells. Feel the balance of fire and water dancing.

Your joints open and close like the winged ones bringing signs from the heavens. Your body, hands, and feet move with awareness along the ancestors' path.

What textures, surges, and voices move through your body? What creative images does your body birth?

Moving Art: Ancestral Messages

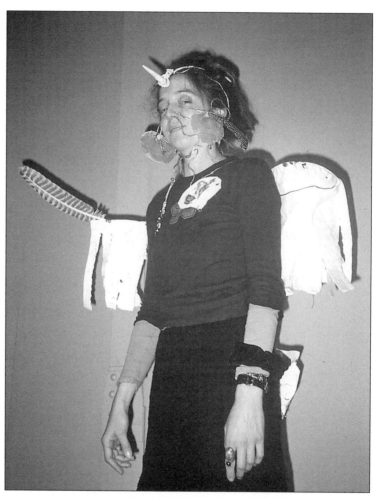 Have an abundant spread of art materials before you. Now take your fresh, anticipating sheet of white paper or raw sculptural materials. Invoke your ancestors.

Receiving Ancestral Messages: Caroline

Give permission to your intuition and your body as you reach for art materials. Embrace the pastel crayon or the oil bar as a channel of visual, textural, and emotional energy. Feel the color. A field of yellow radiates the power of the sun. A thin black line divides or connects. A large swath of red unleashes a primal scream, a bold declaration, or the joy of love.

Track the textures, manipulate shapes, string words of your ancestors. Release the temperatures, sounds, and smells onto the receptive expansiveness of the paper before you. Or take up the sticks, twine, wire, clay, fabric—whatever moves you.

In your hands you hold a life force. What form emerges?

When you feel your creative process is complete, move with the Chi of your art piece. Feel how your creative Chi merges with your dance of life.

Chi Listening and Creativity: Responding to Ancestral Messages

Listening with Chi awareness is another way of freeing creativity. You may listen to the breath of a painting, or the space around your body in dance, or the rhythms of a client's body during massage. There is a dance of energies, an interplay of creative forces.

Now stand before your creation from the previous exploration, "Moving Art: Ancestral Messages" on page 102. Listen to your art piece with your entire body. Listen to its energy, where it is strong or weak, blocked or free, warm or cool, electric or watery.

Now rub your hands together to activate your Chi palms. Close your eyes and extend your Chi palm over your art piece and let it receptively scan from a few inches away. Feel the membrane of energy. Receive its emotions, shapes, temperatures, sounds. Do you hear its ancestral messages?

Ask the ancestors: What more do they want? Do they invite you to reenter the art piece and cut away or apply another layer? Do they want you to use your Chi knife or Chi quill or Chi nourisher? Do they ask for sounds of tearing, scratching, or splashing? Special colors for healing? Special herbs, such as lavender to comfort and caress the surface?

Then go ahead and reenter your art piece. Follow your intuitive body and its ancestral wisdom as you go deeper in creative process.

And when you are finished, rest.

Five Element Alchemy: Foundations

Alchemy in Western psychology is less important as an outdated scientific theory of chemical interactions than as a map of the mind. Alchemists, lacking the tools of modern science, came to understand the chemical interactions of the elements through the projection of their own subconscious processes onto laboratory analyses. If their theories were of little help to science, they offered powerful metaphors for the transpersonal paradigm of the psyche as articulated by C. G. Jung. The processes of burning (fire), dissolving (water), manifesting (earth), evaporating (air), decaying (death), separating (separation of parts), and uniting (harmony of the whole) are none other than the processes by which the mind individuates, Jung's term for psycho-spiritual self-evolution. The alchemists' connection of inner and outer worlds through the elements parallels the Taoist's model for the relationship of the human being to the physical world; moreover, the processes of separation and union generate the dance of Yin and Yang.

Five Element Correspondences

In Traditional Chinese Medicine, alchemical processes are based on the five elements of metal, water, wood, fire, and earth. These elements interact with each other in many ways and depend on each other for balance and harmony.

The five elements are associated with organs and meridians of the body. Metal is connected to lungs (Yin), large intestine (Yang), and nose (sense organ); water to kidneys (Yin), bladder (Yang), and ears; wood to liver (Yin), gall bladder (Yang), and eyes; fire to heart and pericardium (Yin), small intestine and triple warmer (Yang), and tongue; earth to spleen (Yin), stomach (Yang), and mouth.

The elements and their organs and meridians are also associated with a range of emotional challenges and strengths: metal with grief and divine inspiration; water with fear and will-power; wood with anger and growth; fire with withdrawal and joy; earth with worry and centeredness.

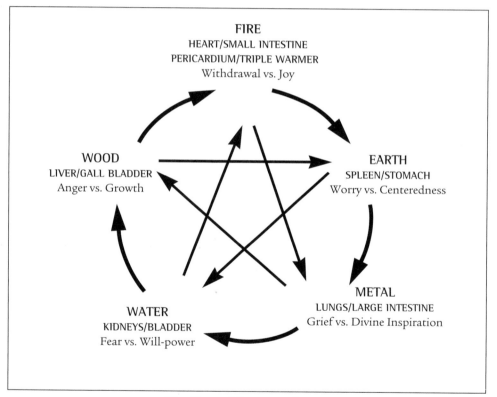

Five Element Correspondences

The elements, organs, and meridians have particular spheres of influence in one's life. Lung and large intestine are about change, letting go, and starting anew. Kidney and bladder are about energy, adaptability, and protection. Liver and gall bladder are about planning, decision making, and action. Heart, small intestine, pericardium, and triple warmer are about interpersonal relationships. Spleen and stomach are about nurturing one's relationship to self and others.

For example: When an acupressurist takes your pulse, the findings of the Yin organs and meridians reveal what is going on with your inner life, whereas the Yang organs and meridians reveal more about your outer life. If there is an imbalance in the lungs, it may mean you are dealing with loss of old patterns and facing new beginnings in your life. If the kidneys show deficiency, it may mean you are exhausted from all the adjustments to the changes. If the liver is excessive, it may reveal that much planning is going into this process. If the heart and pericardium pulses are normal, it may mean that your heart feels fine and your relationships are supportive of you during this time of transition. If the spleen shows excess, it may mean you are spending a lot of time and energy building up your inner resources to cope with the change. The pulses of the Yang organs and meridians would reveal related information, but more directed toward the outer world.

Generative Cycle

Each of these elements is in reciprocal relationship to each other. There is the parent/child relationship, the generative cycle, the cycle around the circle in the direction of the arrows. Refinement of metal liberates water, which nourishes wood, which feeds fire, which makes earth, which generates metal. Conversely, water depends on metal, wood on water, fire on wood, earth on fire, metal on earth.

In the human body, metal manifests through the presence of minerals, such as sodium, potassium, calcium, iron, magnesium, and others. Metal feeds water as sodium and potassium, in balance with other substances, functioning as electrolytes, conductors of electricity. Where metal leads, water follows, maintaining proper balance of fluid within and among the cells of the body. The support of metal in water, of electrolytes in the body's fluids, is essential for life. Disturbances in the electrolyte balance disrupt all the body's functions.

Water's composition in the human body is like the mouth of the river where it meets the sea. Being 0.9 percent sodium chloride (NaCl), the body's cellular fluid saline content is partway between fresh water and the 3+ percent saline content of the ocean.

Water in the body nourishes the metaphorical wood of the body, the structure. The body is about 75 percent water supporting what grows from the fertilized ovum into the structure that moves in the world.

Wood, the body's structure, houses fire, the heat that warms the body to its optimal temperature of approximately 98.6 degrees Fahrenheit. Without fire the body becomes cold, stiff, unable to move. If you have ever experienced hypothermia, you know the necessity of heat, for without it, everything numbs, slows, and ultimately stops, from the brain to the heart, from the muscles and joints to the lungs.

And fire warms earth, the metaphysical and physiological core of the body, the dark, still center, which transforms food taken into the body, releasing minerals (metal) for use by the body.

Balancing Cycle

While the elements are linked in a circle, they also have relationships with the elements across the circle. After the child element comes the grandchild. While the parent/child cycle is the generative cycle, the grandparent/grandchild cycle is the balancing cycle: metal/wood, water/fire, wood/earth, fire/metal, earth/water.

When healthy, the grandparent and grandchild respond to each other in a way that brings greater balance. The grandparent's role is more Yang (directive) in its influence, while the grandchild's role is more Yin (receptive). The grandparent guides the grandchild with intention, while the grandchild influences the grandparent through receptivity.

Cycles of Creativity

Five element alchemy can also be applied to creative process. In terms of the organs, the lungs are the source of inspiration; the kidneys are the keepers of water—the body's fluids and the watery depths of the subconscious mind; the liver is the guardian of action, of conversion of potential into form; the heart is the seat of compassion and creative expression; and the spleen represents the center of the body and the core of the self.

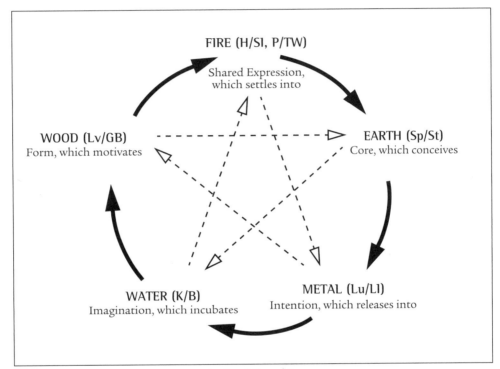

FIRE (H/SI, P/TW)
Shared Expression, which settles into

WOOD (Lv/GB)
Form, which motivates

EARTH (Sp/St)
Core, which conceives

WATER (K/B)
Imagination, which incubates

METAL (Lu/LI)
Intention, which releases into

Cycle of Creativity

In terms of the generative (parent/child) cycle and the elements relative to creativity, metal represents the intention, the idea, the design of creativity, which releases into water, representing the creative sea of the subconscious. Within this sea the intention incubates to grow into creative form, governed by the element wood. Wood motivates the warm and outward moving element fire to share the fruits of creative expression. As fire settles, the process of creative exploration then returns home to center, represented by earth. Then earth, through the union of self (mortal dimension) with Self (immortal dimension), conceives new intention (metal).

As applied to creative process, the balancing (grandparent/grandchild) cycle works in the following ways.

Metal refines the form of wood by redefining its shape and function, as a wooden sculpture requires finer and finer metal tools as its form emerges. Wood influences metal by giving its precision a purpose.

Water directs fire by dousing it, so that it either puts its creative energy into forming new earth or takes a more focused course. Fire influences water by releasing it from inertia to transform from ice to water to vapor. Water reminds fire of its origins deep in the earth (everything comes full cycle), so fire does not think it can burn endlessly on the thrill of connectedness but must take time out to return to the imagination. Conversely, fire reminds water that its imaginings are nothing without connection to the world.

Wood directs earth out of stagnation by the action of its roots. Earth influences wood by grounding and supporting it, so that it may expand and grow with purpose.

Fire directs metal by melting and transforming it. Metal influences fire by giving it a medium for creative expression and reflecting the glow of its passion and power. Fire reminds metal that without passion its intentions are hollow vessels. Metal reminds fire that without intention its passion will fade and burn out.

Earth directs water by shaping its movement. Conversely, water influences earth by softening it so that it opens to new forms, as when moisture is added to clay. Earth guides water's imagination to serve the explorations of self in search of Self. Water gives earth depth of movement in the search.

The Five Elements and Twelve Organ Meridians

The elements correspond to twelve energy pathways or meridians that flow through the body and are governed by the twelve organs. Each organ/meridian is most active during a certain two hour period of the day. See the following chart for a description of the elements in relationship to the organ meridians and their correspondences.

Elements, Meridians, Correspondences

		Metal	Water	Wood	Fire	Earth
Meridian/ Organ	Yin	Lungs	Kidneys	Liver	Heart Pericardium	Spleen
	Yang	Large Intestine	Bladder	Gall Bladder	Small Intestine Triple Warmer	Stomach
Diurnal Cycle	Yin	3–5 a. m.	5–7 p. m.	1–3 a. m.	11 a. m.– 1 p. m. 7–9 p. m.	9-11 a. m.
	Yang	5–7 a. m.	3–5 p. m.	11 p. m.– 1 a. m.	1–3 p. m. 9–11 p. m.	7–9 a. m.
Season		Autumn	Winter	Spring	Summer	Late Summer Season Changes
Color		White or Gray	Blue or Black	Green	Red	Yellow
Climate		Dry	Cold	Windy	Hot	Damp/Humid
Tissue		Skin Body Hair	Bones Head Hair	Tendons Ligaments	Blood Vessels	Muscles
Sense Organ		Nose	Ears Genitalia	Eyes	Tongue	Mouth
Fluid		Mucus	Urine	Tears	Perspiration	Saliva
Emotional Challenge		Grief	Fear	Anger	Withdrawal	Worry
Emotional Strength		Divine Inspiration	Will-power	Growth	Joy	Centeredness
Vocal Sound		Weeping	Groaning	Shouting	Laughing	Singing
Inner Sound		Hsss	Chru	Shhh	Haaa/Eeee	Hooo
Smell		Rotten	Putrid	Rancid	Scorched	Fragrant
Taste		Spicy	Salty	Sour	Bitter	Sweet
Directions		West	North	East	South	Center
Action		Contracts	Descends	Expands	Ascends	Centers

Vessels: Governing (Yang), Conception (Yin)

The Individuality and Interconnectedness of the Elements

The five elements in the circle and the organ/meridian chart appear equal in posture; everything is visually and categorically symmetrical. However, balance among the elements and in their interactions comes from recognizing the unique spirit and scope of each of the elements.

Biochemically, metal comprises a large class of elements in the Periodic Table characterized by being good conductors of heat (fire) and electricity (Chi). In the human body, this can be observed in the nature of the lungs (metal). They govern the flow of Chi (bioelectrical current) in the body by bringing in air and by refining the crude Chi (from food and air) into Chi that can be used by the body. They regulate heat by governing the flow of Chi throughout the body, directly influencing the blood vessels and organ meridians, which, among other functions, maintain the body's warmth.

Water is the most simple, fundamental element, whose presence in the universe is essential to life. When astrobiologists search for signs of life on other planets, they search for it indirectly through signs of the influence of water.

Wood is the organic element, a living being, whose complexity most dramatically exhibits the influence of the other elements: Earth roots it; water sustains it; metal (as minerals) enters it from below; the fire of the sun feeds it from above.

Fire is both empty at the core and at the core of the universe itself. Fire is the "original Chi" of the universe, the impetus of the "big bang" from which the universe as we know it theoretically began.

Earth is gravity acting on matter and sculpting its form. All the elements in potential form reside in earth: metal ready to be shaped; water waiting to emerge; seeds of wood; fire in earth's core.

Five Element Alchemy: Practice

VI

This chapter is about bringing the five elements of metal, water, wood, fire, and earth into your life in a creative and active way through Chi awareness, guided imagery, art, writing, and personal process.

Let the five elements enhance your awareness of Chi flowing through the acu-points. Feel their influences on your organs, senses, and rhythms. Take one element for a period of days and engage its influence in your life. Journey in guided imagery with each element. Meet the spirit and find the animal of each element.

As you live, work, play, and create with each element, be aware of the influences of the other elements meeting, merging, mingling inside of you, nothing in separation, all interlacing in the design that is your life.

The alchemical interaction of the elements in creative process is magical. Feel the spirit of adventure as you journey creatively with and through the five elements.

Acupressure Points

Acupressure is a path in Chi awareness. Explore the Chi pulsing in the caves (Shu) of the acupressure points described for each element. Acu-points have influences that radiate throughout your body. Some are excellent for pain relief, some for relaxation and calming of the mind, some for building energy and immunity, some for relieving physical, energetic, or emotional blockages.

For example, if you have pain in the shoulder joint, congestion in the lungs, or difficulty with stuck grief, Lung 1 (Central Storehouse) is beneficial. Realize that point descriptions included herein are not comprehensive but emphasize the general qualities and creative applications of the points. Be aware that all points on the twelve organ meridians are bilateral. For example, the Lung meridian runs from the shoulder's hollow down the inner arm to the thumb on both the left and the right arms. You can find a point on either or both sides of your body. Because you are using finger pressure and not a needle, point location does not need to be precise. If you are within about one-half inch of a point, your touch affects it.

Locate a point with your index or middle finger, and press in until you connect with the thickness of the flesh beneath the skin. You may also feel the solidity of bone beneath the flesh. Then ease up slowly until you feel like you are reaching just through the layer of skin. Hold this light but connected pressure until you feel the whooshing pulse of Chi (compared to the bounding pulse of arterial blood) moving through the acu-point. Sometimes it takes five seconds for the energy to come in, sometimes a minute or two. Feel the gate opening. Notice how long the pulsing acu-point asks to be held, perhaps just a few seconds, perhaps a minute or more. Notice how your body reacts. Does it calm down, sigh, and relax in comfort as a muscle spasm releases? Does a sense of emotional tension give way to harmony? Or a sense of being exhausted shift to feeling more energized?

Acupressure approached in this gentle way is generally safe and beneficial. However, if you notice any adverse effects, stop.

Acu-points are like good friends to call on. Go to the ones that call to you. Use them as portals to discovery. Be aware of how you respond as you connect with them. Notice shifts in your energy, body, emotions. Notice changes in your relationships with others. Acu-points are powerful tools for enhancing well-being on many levels.

Kaleo asked one of his regular clients after several acupressure massage sessions, "Have you noticed any changes in your relationships with your wife and child?" His client cocked his head in surprise and replied, "Why, yes, there is a lot less tension. There is a lot more openness." Kaleo explained, "Yes, that's because your relationships are mirroring what's happening inside of you."

Metal (Lungs, Large Intestine)

Lung (Yin)

Lu1 — **Central Storehouse**
Portal into the lungs and their emotional terrain. Relieves stuck grief, restores tranquility, brings comfort. Relieves shoulder pain. Benefits the respiratory system. Invites divine inspiration.

Lu7 — **Broken Sequence**
Master point for the Conception Vessel, which influences the creative energies of the seven chakras. Fights colds and flus. Releases repressed emotions.

Lu9 — **Great Abyss**
Source point (balances the Chi in the Lung meridian). Governs and supports the Chi that guides the flow of blood through the vessels.

Large Intestine (Yang)

LI4 — **Joining Valley**
"Tiger's Mouth." Source point (balances the Chi in the Large Intestine meridian). Major pain relief point. Brings calm during stress from external influences. Fights colds and flus.
Avoid during pregnancy.

LI11 — **Crooked Pond**
Stimulates antibody production. Harmonizes blood and Chi. Frees the sinews and joints. Releases stagnation and blockages to creative energies.

LI20 — **Welcome Fragrance**
Cultivates the inner smile. Opens sinuses. Arouses sense of smell.

Living with Metal

During the upcoming days, observe the influence of the element metal in your life. Write your observations and reflections in your journal. Use your awareness to inspire your creative journey. As you work with the element metal, consider the following:

- Organs

  The lungs take in fresh air and extract the oxygen to feed the cells of the body. They take in Chi with the air to transform for use by the body. The large intestine takes fecal material from the small intestine and extracts water to condense feces for elimination. How do your lungs and large intestine feel? Do they take in the new and release the old? Are they congested with grief? Do you do enough exercise so that your lungs and large intestine are cleansed and functioning properly?

- Acu-points

  Hold the Great Abyss of the lungs (Lu9) to help bring balance in relationship to change. Enter the tiger's mouth (Joining Valley/LI4) to alleviate the emotional and physical burdens that saddle your shoulders and neck.

- Color

  How does the color white (or gray or silver) influence your life: in the clothes you wear, in your home or work space?

- Taste

  How do you relate to spicy foods? Notice how spiciness loosens sinus and lung congestion.

- Sense

  How is your sense of smell? Are you sensitive to smells? What is your experience of the associations between aromas and memories?

- Sound

The vocal sound of metal is weeping or sighing; the inner sound is *hsss*. How do your lungs feel when you make the sound of weeping or an inner hissing?

- Tissue

The skin is your third lung. It breathes. How is your skin: color, texture, moisture, temperature? Do you open the pores of your skin through scrubbing away old dead cells? Do you help sweat out old stuck grief through vigorous exercise? Does your skin enjoy being in the temperatures and textures of the air in nature?

- Season

What is your experience of autumn? As the trees let go of their leaves, do you find yourself letting go of things, activities, or emotions that you no longer need in your life?

- Climate

How do you feel in dry climates?

- Mental Aspect

Metal reflects like a mirror. It helps you with clarity. How do you bring structure, focus, and organization into your life?

- Spirit

Consider: The lungs in Traditional Chinese Medicine house the Po, the corporeal soul. This is the part of your spirit that gives life to and depends most directly upon bodily form. It is your animal soul, your soma. The breath is the most immediate link between the Chi that gives life to the body and the Chi that permeates the external universe. When this link is cut, the body dies and the Po descends into the earth.

- Emotional Attribute

What do you want to bring into your life? To let go of? How do you receive divine inspiration in relationship to your life's journey? As you take your last breath, what do you really believe in?

- Emotional and Spiritual Challenge

How do you cope with the changes in your life? Emotions come and go. Notice how you take them in, digest them, and assimilate them. Some you store in your body while others are eliminated. Who and what bring you grief? What do you do when you experience loss? How do you let go? How do you strengthen your belief system?

- Physical and Environmental

Where is grief stored in your body? How does it manifest in your body and in your home? What needs to change in your body or your environment to bring in and let go easily?

- Value

What are your values? What gives you steadfastness and perseverance?

- Strength

How is your day-to-day perseverance, your ability to stay the course, physically, emotionally, spiritually? How are your boundaries and your filters?

- Consideration

How is your breathing? Observe its changes. When does your breathing become tense, rapid, shallow? When is it full, deep, relaxed?

- Cycles

What are you bringing into your life and what are you releasing?

- Time of Day

  What happens to you between 3:00 and 7:00 a. m.?

- Make Lists

  Make a list of the qualities, situations, people, and relationships that bring you clarity and focus. Make another list of those that bring you confusion and lack of focus. Make a third list: Where do you need to strengthen your boundaries, and where do you need to soften them?

- Animal

  What animal do you associate with the element metal?

- Movement

  What movement expresses the nature of metal?

- Landscape

  What natural terrain contains the essence of metal?

- Music

  What musical sound and instrument give voice to metal?

- Chi Hand Techniques

  Notice how the tiger's mouth, Chi knife, and Chi sword express the element metal. What symbol do you draw with your Chi quill to represent metal?

- Creativity

  How are you with design? How can metal support you in your creative expression? Do you need metal to structure and organize your life and strengthen boundaries in relationship to life's demands? Do you need the practice of Chi Kung to open your lungs and bring in fresh Chi and oxygen for overall energy and creative inspiration?

Guided Imagery: Landscape of Metal

Sit or lie in meditation. Feel your breath relax, your body relax, your mind relax. Breathe softly into all the corners of your lungs, bottom, middle, top. Then gently release your breath. Then on an inhalation, ride your breath into an inner landscape. You find yourself in the pristine clarity of mountains lightly dusted with snow. The firmness of cool earth beneath your feet supports you as you explore. A cool dry breeze gently strokes your skin. Smell the fresh, crisp, fine mountain air filling your lungs. Your mind empties of thought and expectation. All your senses are sharp, alert, focused.

You round a bend in the path. Before you lies a crystal clear lake, still as a mirror. Walk up to the edge and peer in. Your true reflection looks back at you. You breathe and it breathes. You smile and it smiles back. Look deeper. Understand that there is hidden wisdom behind this reflection. Then ask it, ask yourself: What do you need to let go of to deepen your life's journey, to open to new possibilities?

As you inhale, your reflection trembles. Feel it reaching into the depths for awareness. What does it bring up to the still surface of the lake to share with you? Discover in your possession a symbol of what you need to release. Feel its weight and texture as you hold it in your hand. Then throw it into the lake. It creates ripples that spread out in circles. What shifts occur in your lungs? Do they sigh or gasp as your reflection quivers and disappears?

Feel the space opening in your being from what you have released. Feel the radiant Chi of the mountains coursing through your body. Inhale divine inspiration—to bring clarity, integrity, focus, and wisdom on your life's journey. Then exhale and return to waking awareness.

Art: Landscape of Metal

Have before you a large sheet of paper, an expansive white, pristine as the snow dusted landscape. You might want to use chalk pastels, their dryness representing the climate of metal. You might want to hear scissors snipping inspiring images from magazines. You might want to paint with metallic pigments or sprinkle with glitter or shape with foil.

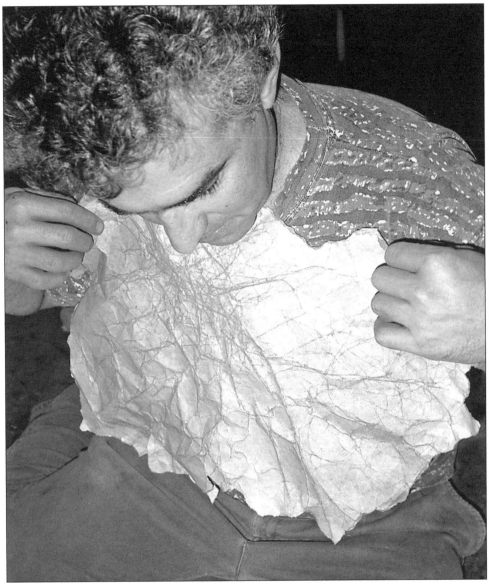

Terrain of the Lungs: Matt

Let your hands breathe the landscape of metal onto the white surface. The paper is your skin, the landscape its features. Layer the lake into the landscape. Layer your reflection into the surface of the lake. Then cast in your symbol of letting go. Do your lungs release a sigh, an emotion? As you inhale divine inspiration, how do you channel it into your landscape? Notice as you create how your breathing changes: its rhythms, its sounds, its depth.

Water (Kidneys, Bladder)

Kidney (Yin)

K1	**Bubbling Well** Drains excessive Chi and siphons earth Chi. Clears the brain and calms the mind.
K3	**Great Ravine** Source point (balances the Chi in the Kidney meridian). Relieves lower back pain, fear, and chronic exhaustion. Tonifies the bones and marrow.
K10	**Yin Valley** Water point of the water meridian. Energetic basin for the watery depths of the subconscious.
K23 K24 K25	**Spirit Seal, Spirit Ruins, Spirit Storehouse** Support the heart by balancing protection and vulnerability, Yang and Yin, fire and water. Help the spirit regain strength, will, and identity in life and leave the body in death.
K27	**Point Mansion** Restores vitality and courage. Strengthens the respiratory system. Ensures that the energy in the meridians flows in the right directions.

Bladder (Yang)

B1	**Eye Brightness** Promotes clarity and vision. Relieves eye problems, sleep disturbances, tension, and headaches.
B42	**Ethereal Soul Gate** Supports and frees the Hun (ethereal soul) to realize life's purpose and balance emotional problems related to the liver (anger, frustration, lack of motivation).
B47	**Will Chamber** Strengthens the Zhi (will) and character (backbone). Supports the will of the ancestors and their gifts. Tonifies kidneys. Relieves low back pain.
B54	**Supporting Middle** Alleviates lower back pain. Relaxes the sinews. Frees and supports the legs and hips for movement.
B64	**Source Bone** Source point (balances the Chi in the Bladder meridian). Receives support and grounding by the earth, which nourishes and strengthens the bones and marrow.

Living with Water

During the upcoming days, observe the influence of the element water in your life. Write your observations and reflections in your journal. Use your awareness to inspire your creative journey. As you work with the element water, consider the following:

- **Organs**

  The kidneys filter the water and waste products from the blood. The adrenal glands sit atop the kidneys, so their health and functioning are closely connected. In Traditional Chinese Medicine the kidneys are the original source of the Yin and Yang energies for the body in the form of the inherited pre-heaven essence (Yin) and the fire (Yang) of the Gate of Life (GV4/Ming Men) housed between them. The urinary bladder stores the water and waste products for elimination. How do your kidneys and bladder feel? Are they healthy or are they overworked, tired, and cramped? Do you drink enough water to flush them properly?

- **Acu-points**

  Feel the flesh and bones of your ancestors living in the earth beneath your feet; then let the nourishing, comforting earth Chi ascend into your body through the Bubbling Well (K1). Let Eye Brightness (B1) bridge your outer eyes and your inner eyes for focus, insight, and clarity in creative expression.

- **Color**

  How do the colors blue and black influence your life: in the clothes you wear, the colors that surround you at home and in the world?

- **Taste**

  How do you like salty foods? Many foods from the sea, such as kelp, seaweed, mussels, lobster, and shrimp, benefit the kidneys.

- Sense

  How are your hearing and your listening? What sources of sound enhance your will-power and what ones drain it? What sounds bring fear into your life and what ones bring support and energy?

- Sound

  The vocal sound of water is groaning; the inner sound is *chru*. How do your kidneys feel when you make the sound of groaning or an inner churring?

- Tissue

  How are your bones and hair? What form of exercise can you do to strengthen the bones and the bone marrow, which produces your blood? In TCM, marrow also comprises your brain and spinal cord. How are your brain and central nervous system? Do neurological messages flow smoothly through your system, or do they get clogged somehow? How do you nurture and support them? Through exercise, meditation, focused mental and physical activity?

- Season

  What is your experience of winter? As the environment goes dormant, do you go more into your inner world, hibernating from intense activity, preferring contemplation and rest? Winter is a time of restoration. Do you give yourself this opportunity?

- Climate

  How do you relate to cold?

- Mental Aspect

  How do imagination, dreamwork, and journeys into subconscious realms help you give shape to your life's journey?

- Spirit

  Consider: The kidneys in TCM house the Zhi, the will. This is the spiritual part of your being that, in alignment with the character of the kidneys, provides the foundation for your will to survive and thrive. The will (Zhi) supports your sense of purpose (Hun, the spirit of the liver). When the Zhi is weakened by fear or exhaustion, there is no strength of will to carry intention into action.

- Emotional Attribute

  How is your will to survive and thrive? Do you have patience? When does fear help you to be cautious, to step back and try to see clearly? How are your reserves of energy to call on when life makes unexpected demands?

- Emotional and Spiritual Challenge

  Who and what cause you fear? What do you dread or avoid? Do you isolate yourself when you are afraid? How can you reach out to others in times of fear?

- Physical and Environmental

  Where is fear stored in your body? How does it manifest? What in your environment brings you fear? What needs to change in your body or your home to make it safe and energized? If you find that little is left of your energy reserves, how can you protect and restore them?

- Value

  How adaptable are you?

- Strength

  How is your patience? How is your stamina?

- Consideration

  How do you feel around water? What bodies of water do you most like to visit? How often do you go there?

- Cycles

  How is your energy level? How does it change with the rhythms of the day, month, seasons?

- Time of Day

  What is your day like between 3:00 and 7:00 p. m.?

- Make Lists

  Make a list of the qualities, situations, people, and relationships that bring you energy and enhance your will-power. Make another list of people or things that undermine your resolve or drain your energy. Make a third list: What actions can you take to enhance what brings you energy and to adjust what drains your energy?

- Animal

  What animal do you associate with the element water?

- Movement

  What movement expresses the nature of water?

- Landscape

  What natural terrain contains the essence of water?

- Music

  What musical sound and instrument give voice to water?

- Chi Hand Techniques

  Notice how the Chi wave, Chi siphon, and Chi rain express the element water. What symbol do you draw with your Chi quill to represent water?

· Creativity

How does creativity shape your inner world, and how does your inner world shape your creative expression? How does the element water support your creativity? Do guided imagery journeys connect you with subconscious images, messages, and guides from your inner terrain? Do you need to spend more time alone, in trancework or the dreamworld?

Guided Imagery: Landscape of Water

Sit or lie in meditation. Feel your breath relax, your body relax, your mind relax. As you sink deeper in relaxation, feel the breath seeping into every corner of your body. Then listen. Listen to the murmurs from the depths of your inner terrain. From deep down water is surging toward the surface. Pristine water bubbles up from a mountain spring to rush as a steep stream down the mountainside, leaping around boulders, gaining volume as waters from other streams and melted snow join it, becoming a wide great river.

Hear in its changing tones and rhythms its patience as it moves through and around obstacles in your inner terrain, its adaptability as it conforms to the shape of the land, its transformations as it changes from ice at the mountain-top to water that runs over the earth to vapor that ascends to the clouds.

As the river widens and slows and opens its mouth to the blue ocean deep in the basin of your pelvis, what sensations do you notice in your lower back? What emotions do you feel as you enter the currents of the unknown? What do you fear as you confront these depths? What does your will-power guide you to explore? How does your imagination challenge you; how does it support you?

Then enter the unknown. Meet the mysteries that await you. What voices do you hear, traveling through the liquid medium of water? Do awesome creatures of the deep tone their ancient secrets? Do ancestors whisper lessons they long to share with you, dreams they hope for you to fulfill? Does the muse sing her inspiration?

Hear the messages echoing with your breath in the caverns of your body. Inhale and feel the awareness from subconscious realms returning with you as you exhale and return to waking awareness.

Art: Landscape of Water

Have before you a large expanse of paper and your chosen media, perhaps watercolor crayons or paints, to express the element water. Then feel the wave of impulses flowing from your brain and spinal cord. Fluid Chi merges with the sea of paper as images bubble up from the watery depths of your subconscious. What realms of water do they inhabit: mountain spring, rushing river, vast ocean, or mighty clouds? What secrets are water and its denizens ready to share through creativity? As shapes and figures emerge, what shifts do you feel in the depths of your body, in the spirit of your will (Zhi), in the marrow of your bones?

Whale Emerging from Watery Depths: Abe

Wood (Liver, Gall Bladder)

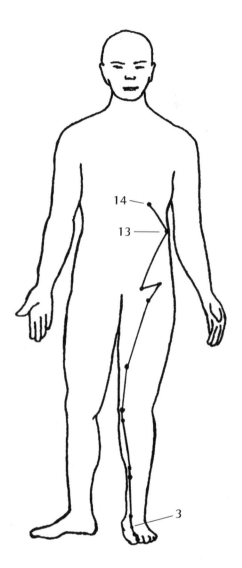

Liver (Yin)

Lv3	**Great Surge** Source point (balances the Chi in the Liver meridian). Promotes the smooth flow of liver Chi, calming the mind and helping to relieve stress, frustration, and repressed anger. Clears toxins and blockages.
Lv13	**Hilltop Gate** Helps move stagnant liver Chi and relieve symptoms of liver invading spleen (nausea, gas, abdominal distention, diarrhea), to balance the wood and earth elements in the body.
Lv14	**Cycle Gate** Promotes harmony between the liver and the stomach (wood and earth). Uplifting for the Hun (ethereal soul).

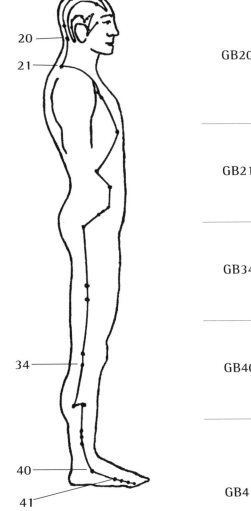

Gall Bladder (Yang)

GB20	**Wind Pond** Alleviates eye problems. Improves visual and mental clarity. Enhances memory and alleviates dizziness. Holding both GB20s until their pulses come into synch helps balance the right and left hemispheres of the brain and harmonize perceptions of one's inner and outer worlds.	
GB21	**Shoulder Well** Helps shoulder and neck problems. Good for lactation in nursing mothers. Supports delivery during childbirth. *Avoid during pregnancy.*	
GB34	**Yang Mound Spring** Major point in the body to soothe and nourish the tendons. Promotes smooth flow of liver Chi. Supports circulation of Chi and blood and relieves pain and swelling in the legs.	
GB40	**Mound Ruins** Source point (balances the Chi in the Gall Bladder meridian). Enhances the GB's mental aspect (sound judgment, decision making, courage in action).	
GB41	**Foot Overlooking Tears** Master point for the Belt Vessel, balancing the upper and lower body, promoting Chi flow through the abdomen, and supporting the cultivation and storage of Chi in the pelvic Tan Tien. Promotes smooth flow of liver Chi. Good for pains that move around the body like the wind in the trees.	

Living with Wood

 During the upcoming days, observe the influence of the element wood in your life. Write your observations and reflections in your journal. Use your awareness to inspire your creative journey. As you work with the element wood, consider the following:

- Organs

    The liver filters the pollutants (oils, fats, metals, drugs) in the blood and breaks them down. The liver also stores many minerals and nutrients for the body. In Traditional Chinese Medicine the liver is the organ most susceptible to disturbance by negative emotions. When it gets upset, its Chi can get stuck, and this can disrupt the flow of Chi in the rest of the body. Because the liver (unlike the lungs, kidneys, heart, and spleen) is not involved in the formation of Chi, but only in the flow and distribution of Chi, it will take what Chi it needs for its own use, ultimately at the expense of the other organs. The gall bladder stores bile that travels through the bile duct into the small intestine to help emulsify the fat products. Stress constricts the bile duct. Laughter and rest keep the bile duct open for bile release. How are your liver and gall bladder? Do they feel flexible, angry, stuck, or tense? How does your diet help or hinder your liver and gall bladder?

- Acu-points

    Let the Great Surge (Lv3) promote the smooth flow of liver Chi for cleansing, energizing, and nourishment; let it transform anger into creative motivation and expression. Hold the Wind Pond (GB20) acu-points as you lie in meditation, and enter into the realm of dreams, intuition, inner mysteries.

- Color

    How do you relate to the color green? Does wearing green motivate you? Do you surround yourself with plants in your living environment?

- Taste

  How do you like sour foods? A bit of lemon or apple cider vinegar in warm water in the morning benefits the liver/gall bladder.

- Sense

  How are your eyes? What do you feed your body, mind, and spirit through your eyes? What images cause you anxiety or enhance motivation?

- Sound

  The vocal sound of wood is shouting; the inner sound is a *shhh*. How does your liver feel when you make the sound of shouting or an inner shushing?

- Tissue

  How are your joints, tendons, and ligaments? How are your nails? Do you have springiness and flexibility in your body? In your life? How do you nourish and support your joints? Wood energy has a strong driving force. Do you exercise with moderation, to bring strength but not injury?

- Season

  How do you feel in the spring? How does spring's surge of creativity and growth affect you? Do you feel more vibrant and energetic? How do you channel your increased energy?

- Climate

  How do you feel in the wind?

- Mental Aspect

  How is your vision mentally and spiritually? How are you with planning, making choices, decision making, and following through?

- **Spirit**

  Consider: The liver in TCM houses the Hun, the ethereal soul. This is the part of your spirit that interacts with the world and gives your life a sense of vision, purpose, and direction. The liver is the organ, and thus the Hun is the spirit, most easily disturbed by negative emotions; such disturbance can easily muddle your clarity in relation to your sense of who you are in the world.

- **Emotional Attribute**

  How is your motivation for growth and self-actualization? Are you energized, like the budding trees in spring? What people, environments, and activities enhance your emotional harmony and your motivation for growth and fulfillment of your life's destiny?

- **Emotional and Spiritual Challenge**

  What makes you angry, frustrated, irritable, stuck? How do you express and release your anger: through vocalization, work, physical activity? What brings you stress and how do you cope with it? Do you take on too many projects and get burned out? Or do you get overwhelmed before you begin? Or do you under-actualize your potential?

- **Physical and Environmental**

  How do you experience stress in your body? In your joints? In your digestion? In tension headaches? How can you transform stress so that the Chi flows smoothly in your body and in your life? How do you make space in your body, your mind, your home, and your environment for new projects?

- **Value**

  How do you actualize your dreams?

- **Strength**

  What drives you to action?

- Consideration

  How can you channel your expansive energy in a way that does not overwhelm others but supports them?

- Cycles

  How can you maintain balance between growth and serenity?

- Time of Day

  Do you sleep between 11:00 p. m. and 3:00 a. m.? If you are awake during this time, on what does your mind focus? Do you find yourself planning and problem solving? What would bring resolution in these areas and restfulness to your sleep?

- Make Lists

  Make a list of the qualities, situations, people, and relationships that encourage growth and expansion of your body, mind, and spirit. Make another list of those that bring you frustration, stress, or discouragement. Make a third list: What actions can you take to enhance the aspects that motivate and support you and reduce those that add frustration and stress?

- Animal

  What animal do you associate with the element wood?

- Movement

  What movement expresses the nature of wood?

- Landscape

  What natural terrain contains the essence of wood?

- Music

  What musical sound and instrument give voice to wood?

- Chi Hand Techniques

   Notice how the Chi brush expresses the element wood. What symbol do you draw with your Chi quill to represent wood?

- Creativity

   How does your creative energy manifest in your work in the world? In your ability to plan and act? How can the element of wood support you in your creative expression? Do you need to feed your urge to grow and learn through taking classes or trying a new project? Do you need to spend more time among the elements in nature to stimulate your vitality, like a tree in spring, burrowing its roots in earth, feeding on minerals and water, soaking up sun? Do you need to plot and plan, or do you need to decide and act?

Guided Imagery: Landscape of Wood

Sit or lie in meditation. Feel your breath relax, your body relax, your mind relax. Your breath is slow and easy. Your eyelids feel heavy but soothing. As your eyeballs rest in their sockets, feel their weight all the way back to the base of your skull at the Wind Ponds (GB20s). Your gaze turns inward. Open your inner eyes and find yourself walking through a forest. You know this forest. You recognize the trees surrounding you. How have the trees worked to create this setting? Do they soften the path with leaves or needles? Do they dapple the sun, scatter the mist, release fragrances? What creatures do they hide in their shadows? Listen to the sound of the wind in the trees, the echo of the secrets of the forest, the hush of your own footsteps.

Then stop and look around. One tree invites you to approach. What kind of tree is it? How long does it live? Is it a fruit tree living only a few decades? Or is it a bristlecone pine sprouted from a seed 5,000 years ago, old as the roots of Traditional Chinese Medicine? What weather has shaped this tree? What creatures has it invited to visit it, eat from it, make homes in it? What does this tree feel like in your body? Feel its core, your core.

How has water given the tree stability to stand and suppleness to flex in the wind? How has metal carved and reshaped it? Feel how the tree loosens the earth with its roots, how it feeds fire with its dead branches.

Its life is a relationship of give and take. This tree knows about vision and purpose: where it is going, where to send its roots and branches, how to scatter its seeds for the future. It has been awaiting your approach. Spend some time with this tree. Harvest its fruit for your own path of growth, expansion, and purpose in the world. Inhale and bring this gift of wisdom inside of you. Exhale and return to waking awareness.

Spirit of Wood: Stephanie

Art: Landscape of Wood

Paper comes from wood and invites you to create on it from your experience of your special tree. Use your chosen media to manifest the tree of your journey. Do you use a brush with a wooden handle? Special herbs, the offspring of wood? Or nuts, seeds, needles, leaves, cones? Do you rub the paper with soft earth, where the tree sends its roots? Or sprinkle it with fiery red and gold glitter? Or nourish it with pools of water? Or slice it with the edge of metal?

What does the life of this tree have to teach you about your own life's purpose? If you were to build a house for yourself in this tree, where you could grow your own roots, sprout your own branches, scatter your own seeds to the world, what would it be like? Go ahead. How do you build it? What materials do you use? Notice the shifts in your body as you build in your drawing.

Fire (Heart, Small Intestine; Pericardium, Triple Warmer)

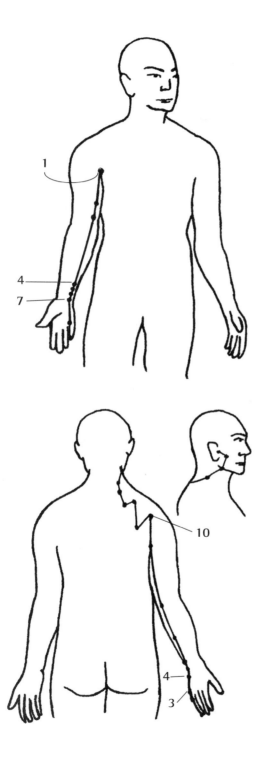

Heart (Yin)

H1	**Supreme Spring** Calms the mind and loosens the chest. Portal for harvesting environmental Chi.
H4	**Spirit Path** For speaking the heart's truth. Helps inspire the spirit of the heart, the Shen, in creative expression.
H7	**Spirit Gate** Source point (balances the Chi in the Heart meridian). Major point for calmness of mind and stillness of spirit. Helps relieve disturbance of the Shen manifesting as anxiety, hysteria, palpitations, insomnia, dream-disturbed sleep, and obsessive thoughts.

Small Intestine (Yang)

SI3	**Back Ravine** Master point for the Governing Vessel, for balancing the seven chakras and supporting one's strength of mind and spirit in relation to the world (backbone). Frees hand, arm, and shoulder for creative expression.
SI4	**Wrist Bone** Source point (balances the Chi in the Small Intestine meridian). Good for wrist, elbow, shoulder, and neck problems.
SI10	**Upper Arm Point** Relieves pain and stiffness in wrist and shoulder. Frees creative blocks.

Pericardium (Yin)

P6	**Inner Gate** Moves stuck blood, Chi, and emotions in chest. Held with TW5/Outer Gate helps communication between inner world and outer reality in guided imagery.
P7	**Great Mound** Source point (balances the Chi in the Pericardium meridian). Enhances intimacy and communication. Calms the mind. Subdues excess emotions in the fire element (hysteria, anxiety, withdrawal, fear of connectedness).
P8	**Labor Palace** Important point for sensing, absorbing, and transmitting Chi. Calms the mind and restores the spirit. Frees the hand for creative expression.

Triple Warmer (Yang)

TW4	**Yang Pond** Source point (balances the Chi in the Triple Warmer meridian). Relaxes sinews. Opens meridian flow in the wrist, arm, shoulder, back of head for creative expression.
TW5	**Outer Gate** Relieves arm, shoulder, and neck pain and headaches. Held with P6/Inner Gate helps communication between inner world and outer reality in guided imagery.
TW15	**Heavenly Crevice** Excellent for shoulder tension and relief from external burdens. Helps open shoulders to express and manifest.
TW17	**Wind Screen** For all ear problems. Clears blockages to hearing, seeing, and speaking.

Living with Fire

During the upcoming days, observe the influence of the element fire in your life. Write your observations and reflections in your journal. Use your awareness to inspire your creative journey. As you work with the element fire, consider the following:

·   **Organs**

In Traditional Chinese Medicine the heart governs the blood. The heart pumps the information and emotions into the river of life throughout your body. The small intestine filters the food products and transports the nutrients into the liver and cardiovascular system to feed the body or moves the waste products into the large intestine for elimination. The pericardium is a firm sac protecting and anchoring the heart, with a cushion of lubricant between them. The triple warmer in TCM is a function that coordinates. It governs the endocrine system and hormones, as well as the distribution, digestion, and elimination processes of the body. How are your organs functioning? Is your circulation good? Does your small intestine successfully filter the information and emotions and feed the heart what it can take? Does the pericardium successfully protect the heart? Are your hormones in balance?

·   **Acu-points**

Hold Spirit Path and Spirit Gate (H4 and H7) to calm and open your heart and speak your truth through creativity. Let Back Ravine (SI3) harmonize your seven chakras for creative expression. Let Inner Gate and Outer Gate (P6 and TW5) balance receiving and giving, inner and outer worlds, gestating and embodying your creativity.

·   **Color**

How do you relate to the color red? What does red mean for you symbolically or metaphorically?

·   **Taste**

How do you like bitter tasting things? Notice how bitter foods stimulate circulation and bring a flush of warmth to the skin.

- Sense

   How is your sense of taste? Does your tongue express your heart's truth?

- Sound

   The vocal sound of fire is laughing; the inner sound is *haaa,* plus *eeee* for the triple warmer. How does your heart feel when you make the sound of laughing or an inner haahing?

- Tissue

   What do you do to benefit your blood vessels? Do you exercise to open them and to strengthen your heart? Do you eat a diet that is moderate in fat? Do you lead a life that is free from excessive stress and tension, which cause chronic vasoconstriction and resultant blood vessel damage?

- Season

   How do you like summer? The day is long and warm. It is easier for circulation to occur in your body. It is easier for the blood warming energy of friendship to flow. Have you ever had a summer love?

- Climate

   How do you feel in the heat?

- Mental Aspect

   How is your intuition?

- Spirit

   Consider: The heart in TCM houses the Shen. The heart is the sovereign organ of the body, and the Shen is the sovereign spirit. As such, the spiritual essences of the other organs are dependent on and governed by the Shen. The Shen animates one's being and provides the spiritual canopy under which the other spirits settle into their functions and their realms. The Shen requires stillness to maintain its residence; thus, if the heart is disturbed, unbalanced, or troubled by excess of emotions, the Shen may become restless and wander, unsettling the whole of one's life. If the heart is in harmony, the Shen shows its health in the glimmer of the eyes.

- Emotional Attribute

  What brings you joy? And how do you share your joy in life? With whom do you share intimacy, trust, and support?

- Emotional and Spiritual Challenge

  Who or what takes your joy away? What makes you feel disconnected and isolated from others?

- Physical and Environmental

  Is your heart happy, heavy, or hiding? How does fire manifest in your body? In your relationships and circle of friends? In your home? The fire of the sun is essential to life, but moderation is essential. Do you protect your skin and eyes from excessive exposure to the sun's radiation? Do you get adequate sunlight to nourish your endocrine system and support hormonal cycles?

- Value

  How much value do you place on your relationships with people?

- Strength

  How do you inspire others?

- Consideration

  What is the relationship between passion and path in your life?

- Cycles

  How do you sustain your heart connectedness through the ups and downs of relationships?

- Time of Day

  What is your day like between 11:00 a. m. and 3:00 p. m. and between 7:00 and 11:00 p. m.?

- Make Lists

  Make a list of the qualities, situations, people, and relationships that bring you joy, intimacy, and community. Make another list of those that cause you to lose trust in others, have heartbreaks, dampen joy, withdraw, and disconnect. Make a third list: What can you do to strengthen healthy connections and to transform dysfunctional ones in your life?

- Animal

  What animal do you associate with the element fire?

- Movement

  What movement expresses the nature of fire?

- Landscape

  What natural terrain contains the essence of fire?

- Music

  What musical sound and instrument give voice to fire?

- Chi Hand Techniques

  Notice how the Chi vibrator and Chi blaster express the element fire. What symbol do you draw with your Chi quill to represent fire?

- Creativity

  How do you express and exhibit your feelings and creativity? How can the element of fire support your creative expression? What people and relationships stimulate your creative energy? Do you need to bring your creativity out into the world and share it with others? Sometimes sharing creative self-expression can feel intimidating but is also necessary in order to bring our personal growth to the next level. Sharing may take various forms. It may be in the form of critique: honest feedback about how others respond to our creative endeavors. If you seek critique, make sure it is shared in a supportive and constructive environment. Sharing may also take the form of process: What insights, dreams, discoveries surface from sharing your creativity journey with others?

Guided Imagery: Landscape of Fire

Sit or lie in meditation. Feel your breath relax, your body relax, your mind relax. Feel your inhalation expanding your lungs and chest and massaging your heart, your exhalation relaxing and releasing. As you breathe in and out, your heart continues its rhythmic steady pumping, working with your lungs to bring fresh oxygen and Chi to every cell in your body. As your breath calms, feel the beating of your heart also calming.

Find yourself walking easily, comfortably, alone down a path in the forest. It is indigo twilight, time for you to find a place to rest. You find a place among the trees, gather wood, and build a fire. Listen to the crackling of fire devouring wood. See the red glow of dancing flames. Smell the luscious smoke.

Fire is about warmth, connectedness, shared journeys. What others do you invite to join you around this fire? As they arrive, one by one, observe your connection with each of them. How does your heart feel as you enjoy the intimacy of their company?

The heart opens onto the tongue: What does your heart need to voice in order to deepen your connectedness? Do you need to express this to one or to all? Notice how your heart shifts in response to your interactions. This is your heart's domain: the realm of intimate sharing. How does sharing feel? How do the others respond? What do you need to do in this moment to complete the circle?

When you feel satisfied with your interactions, how do you take your leave from the circle? Then return through the forest to the rhythm of your heart and the rising and falling of your breath. You are back in waking awareness.

Art: Landscape of Fire

With your abundance of art supplies, invite the energies of those who joined you in the fire circle to join you in creativity. What colors and textures bring the fire to life? How do you evoke the figures around the fire? What materials do you use to show connectedness? Allow your creative Chi to flow through your Chi palms and express your interactions with these others, your sharing of your heart's truth. Notice the sensations and emotions shifting in your heart as you create. As you interact in the world, notice shifts in your relationships with others.

Yasmin's Journal

In our "Chi and Creativity" class, I made this fur hat and cape as creative manifestations of my connectedness and intimacy with my great-grandmother, Valiama. Born in Martinique of East Indian heritage, she settled in Trinidad and Tobago, in the West Indies in the early 1900s. She made a considerable livelihood with her skill as a masseuse during a time when people did not realize the healing powers of massage.

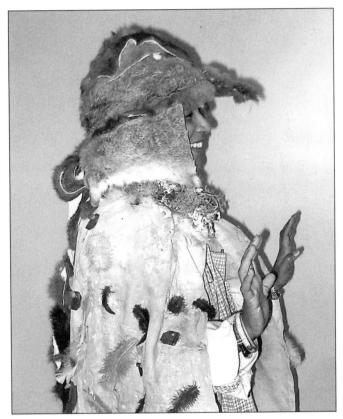

Transmitting Matriarchal Wisdom: Yasmin

I have always felt a deep connection to her because of her revolutionary pioneering spirit. I believe deeply that my connection to her during our guided imagery in class answered questions that I had felt I knew the answers to but could not vocalize.

Earth (Spleen, Stomach)

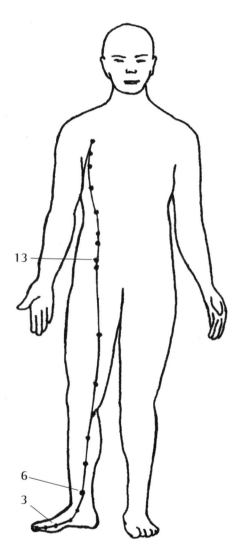

Spleen (Yin)

Sp3	**Supreme White** Source point (balances the Chi in the Spleen meridian). Tonifies spleen, resolves dampness, and relieves gastrointestinal imbalances. Supports spleen's mental function (clarity, concentration, memory, mindfulness).
Sp6	**Three Yin Meeting** Meeting point of Kidney, Liver, and Spleen meridians. Tonifies the spleen and kidney and promotes the smooth flow of liver Chi. Calms the mind and anchors the Yi (thought/intention).
Sp13	**Mansion Abode** Relieves pelvic tension and related emotional constriction. Good for circulation of the blood and Chi in the lower abdomen.

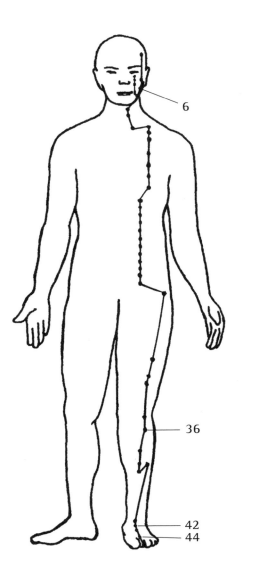

Stomach (Yang)

	Jaw Chariot
St6	Relaxes the masseter muscle, alleviates TMJ tension, and opens the jaw to free the voice.
	Leg Three Miles
St36	Good for tonifying blood and Chi, invigorating the body, and relieving fatigue.
	Surging Yang
St42	Source point (balances the Chi in the Stomach meridian). Tonifies the stomach and spleen. Calms the mind and grounds the spirit. Encourages adaptability and moving forward.
	Inner Courtyard
St44	Relieves pain along the meridian. Helps emotions and energy descend and ground.

Living with Earth

During the upcoming days, observe the influence of the element earth in your life. Write your observations and reflections in your journal. Use your awareness to inspire your creative journey. As you work with the element earth, consider the following:

- Organs

  The spleen is the largest lymph node in the body and filters the by-products of the lymph system. It also filters the blood, puts antibodies into the blood, and makes bile salts for the liver. In Traditional Chinese Medicine it is responsible for the transformation and transportation of food and fluids ingested for use by the body. The stomach is a vat of hydrochloric acid especially designed to digest protein. It also digests new information and, if overloaded, may react adversely with gastric discomfort, ulcers, or acid reflux. In TCM the stomach is said to be responsible for the rotting and ripening of food. Does your stomach digest protein and information well? Does your spleen cleanse your lymphatic and cardiovascular system well and support your physical and emotional immune system? Does it create a healthy environment for the transformation of what you consume?

- Acu-points

  Be invited into Mansion Abode (Sp13) to discover mysteries and emotions that reside in the cavern of the pelvis. Feel the Inner Courtyard (St44) releasing worry and distractedness into the earth and centering and grounding you as you stand in meditation.

- Color

  How does the color yellow influence your life?

- Taste

  How do you like sweet tasting substances? Notice how a bit of sweetness brings comfort.

- Sense

  How sensitive is your mouth? Does what you eat drain, clog, or nurture you?

- Sound

  The vocal sound of earth is singing or humming; the inner sound is *hooo*. How does your spleen feel when you make the sound of singing or an inner hooting?

- Tissue

  How are your muscles and how do you care for them? Are they healthy or weak? Does the exercise you do bring a balance between muscular strength and flexibility?

- Season

  How do you feel during the times when the seasons are changing, during the solstices and equinoxes? How do you feel at harvest time?

- Climate

  How do you feel in humidity and dampness?

- Mental Aspect

  How is your ability to synthesize? How are your memory and concentration?

- Spirit

  Consider: The spleen in TCM houses the Yi, reflection/intention. The Yi is the spirit of thought, the part that contemplates, originates ideas, memorizes information, and creates the mental blueprints by which you construct your life. If the Yi becomes unbalanced, productive cognition may degenerate into pointless worry, distractedness, and obsessive thoughts. Meditation is both the expression of a healthy Yi and a remedy for a disturbed Yi. Chi awareness practice benefits from, as well as helps cultivate, a healthy Yi, as Yi sets the intention, which Chi follows.

- **Emotional Attribute**

  What makes you feel centered and grounded? What promotes your sense of self and of Self? What cycles, routines, and rituals support you? How do you nurture your emotional and spiritual growth? What role does meditation play in your life?

- **Emotional and Spiritual Challenge**

  Who and what bring you worry, anxiety, distress? How do you sabotage yourself?

- **Physical and Environmental**

  Do you like your body? Do you like your home? What needs to change in your body or your home to make it grounded, safe, comfortable? How are your eating habits? What foods nourish you and what foods drain you? What do you need to do to strengthen and maintain your physical, mental, and emotional centers? What nice things do you do for your body, your home, your self, your Self?

- **Value**

  How is your center: your body, your mind, your home, your family?

- **Strength**

  What do you do to nurture yourself? To nurture others?

- **Consideration**

  How introspective are you? How well do you know yourself? Your Self? How does self-awareness affect your relationships?

- **Cycles**

  What do you do to bring balance and harmony through the shifting cycles of your life?

- **Time of Day**

  What is your day like between 7:00 and 11:00 a. m.?

- Make Lists

  Make a list of the qualities, situations, people, and relationships that center, nurture, and ground you. Make another list of those that cause you to get pulled off center, to lose your sense of self. Make a third list: What can you do to bring integration in you, to strenghten the things that support and to transform those that undermine your sense of self?

- Animal

  What animal do you associate with the element earth?

- Movement

  What movement expresses the nature of earth?

- Landscape

  What natural terrain is the quintessence of earth?

- Music

  What musical sound and instrument give voice to earth?

- Chi Hand Techniques

  Notice how the Chi nourisher and kneading Chi express the element earth. What symbol do you draw with your Chi quill to represent earth?

- Creativity

  How can the element earth support you in your creative expression? Do you need to change your ingestion of earth's bounty—food—for greater health and creative energy? Do you need to spend more time in meditation? Or near hearth and home? How do you use your creative gifts to nurture others?

Guided Imagery: Landscape of Earth

 Sit in deep relaxation. As your breath slows and deepens, filling your lungs, then releasing, feel yourself held in the lap of the earth. Close your eyes.

Then open your inner eyes and find yourself sitting on an earthen floor among moist cave walls. Feel the comfort and support of the earth beneath you. The cave echos with your own thoughts, and you settle into meditation.

Feel the rhythms of your body, your breath entering and exiting, heart beating, digestive system processing. Your spleen and stomach transform not only food but thought, and you find your thoughts becoming quiet, harmonious, content.

As you enter the rhythm of centeredness, the fluctuations of stillness, you feel everything contained within this moment, within this earth cave, within the cave of your mind. You taste the sweetness of integration.

As you sit sweetly in meditation, hold this question: What do you need to do to bring integration more fully into your life as you walk on this earth beyond the home of the cave? How can you turn the cave inside-out, to bring the spirit of the cave into the world?

As you prepare to rouse from meditation and leave the cave, carry your question with you as you go. Let it incubate in the cave of your subconscious. You are the cave.

Then return from the cave within to waking awareness.

Art: Landscape of Earth

From your abundance of art supplies, prepare to create the cave. First sit in meditation and reenter the abode of the cave. Let the smell of solitude and the echo of your breath against the cave walls guide you deep within. When you feel centered in this place, allow the earth Chi to move through you and to bring the spirit of the cave into the world of creativity.

Do you smear paper with clay to make an earthen floor? Or do you sculpt a cave big enough to sit in from wire mesh and line its walls with skins of rice paper?

Notice how your body feels as you create. Do your spleen and stomach feel harmonious and contented? How are they digesting your awareness of yourself, your relationship to creativity, your quest for holding your center in the midst of life's fluctuations?

Grounding and Centering in Earth: Ruth

Five Element Alchemy: Integration

Internal Alchemy, Breath Awareness, and Creativity

Alchemy can facilitate a deeper understanding of the relationship of the inner and outer worlds, as the five elements dance in the flow of breath, Chi, and creative images. Travel with the breath into your internal organs related to the five elements. Explore their domains. Meet their guardian animals. Then invite your discoveries to join you in creativity.

Benefits of Tan Tien Breathing for Your Internal Organs

- *Mindful Tan Tien breathing introduces and connects your mind to your internal organs,* which have served you well for so long. When your mind befriends your body, the relationship is reciprocal. The increased gratitude and appreciation for one another help the body and mind cooperate and function more efficiently.

- *In Tan Tien breathing your breath fills all the corners of your lungs and massages and exercises the internal organs,* cleansing them and nurturing them with fresh blood, nutrients, oxygen, and Chi. The five elements and their organs—metal/lungs, water/kidneys, wood/liver, fire/heart, and earth/spleen—function more efficiently and harmoniously.

- *You may also get in touch with emotions that have been repressed in your belly and internal organs.* These may have originated in a past life. They may come from your life in your mother's womb, where you were fed nutrients, oxygen, Chi, ideas, and emotions through the umbilical cord. Their source may be in your birthing or childhood years. In Chi Nei Tsang getting in touch with these hidden emotions is an important part of healing the body, mind, and spirit.

- *The pelvic Tan Tien is a place of creative potential, conception, gestation, and birth.* Many visual and performing artists, bodyworkers, and Chi Kung practitioners have experienced the enormous potential, power, creative instincts, and intelligence residing in the Tan Tien. Through Tan Tien organ breathing, this intelligence is brought into connection with that of the five element organs and their respective spheres of creative influence.

Chi Awareness: Tan Tien Organ Breathing with a Partner

Find a partner to work with and choose a quiet setting. Notice the balance of the five elements in this setting.

As you stand or sit, your partner places his or her palms on your middle back. Your lungs are very large and fill much of your upper and middle back beneath your shoulder blades and ribs. As you engage Tan Tien breathing, feel the inhalation and exhalation filling and emptying your pelvis and entire waist area. Feel your breath as a wave gliding gently within the cylinder of your ribcage, as you inhale into the bottom, then middle, then top of your lungs, then exhale from top, to middle, to bottom. Bring your inhalation into the back of your ribcage as your sternum bone and the top of your ribcage stay relaxed. Feel your lungs expanding and pressing into the inner lining of the back of your ribcage. Feel them pressing into your partner's receptive palms. Then exhale and rest.

Next, your partner places his or her palms on your lower back to cover your kidneys. Each kidney is about half the size of your fist and is mostly protected by the lower ribs of your back. Engage Tan Tien breathing. Bring your inhalation into your lower back. Feel your kidneys expanding and pressing into the inner lining of the lower ribs of your back. Feel them pressing into your partner's receptive palms. Then exhale and relax.

Next your partner places his or her palms on the upper right front and side of your abdomen to cover your liver. The liver is a large dense organ mostly protected by your right front lower ribs. Engage Tan Tien breathing. Bring your inhalation into the right front and side of your ribs. Feel your liver expanding and pressing into the inner lining of your right lower ribs. Feel it pressing into your partner's receptive palms. Then exhale and relax.

Next your partner places his or her palms on the upper left center of your chest to cover your heart. The heart is about the size of your fist. It is protected by a stiff sac, the pericardium, which anchors, lubricates, and cushions it, and by the bony shell of your ribcage and sternum. Engage Tan Tien breathing. Bring your inhalation into the front upper left chest as your sternum bone and the top of your ribcage stay relaxed. Feel your heart expanding and pressing into the inner lining of your upper ribcage and breastbone. Feel it pressing into your partner's receptive palms. Then exhale and relax.

Next your partner places his or her palms on your upper left abdomen to cover your spleen. The spleen is tucked in its cave, behind the stomach, in your upper left abdomen back behind the lower left front ribs. Engage Tan Tien breathing. Bring your inhalation into the lower left front ribs. Feel your spleen expanding and pressing into the inner lining of your lower left ribs. Feel it pressing into your partner's receptive palms. Then exhale and relax.

Now, alone, engage Tan Tien breathing. As you execute one full, relaxed breath, feel your breath and Chi traveling from your lungs throughout your body, filling and feeding your kidneys, liver, heart, and spleen on the inhalation, cleansing and relaxing your organs on the exhalation. Feel breath and Chi circulating from metal to water to wood to fire to earth, one full cycle of breath completing one full alchemical cycle. Go ahead and breathe through the organs for several cycles. Practice slowly, allowing your mind to be aware but relaxed. As your mind relaxes into the cycle, your Chi and your body follow.

As your breath and Chi gently travel into each organ—lungs (metal), kidneys (water), liver (wood), heart (fire), spleen (earth)—feel your breath, Chi, and each organ becoming one.

Observe your organs and their elements feeling more and more in balance, as they are noticed and nurtured. On the next inhalation, feel your breath exuding from the lungs, spreading throughout your entire body, and pressing into the inner lining of your skin, filling the entire organ of your skin as if it were a balloon. Then relax and feel the pores of your skin opening as your exhalation moves through the layers of muscle, fascia, and then skin to cleanse your entire being. Any stagnant Chi, thoughts, or emotions simply release into the earth.

Feel your attention returning back to your quiet setting. Your partner awaits you. When you feel ready, repeat this exercise, trading places with your partner.

Guided Imagery: Your Inner Body and the Five Elements

Sit or lie in meditation. Feel the breath filling your lungs and nourishing you on the inhalation, relaxing you on the exhalation. As you engage Tan Tien breathing, feel your entire waist area and pelvic basin expanding as you inhale, then contracting as you exhale. Allow your breath to take you gently but deeply into the domain of your inner body.

Breath of Metal: Inhale and your breath turns to metal, molten metal coursing through your bloodstream, filling your entire body, then cooling and casting an inner sculpture. What form of metal glistens in your inner body: copper, bronze, iron, gold? Listen. The ringing of a Tibetan bowl gently dissolves the mold of your skin, revealing the inner form. Let this form lead you on a journey deeper into its domain. Then when you are ready to return, exhale and rest.

Breath of Water: Inhale and your breath becomes liquid. Water flows throughout your body, washing and cleansing every joint, socket, aperture, and pore. Water glides over, under, through the fascial layers, ribs, organs, extremities. Observe the temperature of the water, its clarity, its composition. Is it saline or fresh, boiling geyser or cool mountain stream, fresh snow or gentle rain? Let water transport you on a journey deeper into its domain. Then when you are ready to return, exhale and rest.

Breath of Wood: Inhale and your breath turns into wood filling your entire inner body. What presence does it assume? Is it bending willow, spreading banyan, or solid oak? Does it sprout thick roots from your legs and extend its branches through your arms? Feel your skin shimmering like leaves. See the light splattering through the leaves. See the leaves turn red, yellow, brown, then fall gracefully within your body. As they flutter to the ground, allow them to take you on a journey deeper into their domain. Then when you are ready to return, exhale and rest.

Breath of Fire: Inhale and your breath fills your body, pressing the inside of your skin. Feel warmth surging through fascia and muscles, joints and organs, your entire body invigorated. Warmth licks each cell inside the sheath of your skin. Feel the glow of your interconnectedness with everything within and beyond you. Let the warmth of fire transport you on a journey deeper into its domain. Then when you are ready to return, exhale and rest.

Breath of Earth: Inhale and your breath turns your body into earth. Is earth like an avalanche raking or mud sludging through your body? Is it the hot sand of the desert or the moist humus of the rainforest? What is the sensation of earth in your body? On the next exhalation, let go and sink into earth. She now covers you. How does it feel to be fully embraced by Gaia? Feel her draw you down deep on a journey into her domain. Then when you are ready to return, exhale and rest.

Journaling and Art: Your Inner Body and the Five Elements

Write in your journal: What was your experience of the breath and the elements cycling through your body? What images did you experience? Which element felt most powerful? Which landscape felt most like home? What does this affinity tell you about your relationship to the element?

Now do a collage/drawing of yourself as the embodiment of this element. What colors, textures, images do you combine to create your inner experience on the outer landscape of paper?

Guided Imagery: Your Five Element Animal Guardians

Sit or lie in meditation. Feel the breath entering your lungs softly and fully, then releasing. As you engage Tan Tien breathing, feel your breath gently embracing and caressing your internal organs. Feel its caress take you into deep relaxation. Feel the comfort of your internal organs as they are nurtured by your breath. Each breath brings you deeper into a peaceful rest.

Feel the breath filling your lungs. Hear its sound coming and going. Does the Chi of metal fly you high into the heavens or lift you among mountain peaks? Look around. There are traces of life. What animal resides in this landscape? What animal is the guardian of metal coming to inspire you?

Then feel the breath moving into your kidneys. Hear its sound flowing through them. Does the Chi of water take you deep beneath the sea, or flow through you like a stream, or flood you like a desert thunderstorm? What animal is the guardian of water coming to bring you strength of will?

Then feel the breath moving into your liver. Hear its wind resounding there. Does the Chi of wood wander like tracks into the deep forest, or climb high into branches, or burrow into the bole of a tree? What animal is the guardian of wood coming to bring you motivation and purpose?

Then feel the breath moving into your heart. Hear its power surging there. Does the Chi of fire dance like the noon sun on desert sand, or warm you like a campfire, or shock you like a bolt of lightning? What animal is the guardian of fire coming to bring you connectedness, intimacy, and joy in living?

Then feel the breath moving into your spleen. Hear its sound echoing there. Does the Chi of earth take you into your own deep core, or shift in you like a landslide, or shelter you like an earthen cave? What animal is the guardian of earth coming to bring you groundedness and centeredness?

Now within the domain of your inner body, invite the animals of all the organs to join you. Crawl, growl, dance, and howl with them. Slice with them through the undergrowth. Swim with them through the river. Den with them in the log. Leap with them through fire. Burrow with them in earth. Penetrate to the depths of your being—to a place that is both powerful and safe, like a sacred circle in the center of your soul. And when your journey is complete, rest.

Journaling and Art: Five Element Animals

In your journal describe which animals represented the organs and their elements. How did it feel to explore with them? Which animal and its organ and element feel most alive in you today? Invite this animal to express its creativity through art. Does it paint its colors and patterns on your skin? Does it build its shell, nest, or den through sculpture? Does it create with its element on paper? As the animal paints, scratches, and claws the colors, textures, and symbols of your symbiotic discoveries, you are one.

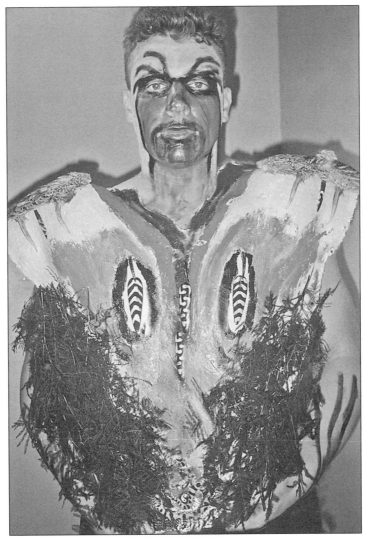

Alchemy with Panther: Paul

Harmonizing the Five Element Emotions

The following exploration helps to clear excessive negative emotions and bring in positive emotions associated with the elements. Through awareness and use of your Chi palms, breath, vibration, sound, and other senses, you can feel the quality of Chi in each of the five element organs and affect it.

Go to a place where the five elements are strong and healthy. An especially supportive setting might be by a stream in the woods on a warm sunny day. You can also create a strong five element ambience indoors by bringing the five elements around you. For example, you might have five small bowls holding representations of the five elements. Or you might sit by a fountain with a healthy plant and a candle.

Chi Awareness: Harmonizing the Five Element Emotions

 In your chosen setting, do the following Chi awareness exercise, exploring the five elements in sequence and resting quietly for a few moments between them to allow the effects to sink in.

Sit comfortably in meditation and engage Tan Tien breathing. Rub your palms together. Feel them filling with Chi. What do you feel: tingling, pulsing, coolness, warmth, vibration? Feel your Chi palms sensitized, aware, ready to explore.

Metal

Use your Chi palms to scan your lungs beneath the ribs of your chest. What do they feel like? Understand that the lungs hold excessive grief. Feel the vibration of this emotion. Connect with it; then on the next inhalation, encourage the vibration to move into your throat. On the next exhalation, let it release through your throat to make the vocal weeping or heavy sighing sound of metal. Your sound is very personal. What is it? Let it release from your lungs through your skin. Let it bring to the surface any negative emotions stuck in the lungs, perhaps old grief or ancient sorrow. Notice the climate of grief, perhaps too dry, empty of tears. Notice the smell, perhaps rotten from grief having lingered too long. Notice the taste, perhaps overpoweringly pungent.

With your Chi palms connect with the vibration of the negative emotions in your lungs. Brush or rake the negative Chi away as you exhale a quiet *hsss* tone. How does it sound? Is it like wind whistling through the feathers of a diving falcon? Or a breeze rustling the dry grass of autumn? Or a gust rounding the corner of a tunnel? Feel it echo in your lungs as the old murky Chi releases. With your Chi palms send the old Chi to the earth. Keep cleansing until your lungs feel clean. Then use your Chi knife to sever your connection to the old Chi.

Then with your Chi palms feel the fresh Chi from the heavens, earth, and environment. Use your Chi nourisher to harvest this Chi and feed it into your lungs. Feel the divine inspiration and clear intention of strong lung Chi. What form does this inspiration take? An archetype, an animal, a force of nature?

When your lungs feel clear and well nourished, check them by making your lungs' vocal sound (sigh). How has the sound changed? How has its vibration in your lungs shifted?

Feel the climate of the lungs, dry, but moistened with a light mist. See the clarity and smell the freshness of the air. Taste the gentle spice. And then rest.

Water

Use your Chi palms to scan your kidneys in your lower back just above your waist and beneath your ribs. What do they feel like? Understand that the kidneys hold excessive fear. Feel the vibration of this emotion. Connect with it; then on the next inhalation, encourage the vibration to move into your throat. On the next exhalation, let it release through your throat to make the vocal groaning sound of water. Your sound is very personal. What is it? Let it release from your kidneys through your skin. Let it bring to the surface any negative emotions stuck in the kidneys, perhaps fear, dread, or exhaustion. Notice the climate of fear, perhaps so cold that nothing moves. Notice the smell, perhaps putrid and rank from fear having pooled too long. Notice the taste, perhaps salty as the cold black sea.

With your Chi palms connect with the vibration of the negative emotions in the kidneys. Brush or rake the negative Chi away as you exhale a quiet *chru* tone. How does it sound? Is it like a river rubbing against its banks in the bottom of a canyon? Or cascading over a rocky precipice? Or waves of a sea licking the shore? Feel it echo in your kidneys as the old brackish Chi releases. With your Chi palms send the old Chi to the earth. Keep cleansing until your kidneys feel clean. Then use your Chi knife to sever your connection to the old Chi.

Then with your Chi palms feel the fresh Chi from the heavens, earth, and environment. Use your Chi nourisher to harvest this Chi and feed it into your kidneys. Feel the strength of will and perseverance of strong kidney Chi. What form does this strong will take? An archetype, an animal, a force of nature?

When your kidneys feel clear and well nourished, check them by making your kidneys' vocal sound (groan). How has the sound changed? How has its vibration in your kidneys shifted?

Feel the climate of the kidneys, cool, but not too cool, warmed by a healthy fire of the Gate of Life. See the clear blue and smell the clean scent of flowing water. Taste the hint of salt. And then rest.

Wood

Use your Chi palms to scan your liver in your right front side tucked behind your lower ribs. What does it feel like? Understand that the liver holds excessive anger. Feel the vibration of this emotion. Connect with it; then on the next inhalation, encourage the vibration to move into your throat. On the next exhalation, let it release through your throat to make the vocal shouting or exasperated sound of wood. Your sound is very personal. What is it? Let it release from your liver through your skin. Let it bring to the surface any negative emotions stuck in the liver, perhaps anger, frustration, irritation, or stress. Notice the climate of anger, perhaps wild raging wind whipping everything into chaos. Notice the smell, perhaps rancid from anger having fermented too long. Notice the taste, perhaps so sour it makes you pucker.

With your Chi palms connect with the vibration of the negative emotions in the liver. Brush or rake the negative Chi away as you exhale a quiet *shhh* tone. How does it sound? Is it the sound of spring wind scraping against tree branches? Or a smooth wooden staff whipping through the air? Feel it echo in your liver as the old sickly Chi releases. With your Chi palms send the old Chi to the earth. Keep cleansing until your liver feels clean. Then use your Chi knife to sever your connection to the old Chi.

Then with your Chi palms feel the fresh Chi from the heavens, earth, and environment. Use your Chi nourisher to harvest this Chi and feed it into your liver. Feel the purposeful growth and motivation of strong liver Chi. What form does this growth take? An archetype, an animal, a force of nature?

When your liver feels clear and well nourished, check it by making your liver's vocal sound (shout). How has the sound changed? How has its vibration in your liver shifted?

Feel the climate of the liver, a light spring breeze that clears and cleans without disturbing. See the fertile green and smell and taste the piquancy of new growth. And then rest.

Fire

Use your Chi palms to scan your heart and its protector, the pericardium, beneath your ribcage in your chest. What do they feel like? Understand that the heart holds excessive isolation. Feel the vibration of this emotion. Connect with it; then on the next inhalation, encourage the vibration to move into your throat. On the next exhalation, let it release through your throat to make the vocal laughing sound of fire. Your sound is very personal. What is it? Let it release from your heart through your skin. Let it bring to the surface any negative emotions stuck in the heart, perhaps isolation, loneliness, hysteria, or intolerance. Notice the climate of isolation, perhaps the stifling heat of confinement. Notice the smell of loneliness, perhaps scorched as the desert noon. Notice the taste, perhaps the bitterness of neglect.

With your Chi palms connect with the vibration of the negative emotions in the heart. Brush or rake the negative Chi away as you exhale a quiet *haaa* tone. How does it sound? Is it like an inner whisper of satisfaction? Or the voice of fire purging dry brush? Or the echo of smoke ascending a chimney? Feel it echo in your heart as the old dull Chi releases. With your Chi palms send the old Chi to the earth. Keep cleansing until your heart and heart protector feel clean. Then use your Chi knife to sever your connection to the old Chi.

Then with your Chi palms feel the fresh Chi from the heavens, earth, and environment. Use your Chi nourisher to harvest this Chi and feed it into your heart and pericardium. Feel the connectedness, enthusiasm, and joy for life of strong heart Chi. What form does this connectedness take? An archetype, an animal, a force of nature?

When your heart and pericardium feel clear and well nourished, check them by making your heart's vocal sound (laugh). How has the sound changed? How has its vibration in your heart shifted?

Feel the climate of the heart, warm, but not too warm, tempered by the fresh cool liquid that balances fire with water. See the vibrant red and smell the smoky aroma. Taste the dash of pepper. And then rest.

Earth

Use your Chi palms to scan your spleen in your left side tucked behind your lower ribs. What does it feel like? Understand that the spleen holds excessive worry. Feel the vibration of this emotion. Connect with it; then on the next inhalation, encourage the vibration to move into your throat. On the next exhalation, let it release through your throat to make the vocal singing or humming sound of earth. Your sound is very personal. What is it? Let it release from your spleen through your skin. Let it bring to the surface any negative emotions stuck in the spleen, perhaps obsessive worry, excessive sympathy, or a feeling of being ungrounded and off center. Notice the climate of worry, perhaps a thick sluggish humidity. Notice the smell of worry, perhaps the heavy perfume of overripe fruit. Notice the taste, perhaps sickeningly sweet.

With your Chi palms connect with the vibration of the negative emotions in the spleen. Brush or rake the negative Chi away as you exhale a quiet *hooo* tone. How does it sound? Is it like the hooting of a great horned owl? Or the "whoa" that slows a horse? Or the snoring of a bear in its cave? Feel it echo in your spleen as old grungy Chi releases. With your Chi palms send the old Chi to the earth. Keep cleansing until your spleen feels clean. Then use your Chi knife to sever your connection to the old Chi.

Then with your Chi palms feel the fresh Chi from the heavens, earth, and environment. Use your Chi nourisher to harvest this Chi and feed it into your spleen. Feel the centeredness, groundedness, and nourishment of strong spleen Chi. What form does this centeredness take? An archetype, an animal, a force of nature?

When your spleen feels clear and well nourished, check it by making your spleen's vocal sound (hum). How has the sound changed? How has its vibration in your spleen shifted?

Feel the climate of the earth, a pleasingly tropical humidity perfused with light tradewinds. See the rich golden earth hues and smell the fragrant air. Taste the juicy ripe fruit. And then rest.

Completion

When you have finished, sweep your arms out and up overhead to gather Chi. Feel the temperature and vibration of this Chi from the heavens. Then feed this Chi with your Chi palms into your crown. As it enters your crown, feel how it diffuses to permeate your brain. Feel it descending the inner walls of the energy cylinder at your body's core.

As your Chi palms move down your face and reach the level of your third eye, connect with the inner vibration of the triple warmer sound, *eeee*. Make this quiet inner sound, *eeee,* and move its vibration down the front of your face and torso with your Chi palms. Feel its vibration resonating through the triple warmer, and release it from your body through your hands into the earth. And then rest.

Journaling and Art: Harmonizing the Five Element Emotions

 Write in your journal: What emotions and sensations did you find in each organ, and what sounds did you hear and make? How did they shift?

Then from your abundance of drawing supplies, create your experience.

How do you embody your senses and emotions? What color is the vibration of your lungs? How do you dust your paper with the dry climate of metal? How dense is fear? What do you use to add the smell of brine? What does a sour taste look like? What color is anger? What is the shape of laughter, the texture of *haaa*? How do you center your drawing? What path does old grungy Chi make as it releases into the earth? What is the stroke of gathering Chi and the rhythm of its descent through your core? What shifts in your body occur as senses and emotions surface in your drawing?

What Chi hand techniques do you use? For metal does your Chi knife cut through old stuck grief or your tiger's mouth rip it out? For water do you sprinkle your drawing with the patter of rain or caress it with your Chi wave? For wood does your Chi brush sweep away old clogged repressed anger, then your Chi nourisher encourage new growth? For fire does your Chi vibrator brighten dull, lifeless areas of your drawing, or does your Chi quill etch symbols on the walls of your heart? For earth does your Chi paw knead and coax into movement what is constricted from excessive thinking, or does your Chi nourisher feed and reinvigorate a tired, drained region of your drawing? How does your body change with the work of your hands in your drawing?

You may want to use healing herbs and special media in your drawing to support symbolically the cleansing and nourishing of each element, organ, and associated emotions. For the lungs use horehound to open congested passages, curry or peppermint to add spice, comfrey as a salve to apply to the skin of your drawing, glitter to add metallic brilliance. For the kidneys use borage or kelp to restore exhausted adrenal glands, seaweed for fertile growth in the rich ocean of your drawing, a bone for etching symbols, massage oil to create waves. For the liver use bamboo shoot to detoxify, lemon grass to revitalize, a twig for drawing, fertile dirt to sow seeds of new growth. For the heart use cinnamon to stimulate circulation, rose petals for intimacy, a touch of chili pepper for a bitter taste, fire to scorch paper. For the spleen use ginger to relieve excessive dampness, hops for stimulating a healthy appetite, raisins for sweetness, dirt to ground and center, fragrant flower petals to spread a field of rich yellows and golds. Notice, as you apply herbs and materials to your drawing, how does your body respond?

Alchemy and Personal Identity

You may find yourself connecting strongly with some elements and feeling more distance from others. We have all of the elements in us in different balances. Just as one person has more luminous skin than the next, another larger bones, another looser tendons and ligaments, another more elastic blood vessels, another bulkier muscles, so each person will have a different balance of the elements in his or her personality and constitution. This is not about "typing" yourself according to the elements, but witnessing the alchemical process of your life according to their interwoven influences.

- **You and Metal**

Perhaps a dominant element for you is metal. Metal is stable and enduring. It is precise, sharp, definite, unequivocal. The mind of metal is as keen as the edge of a blade. Metal represents clarity about what you perceive, think, and do. It manifests in your life as organization, neatness, strong opinions, a well-defined value system, and intolerance for that which is wishy-washy, sloppy, or ill-defined. But an overly rigid inner structure can create alienation. The negative emotion associated with metal is grief. This can be excessive grief that comes from loss or from having severed association with others and with your own softer, more pliable inner core. The positive inner experience of metal is divine inspiration manifesting as faith in self, in your higher spiritual source, in the meaning of your life's journey. If the influence of metal can turn like a mirror to reflect your own true nature rather than wield an iron cage of unrealistic values and expectations, then it can reveal the whisper of the divine voice that echos within.

- **You and Water**

Or perhaps you feel a strong influence of water. Water is supple on the outside, adapting to various geographical and climatic conditions, forming springs, lakes, rivers, ponds, seas, changing from ice to liquid to vapor as temperatures rise. Yet its essential quality never changes. It is always itself at the core basic H_2O. Although it is adaptable, it persists over time. Its strength is in its patience and flexibility. Water is creative in its ability to adjust to changing circumstances. Its strength is by nature gentle, but combined with other forces, such as wind or precipitous landscape, water can have formidable power. Just witness the Grand Canyon of the Colorado River. The negative emotion associated with water is fear, the positive will-power. Water experiences confinement by earth, yet its strength over time asserts its will to survive and transcend, as it washes away the river banks or carves deep gorges in rock. If water is strong in you, you may find a vulnerability to stagnation, like a frozen landscape, but also a deep reserve of will that helps to overcome inertia. You may find a strong attraction to the inner journey and the realms of the imagination, for water's time is winter, a time of hibernation for the world of nature, a time of introspection and incubation of creative ideas for the world of the psyche.

- **You and Wood**

Or perhaps you feel a strong influence of wood. Wood is assertive, active, moving, like the spring sapling climbing toward the sun. Wood is stubborn, dominant, unwavering, like the big old oak on the hill. It takes a strong stance, has definite opinions. The negative emotion associated with wood is anger; the positive emotion is growth. Wood is intolerant of that which gets in its way. It pushes aside earth with its roots, and its branches spar with other branches as it struggles upward. Wood is going somewhere, doing something, manifesting in the world, so if wood is a dominant element in you, you probably have a strong vision of the future and a strong motivation to convert that vision into action. Wood seeks new depths and new vistas; it longs for adventure and new experiences. Is freedom more important to you than predictability, adventure more important than comfort?

- **You and Fire**

Or perhaps you feel a strong influence of fire. Fire is the element of the heart, the passion of human connectedness. Is intimacy top priority on your list, not only in being paired with another, but also in your relationships at work and play? Do you seek a career that feeds the flames of your longing to connect with others? In your free time do you love to share the joy of play? Fire is an element with drama, with a flare, not at all afraid to express itself. Are you an eager and sensitive communicator? The negative emotion associated with fire is withdrawal, the positive joy. Does your joy in life come from intimacy with others, and does isolation leave you empty as a fire with nothing left to burn?

- **You and Earth**

Or perhaps you feel a strong influence of earth. Earth is warm, moist, nurturing, holding everything in its lap. It is quiet, mostly Yin in nature, friendly, bountiful, and caring. If you have a strong earth element, you like bringing others together, reflecting the archetype of the earth mother. The negative emotion associated with earth is worry, the positive centeredness, groundedness. A strong earth element might make you prone to worry about that which is within your sphere of influence. But earth is the home, the center, where all things and all beings return. The earth influence is like gravity drawing people together, not so much with the charisma of fire, but with the comfort and security of home. As earth harbors all beings, so a strong earth element makes you a good mediator. Earth is accepting of self and others.

Journaling and Art: You and the Five Elements

In your journal describe which element or elements you most strongly identify with and in what times and circumstances. Which do you feel are lacking in you? How does your particular relationship to the five elements support you? Where do you need to cultivate more balance, dialogue, and integration among them? Realize that the influence of one element suggests the secondary influence of the others. How do all the elements come together beneath the surface, representing the eternal alchemical cycle of change?

Then go to your abundance of drawing supplies. You may want to include the metal blade of your favorite knife, water from a sacred spring, a stick from your totem tree, candles from your altar, earth from a quiet cave.

When you are ready, how do you begin? What elements do you use in your opening ritual? Do you light a candle, ring a Tibetan bowl, or dip your fingers in sacred water?

As you stand in your creative space, feel the vessel of your body. Chi and breath enter; mind expands. Breath releases; mind lets go. Along with your breath, colors, sounds, images, and space come and go. As breath explores your inner being, what element does it find? Metal, water, wood, fire, earth? What form does it take? Go deeper still. How many layers does breath discover? As breath touches your center, your core, what dominant element resides there? What sensations do you feel? What emotions does the element bring? What strengths and vulnerabilities accompany it? How do you feel toward this element? Does it burden you and delight you, disappoint you and encourage you? How can you embrace both the shadow and the light of this element?

When you are ready, let this element flow through you into art.

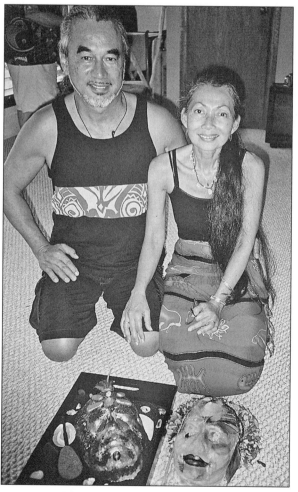

Fire and Water: Dane and Pam

Five Element Dialogue

The influence of the five elements is not just about each individually but about all in relationship. One way to look at the elements in your life is to consider a relationship between two and note how they are linked in the generating or in the balancing cycle. Of course, underlying this dialogue between two elements is the influence of the other three.

Journaling and Art: Dialogue of Two Elements

 ### Your Life's Patterns and Two Elements

The dance between what two elements has been most prominent in your life? When you look at your life's path, what partnership of forces has most strongly shaped it?

For example, fire and earth are parent and child in the generative cycle. Earth makes you a nurturing person whose priority is community. You like bringing people together and creating a warm and comfortable place for gatherings. But you do not stay home waiting for people to come to you. The influence of fire moves you out into the world, where you make connections with people and invite them into your community. Your fire element is quiet and your earth element is warm, like the embers in the hearth at the center of the home.

Or perhaps the relationship is across the circle in the balancing cycle, for example, fire and water: Fire inspires you to spend time in community and connect with people, while water moves you to take time alone and to connect with yourself and others deeply. You find that a balance between these two elements is core to your well-being.

Whatever elements you identify, consider how the dance of elements has affected the shaping of your life. How does your awareness of alchemy affect your understanding of your life's journey?

Then take out mixed media drawing supplies and paper. Express creatively the dance of the two elements.

Your Current Issue and Two Elements

Consider an issue that concerns you at this time in your life. The dance between what two elements is most prominent?

For instance, perhaps you are planning a career move. You have been doing a lot of creative inner work around this and have been incubating both your discontent with where you are and your desire to change. This part of the process is dominated by the element water. As your decision emerges, you begin taking steps, like getting training and doing volunteer work, to prepare you for your move. This part is dominated by the element wood.

Whatever your issue and the elements you identify, observe how the elements are interacting. How does your awareness of alchemy affect your understanding of your issue?

Then take out mixed media drawing supplies and paper. Express creatively the dance of the two elements.

Earth and Fire: Shari

Five Element Interaction

Each element manifests its influence in one's life in its own way. And as one exerts its influence, it affects the others. The following diagram presents the elements in action and their spheres of influence.

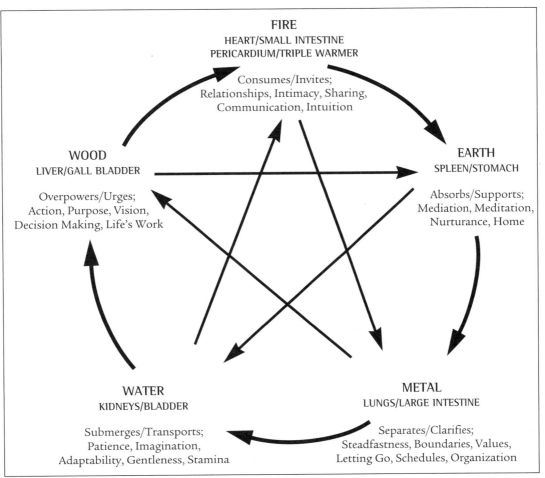

FIRE
HEART/SMALL INTESTINE
PERICARDIUM/TRIPLE WARMER

Consumes/Invites;
Relationships, Intimacy, Sharing,
Communication, Intuition

WOOD
LIVER/GALL BLADDER

Overpowers/Urges;
Action, Purpose, Vision,
Decision Making, Life's Work

EARTH
SPLEEN/STOMACH

Absorbs/Supports;
Mediation, Meditation,
Nurturance, Home

WATER
KIDNEYS/BLADDER

Submerges/Transports;
Patience, Imagination,
Adaptability, Gentleness, Stamina

METAL
LUNGS/LARGE INTESTINE

Separates/Clarifies;
Steadfastness, Boundaries, Values,
Letting Go, Schedules, Organization

Five Element Interaction

Now that you have spent time living with each of the elements, consider how their interwoven patterns of influence manifest in your own life. Select an important issue you are working on in your life right now. It may be the same issue as in the above exercise "Journaling and Art: Dialogue of Two Elements" on page 173. Perhaps it is making a job change, beginning a new relationship, starting a new practice, moving from your current residence. Consider the five elements and how they affect your process.

Example: Alchemical Transition

Jim is a forty-five-year-old college professor thinking about making a career change. He is tired of teaching college English, even though he loves literature and finds working one-on-one with students inspiring. He hates being up in front of a lecture hall. He'd much rather be working with a promising young poet on refining technique or sitting up late writing scholarly articles. But his tenured position is hard to quit. He lives in a lovely small city that he does not want to leave. And his current girlfriend of two years likes him in his niche.

- Earth

Jim finds himself up late at night, no longer writing, but staring into the hearth fire worrying. If he leaves, he loses so much. If he stays, he will never find his true path. But what is that? His inconsolable worry begins to affect his rhythms. He begins eating irregular meals and sleeping irregular hours. His girlfriend leaves him because she says he is "no longer present in the relationship."

- Metal

He begins to try to clarify his dilemma. He reads books on "work with passion" and "earning less and living more." He begins making lists of expenditures, skills, interests, what he likes about himself, and what he wants to change.

- Water

He explores his inner terrain through hypnotherapy. He joins a men's group that's theme is "creative expressions of your personal myths," and he writes a play portraying the figures of his inner life.

- Wood

He makes a decision to become a psychotherapist and enrolls in a master's degree program at an alternative university across the country. He packs up his books and moves.

· Fire

He discovers his heart connection to others and ultimately uses his English skills to guide clients in their therapeutic journeys, with individuals through creative writing, and with groups through dramatic portrayal of the archetypes of their collective mythologies.

Journaling: Your Five Element Interaction

 What is your chosen issue? Refer to your responses to the questions about living with each of the elements (*see* Chapter VI, "Five Element Alchemy: Practice" on page 113), as you consider each element individually and how it influences you and your issue:

· How does your relationship with each element help or hinder you?

· What element's influence do you need more of in your process?

· What element's influence do you need to transform?

· How does each element affect the next along the generative cycle?

· How does each element affect the other across the balancing cycle?

Go into the metal element to look for the strength and endurance to weather this. What in your value system or in your spiritual inspiration can you draw on for support? What do you need to bring into your life? To let go of? How can metal help you bring clarity and discernment? To whom or what can you reach out for steadfast support?

Go into the water element. Listen to the deep current of your inner body, the voices of your subconscious mind. How can you find the patience and adaptability to weather this? Which qualities of water can help you? Do you need to spend time at the ocean? To whom or what can you reach out for help in confronting your fears and strengthening your will-power?

Go into the wood element. How are you growing as a person through this process? Can you accept your frustration and use it to motivate you? How can wood help you make plans and decisions? What options can you create to carry them out? To whom or what can you reach out for encouragement as you move forward and make changes?

Go into the fire element. What do you feel? How can you express these feelings? Which qualities of fire can help you? What brings you joy through this process? To whom or what can you reach out for intimacy, trust, and love?

Go into the earth element. What in your body, your home, your life is throwing you off balance, making you feel ungrounded and worried? How can earth help you? How can you nurture yourself and your core? What form of meditation can you do to bring stillness and clarity? To whom or what can you reach out for nurturing and caring?

Art: Five Element Interaction

Then prepare to do art in response to your five element work with the selected issue. Before you begin, consider:

- What media do you want to use for creative expression?

- What elements are involved in the preparation, tools, and materials for your creativity?

- What senses do they stimulate?

- What parts of your body are engaged in the creative work?

- What Chi hand tools deepen your work with the elements through art?

Now set your intention to free all the elements within you to move through you in creative expression. As you create, feel the precision of metal as it guides your hand to create detail. Feel the fluidity and adaptability of water as it surfaces from the depths of your imagination and alters its course to bring together intention and action as they meet in creative form. Feel the expansiveness of wood encouraging you to reach in all directions as you move into action. Feel the passion and joy of fire as you create. Feel fire stirring in you as desire to share your creation with others. Feel the centeredness of earth as you consider your creative piece. Feel the receptivity of earth as you allow the hand of the creative form to reach back toward you, to penetrate your core, art and artist transforming together through creative dialogue.

How did you feel before you began? How are you changing? Who are you now?

Feline Alchemy: Annalisa

Five Element Medicine Wheel

The five elements can help you understand yourself, your issues, your relationships, your life's process. They are allies whispering secrets to you for deeper understanding. They are archetypes manifesting within and around you.

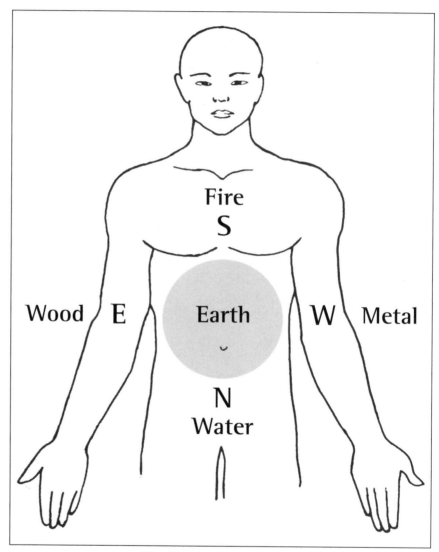

Five Element Medicine Wheel

A Medicine Wheel is a life circle. The Five Element Medicine Wheel is a model you can use to guide you on further journeys. It is based on the Traditional Chinese Medicine model of the elements in relationship to the four directions:

west/metal, north/water, east/wood, south/fire, and center/earth. This arrangement with south at the top is also the map to access the organs and their elements in your body. If the diagram is the abdomen of your body facing outward, center/earth is the domain of the spleen and stomach; west/metal is at the left side of your abdomen, associated with the lungs; north/water is at the bottom, the relative location of the kidneys and bladder; east/wood is on the right side of your abdomen, where the liver and gall bladder reside; south/fire is at the top, the realm of the heart and heart protector (pericardium).

Guided Imagery: Journey from the Center to the Four Directions

You begin at and return to the center, the earth, the core, in a setting that feels powerful and safe. With this awareness, sit or lie in meditation.

Earth: The Center

Engage Tan Tien breathing. Inhaling, feel your breath filling your center. Feel your girth and pelvis expanding with the inhalation, releasing with the exhalation. Feel your stomach and spleen nurtured with Chi.

You find yourself on a path that you know will lead you to a special, personally powerful area of earth, like the sacred circle of a special dream. What is this place?

As you walk, feel your inner eyes gently closing. Let your feet guide you. Listen to the earth with the soles of your feet. Let the earth speak to you and guide you on the path until you come to an area that calls you to be still: the center of the center. Sit down and open your inner eyes.

Where do you find yourself? Take in your environment with all your senses. What do you feel physically, emotionally, intuitively? What message awaits you in the center of your being? What form does it take? Who delivers it?

Thank this place for supporting, empowering, and centering you as you begin your next journey.

Journey to the Realm of Metal

Engage Tan Tien breathing. Inhaling, feel your breath filling your center. Feel your girth and pelvis expanding with the inhalation, releasing with the exhalation. Now feel your lungs filling with Chi.

You start from your earth place and head west, into the terrain of metal. What is this landscape of metal like? What structures and landforms do you find? What smells, temperatures, and textures ride the air? What is the light like in this land of the setting sun? What message reflects back to you from the domain of metal in your torso's left side? What form does it take? Who delivers it?

When you are ready, return along the path to your earth place in the center.

Journey to the Realm of Water

Engage Tan Tien breathing. Inhaling, feel your breath filling your center. Feel your girth and pelvis expanding with the inhalation, releasing with the exhalation. Now feel your kidneys and bladder revitalizing with Chi.

You start from your earth place and head north into the domain of water. How does water make its power and presence felt in this landscape? What sounds do you hear? What is the light like in this land of the summer sun, and how does water affect the light of this place? What secrets does the water hold? What message awaits you in the depths of your torso? What form does it take? Who delivers it?

When you are ready, return along the path to your earth place in the center.

Journey to the Realm of Wood

Engage Tan Tien breathing. Inhaling, feel your breath filling your center. Feel your girth and pelvis expanding with the inhalation, releasing with the exhalation. Now feel your liver cleansing with Chi.

You start from your earth place and head east. You are entering the domain of wood. How does wood dominate this landscape? What movement is happening here? How does wood filter the light in the land of the rising sun? How do you lose and find your path through this terrain? What message awaits you in the right side of your torso? What form does it take? Who delivers it?

When you are ready, return along the path to your earth place in the center.

Journey to the Realm of Fire

Engage Tan Tien breathing. Inhaling, feel your breath filling your center. Feel your girth and pelvis expanding with the inhalation, releasing with the exhalation. Now feel your heart pulsing with Chi.

You start from your earth place and head south. You are entering the realm of fire. What is the light like in the land of abundant sun? How does fire dominate this landscape? Feel the excitement of fire, its drama, its daring. Feel the tingle of heat on your skin. Feel the awe of warmth in your heart urging you to speak. What message emerges? What form does it take? Who delivers it to you?

When you are ready, return along the path to your earth place in the center.

Journaling and Art: Five Element Medicine Wheel

 What was your experience of the earth center and the landscape of each of the four elements? Where did you feel at home, where did you feel strange, and where would you like to spend more time? What messages did you receive?

Now from your abundant art supplies, create your experience of the center and each of the landscapes in the Five Element Medicine Wheel. You can combine these in one drawing or make five separate ones. You may be inspired by your muse to join them together like a hub with spokes, layer them on top of each other like a book of maps, or shape them into a mandala.

Five Element Mandala: J. L. S.

Art: Alchemical Vessel

The Five Element Medicine Wheel represents the dialogue between your inner world and the world of your external experience. The five elements are always in interaction, as is the Chi inside your body and the Chi of the universe beyond.

Now take a container to represent your body. Let the inside of this container represent the realm of your body, mind, and spirit. Let the outside represent your interface with the world.

Cut, shape, add to, or delete from your container until it creates the feeling of your body in this moment.

Then using paint, adornments, and collage, dialogue with the inside and the outside of the container at the same time. Notice how the inner being relates directly with the outer being. Which of the five elements appear and how? What does your vessel show you about how your inner realm and your outer world interface?

Alchemical Vessel: Jamie

VIII

Chi and Meditation

Chi awareness applied to meditation is about quieting your outer being and listening to your inner being to discover its rich and dynamic universe. The deeper in you go, the stronger your experience of interconnectedness with the Chi of the heavens, earth, and environment.

Meditation postures emphasize awareness of the flow of Chi in the body. For beginning breath awareness or for depth of surrender during guided imagery, lying meditation may be most beneficial (*see* "Lying Meditation: Exploring Tan Tien Breathing" on page 47). In this chapter you will learn a widespread practice in Chi meditation called Zhan Zhuang, which means to stand like a tree, a stake, or a staff. If there are times when sitting meditation is preferable to standing, you can apply many of the principles of Zhan Zhuang to your sitting meditation posture (*see* "Sitting Meditation with Zhan Zhuang Awareness" on page 192).

Zhan Zhuang Meditation

Zhan Zhuang meditation cultivates strength, alignment, and wisdom. It means finding balance between Yang and Yin: strength and vulnerability, masculine and feminine, work and play, technique and discovery. Feel yourself like a tree, reaching skyward but grounded, expansive but centered, vital but quietly aware.

Bring your journal with you to each session of Zhan Zhuang, and write or sketch your observations and inner discoveries. Notice the subtleties: the difference between an ache that can be melted with breath awareness and one that requires adjustment or medical attention, between old familiar patterns of imbalance and true balance within the scope of your body's natural capacity (for example, for most of us, one foot is larger than the other, one hand stronger than the other).

You can begin by doing Zhan Zhuang five minutes a day and build up by adding five minutes each week to your daily practice until you can stand comfortably for thirty minutes. As you practice, notice where you feel fatigue on the one hand, or restlessness on the other, the two primary hindrances of standing meditation. Remember to "hang loose" and never go into pain; adjust your practice to accommodate your body. At times during Zhan Zhuang, as the Chi moves through your body, you may find yourself belching, passing gas, perspiring, trembling, laughing, or becoming tearful, restless, nauseous, or dizzy, so sit down and take a break if you need to! Zhan Zhuang is not about competition with yourself or anyone else. It is about Chi awareness, about self-awareness.

Zhan Zhuang Meditation: Posture and Alignment

1   Stand in meditative awareness. Feel your entire body comfortable and aligned. Feel your breath comfortably entering and exiting, each breath long, slow, and deep. Your breath is relaxed, your body relaxed, your mind relaxed.

2   Let your waist area and the basin of your pelvis expand on the inhalation and contract on the exhalation, as your breath softly but fully enters the lower, then middle, then upper lobes of your lungs. Allow it to seep into every corner of your lungs on the inhalation and release on the exhalation. You are engaged in Tan Tien breathing.

3   Let your mind travel to the bottoms of your feet. The Chi will follow your mind. Feel each foot spreading on the ground. The foot is precious. It is where your body sinks into the body of the earth.

4   Let your body rock back and forth, side to side, circle one way then the other, undulations diminishing until you find your center. Find the place of balance on the nine points of the bottom of each foot: the pads of the five toes, the two balls, the mid outer arch, and the center of the heel.

5   Allow your ankles to relax and feel your lower leg bones stacked over the bones of your feet. Feel your knees relaxed, the thigh bones balanced on the shin bones. Feel your hips relaxed, the heads of the thigh bones fitting in the sockets of the pelvis. As your leg bones stack and balance, let the weight of your flesh descend, and feel how these bones settle comfortably and snugly in alignment. Let your pelvis gently rock back and forth, side to side, circle one way then the other, undulations diminishing until you find that place where your pelvis is supported by your legs in comfort, balance, and stability.

6   Feel your pelvis centered over your legs—the wings of your pelvis spreading away from each other, the sitting bones dropping down toward the earth, the "V" of the sacrum also sinking downward. Let the groins remain so soft that, if you put your fingertips there, they feel like they are being swallowed into the soft hollows of your groin creases. Let your perineum, that soft spot at the base of your torso between anus and genitals, be soft, supple, arcing gently upward, then releasing, in rhythm with your breath.

7   Feel the spine stacking vertebra by vertebra over the sacrum—the five lumbar vertebrae of the lower back, the twelve thoracic vertebrae of the middle back, the seven cervical vertebrae of the neck, with the disks like porous sponges between them. Feel how your ribs extend from your spinal column and wrap around to the front of your torso to attach to the sternum bone and form your ribcage. Let your spinal column with its ribcage gently rock back and forth, side to side, circle one way then the other, undulations diminishing until you find that place where you feel your spinal column and ribcage comfortably balanced and stable over your pelvis. You may find yourself shifting your pelvis, knees, and ankles into more comfortable alignment.

8   By softening your chest and the fronts of your shoulders, allow the lower ribs to draw down toward the belly in front, so that your breast bone points like an arrow toward the navel. Feel your ribcage floating, centered, and balanced over your pelvis.

Kaleo in Zhan Zhuang, Big Island of Hawai'i

9   Feel the indentation at the front of each shoulder, between the upper arm and chest muscles, the delto-pectoral groove or shoulder's hollow (Lung 1). It is the place between the upper ribs and the shoulder joint where, if you press your fingers in, they begin to disappear. This is the groin of the upper body. Feel this place melt and your armpit open. Imagine a small pearl nestling in each armpit.

10 As you find yourself gently swaying with the rhythm of your breathing and connecting deeply with your center, feel the ball and socket joints of your shoulders aligning with the ball and socket joints of your hips.

11 Feel your shoulder blades (scapulae) drawing downward, as your arms hang lightly from your shoulders. Your arms may rotate softly inward, so that your palms face backward, or your palms may face your sides. Feel the joints of your fingers opening toward the earth. Let your hands be graceful and relaxed. Let the weight of your flesh hang from your bones and sink toward the earth.

12 Feel the back of your neck lengthen. Without pinching the back of your neck, let your head rock back and forth, side to side, circle gently one way then the other, until you find the place of relaxed balance and stability between your throat and your cervical vertebrae, that place where your head feels most comfortably supported by your neck. Now as you inhale, feel the space opening between the top cervical vertebra, the atlas, and the occiput, while maintaining softness in your chest.

13 Feel the tip of your tongue nestled behind your upper teeth against the roof of your mouth. Feel the muscles of your face and the sides and back of your skull soften. As you inhale, feel your skull lifting toward the heavens. Feel and hold the extension of your spine as you exhale, and let the weight of the flesh of your skull hang and sink toward the earth.

14 Bring your awareness to the crown of your head, that place where the fontanel of the infant remains soft and open for the first few months of life until the sutures of the skull begin to close. Breathe and feel the warth of your breath softening that place, inviting the sutures to open again. Feel the crown of your head pulsing.

15 Now let your eyes stare straight ahead of you, seeking their own level, in soft focus, looking at nothing, but seeing everything, like a tiger hunting. To achieve soft focus, let your eyeballs rest softly in the wells of their sockets. Notice how your peripheral gaze widens as the tunnel vision of pinpoint focus gives way to the broad horizon of soft focus. Or you may gently close your eyes, turning your gaze inward.

16 Now let your entire body surrender to this position. If you feel any areas of tension, observe if your position is balanced and aligned and make any adjustments needed. Then on the inhalation bring your breath into the area of holding and on the exhalation release it. Feel your muscles and joints supple, soft, and relaxed.

17 Feel how your bones are stacked from your feet to your head in a very comfortable, stable, grounded way. Feel how the weight of your flesh hangs from your bones and sinks toward the earth.

18 Inhale and receive the Chi beneath you from the earth, above you from the heavens, and around you from the environment. Let each breath take you deeper, into the core of your being. Exhale and dissolve like the wind into intimate oneness with the universe that supports you.

Sitting Meditation with Zhan Zhuang Awareness

There may be times after a long day on your feet when you prefer sitting to standing meditation. Many of the principles and guidelines of Zhan Zhuang standing meditation can be applied to sitting meditation.

Sit on a chair near its edge. Sit erect, keeping the natural concave curve in your lower (lumbar) spine. If your feet do not reach the floor, place a folded blanket or pillow beneath them for support and anchoring. Align your joints to create ninety degree angles at the ankles, knees, and hips. Hang your hands at your sides, cup them in your lap, or place them on your knees. Lengthen the back of your neck so your head balances easily and lightly and your crown opens. Let your eyes be gently closed or gaze softly at the earth before you.

Engage Tan Tien breathing. Let your body rock on your chair, back and forth, side to side, circle one way then the other, undulations diminishing until you find your center. Feel yourself connecting with the earth beneath you through the soles of your feet and perineum, with the heavens above you through your crown, and with the environment around you through all your senses.

Journaling: Your Experience of Zhan Zhuang

 After your practice of Zhan Zhuang, record in your journal: duration of your sessions (avoid competition with yourself, just observe); reactions to internal and external influences and fluctuations; body/mind/spirit discoveries.

What was your body's habitual alignment prior to the practice of Zhan Zhuang? How is your alignment changing as a result of your practice? Where in your body do you feel difficulty during Zhan Zhuang meditation? How have you been adjusting to accommodate your body's vulnerabilities and to cultivate its strengths?

Zhan Zhuang Body Collage: Savita

Art: Your Body in Zhan Zhuang

 Before practicing Zhan Zhuang, feel your inner body. Is it vibrant or dark, contracted or expansive? Now choose a color, of pencil, ink marker, or pastel, that describes your inner body. Lie on a large sheet of paper, and have a partner trace a partial (for example, ribcage or pelvis) or complete outline of your body with this color. Then, using magazine images, collage within the outline of your body the colors, shapes, intuitions, and words of how you feel inside your body.

Put the drawing aside. Then practice Zhan Zhuang and observe your inner body. Feel how it shifts. When you are ready, choose a color that describes your body. Lie on a large sheet of paper, and have a partner trace a partial or complete outline of your body with this color. Then, using magazine images, collage the colors, shapes, intuitions, and words of how you feel inside your body as a result of Zhan Zhuang.

Place the two drawings side by side and compare them. What shifts in your inner body do they reveal? How is Zhan Zhuang affecting you?

Strength and Surrender

Zhan Zhuang builds balance, strength, inner stillness, and stamina. It helps you center and ground with the earth and open to heaven. It cultivates internal and external harmony.

Zhan Zhuang Meditation: Strength and Surrender

Stand (or sit) in Zhan Zhuang meditation. Close your eyes and align your body. Find your center and focus your attention. Your breath becomes a cycle of Yang and Yin, inhalation and exhalation. Inhaling, draw the Chi up from the earth; exhaling, give it back, releasing tension along with breath back into the earth. On the inhalation receive strength and on the exhalation surrender effort in a cycle of Yang and Yin.

Is there an image, feeling, or presence that you associate with strength? With surrender? Let each manifestation of strength, then of surrender, grow stronger and more tangible as your meditation deepens. Let each come and go, one flowing into the other in a gentle dance.

Journaling, Art, and Story: Strength and Surrender

 In your journal make a list of your attributes, roles, and life's experiences that reflect your quality of strength. Then make a list of those that reflect your quality of surrender.

Compare the two lists. Are there ways in which they overlap? How do strength and surrender manifest separately at different times, and how do they depend upon each other? How do they dance like the archetypal properties of Yang and Yin?

During Zhan Zhuang, how do you experience strength and surrender? What do you feel in your body? What images emerge? Do Yang and Yin feel balanced, and if not, how can you use the breath to balance strength and surrender?

Create a collage/drawing or mask-sculpture that shows how strength and surrender overlap, manifest separately, or connect in the Yin and Yang of the breath.

Write a story or poem depicting the dance of strength and surrender through a persona. Does Yang evolve into Yin or Yin into Yang? Is their relationship circular or linear, static or dynamic, negotiable or absolute?

When you are finished, consider your relationship to the persona. What does he or she have to teach you? How can you wear the lessons in your life?

SAMURAI
by Elise

Three hundred years ago
watching the sun advance upon the sea:
a man with sinews of bear and mind of Buddha

These arms make steel catch the sun just so
Blood like red honey sticks to my fingers
Men tug my sleeves
Women swoon for my sweaty thighs

All who know me bow their heads

I am free to leave
pride, youth, grief, hope, love

Breath alone
naked to the mountain

Samurai by Kaleo (totem mask, 40″h x 36″w x 12″d)

Chi Gauge

Chi awareness is about the balance and integration of Yin and Yang and of the physical, emotional, mental, and energetic bodies.

Do the following Chi Gauge exercises with a partner. Remember that the point is not to see who is stronger, but to gauge your own strength under differing circumstances and to observe the lessons. When you have finished each exploration, trade roles and repeat.

Chi Gauge: The Chi of Emotions

Your partner stands by as you stand (or sit) in Zhan Zhuang. When you feel aligned and centered, extend your arm in front of your chest and reflect on someone who has saddened you, disappointed you, or drained your energy. Observe how your flesh, organs, and energy tend to lose their tone and prolapse. As you reflect on this experience of sorrow or weakness, have your partner press down on your extended arm. Observe and gauge your physical and energetic strength. Release your arm and pause.

Now extend your arm and think of someone who makes you happy or strong, perhaps a mentor, friend, or spirit guide. Bring this uplifting image into your body. You may notice joy in your organs, posture, facial expression. As you connect with this source of inner support, have your partner press down on your extended arm. Observe and gauge your physical and energetic strength. Notice the difference.

Notice how positive emotions and thoughts actually build your Chi, physical strength, and emotional harmony. How can you apply in daily life what you learned in this exploration?

Chi Gauge: Strength of Muscles, Chi, and Intention

Muscular Strength

Your partner stands by as you stand (or sit) in Zhan Zhuang. When you feel aligned and centered, extend your dominant arm in front of your chest and make a fist. As your partner presses down on your hand, try to keep your arm up with physical strength. Gauge your muscular strength.

Strength of Chi

Return to Zhan Zhuang with your arms at your side. Relax and use your mind and your breath to guide the Chi spiraling up from the earth, through the Bubbling Well (Kidney 1), up each leg, and into your pelvis. Center it in your pelvic Tan Tien. Then raise your dominant arm and look at your hand. Feel how the Chi gathers in your hand. Now have your partner press down on your hand. Gauge your energetic strength.

Strength of Chi with Intention

Remember that Chi follows your intention. Return to Zhan Zhuang with your arms at your side. Relax and use your mind and your breath to guide the Chi spiraling up from the earth, through the Bubbling Well (Kidney 1), up each leg, and into your pelvis. Center it in your pelvic Tan Tien. Then raise your dominant arm and look and point at something on the wall across the room. Staying relaxed, use your mind to spiral the Chi up through your spine, shoulder, and arm, to shoot out through your Chi fingers, like water gushing from a hose. Feel your gaze and intention guide the Chi across the room to touch your target. Now have your partner press down on your hand. Gauge the strength of your Chi combined with intention.

How can you apply what you learned here about intention and Chi? During massage, do not look at your hand. Look beyond your hand, into the layers of fascia, into the bones, or into the internal organs, and massage with Chi and intention. In martial arts, look through your opponent. How can you apply this awareness in daily life situations? If you have a goal, look and strive toward it. Do not allow your Chi and your intention to be distracted.

Chi Gauge: Harvesting Earth Chi

Your partner stands by as you stand naturally and comfortably with no special effort. Have your partner gently push you from each side, while you try to maintain your stance. Notice the relative centeredness and groundedness of your posture. Feel where you are vulnerable, unsteady, or easily uprooted. Feel where you are steady and strong.

Then pause.

Now stand with intention in Zhan Zhuang. Let your body rock back and forth, side to side, circle one way then the other, undulations diminishing until you find your center. Find the place of balance over your feet, through your feet. Let the weight of your body sink and feel yourself grounding in the earth.

Feel your breath comfortably entering and exiting, as your entire waist area and pelvic basin expand on the inhalation, contract on the exhalation. Allow your breath to be full but soft, as it enters into all corners of your lungs, then releases, in Tan Tien breathing.

Have your arms relaxed and gently extended in front of your waist with your palms facing down. Let your legs be relaxed and supple, and your perineum relaxed and open. As you inhale, feel your body sinking into the earth. Feel the Chi palms of your hands and the soles of your feet spreading open to earth. Feel your palms, your soles, and your perineum suctioning up earth Chi. Your extremities strengthen and fill with Chi (Regulator and Bridge Vessels). The center of your body opens and fills with Chi (Governing, Conception, Belt, and Penetrating Vessels). As you exhale, feel stakes of energy from your feet driving into the earth. As you breathe, feel earth Chi supporting and strengthening your personal Chi as it courses throughout your entire body. Continue harvesting earth Chi into your body for nine cycles of breath.

Then have your partner gently push you from each side, while you maintain your stance. How has earth Chi grounded, centered, and strengthened you?

Journaling and Art: Chi Gauge

 How did your body feel in the Chi Gauge exercises when Chi felt lacking or unhealthy? Where in your body did you feel sad, weak, drained, or unbalanced? Draw this energy. What is its color and shape?

How did your body feel in the Chi Gauge exercises when Chi felt supported, joyous, uplifted? When earth Chi was flowing through you with intention? Where in your body did you feel strong and centered? Draw this energy. What are the color and texture of your core strength? What are the shape and color of the stakes of Chi from your feet driving into the earth? What is the density of earth Chi? What is its rhythm as it flows through your body? What form does it take?

What can you do to bring more supportive, positive, strengthening energy into your daily life?

Kaleo's Journal: Teaching in the San Francisco County Jail

Elise has worked for the past twenty-four years as a Registered Nurse in the San Francisco County Jail. I also taught there part-time for five years. We often saw each other. Being in the jail was a lesson in Yin and Yang balance. We quickly learned to have a realistic understanding of our strengths and vulnerabilities. We needed to be grounded and centered and have strong protective Chi but, at the same time, keep our hearts open, for there were many moments for compassionate action. For this, we drew on our daily practice of Chi Kung, Tan Tien breathing, Zhan Zhuang, and harvesting earth Chi.

Elise and I wave to each other, as she nurses in the lower tier and I teach in the upper. Class begins. The heavy metal door bangs shut. My art and meditation students, maximum security psychiatric inmates dressed in orange jail attire, join me in the trapezoidal room. The soothing light peach paint does not disguise the thick cement blocks of the walls, the thick paned observation windows, the glaring fluorescent lights. There is an element of safety within the element of intensity.

Benito's head hangs down in the cave of his chest, as if he'd like to withdraw into the shell of his sweatshirt like a turtle. He says nothing through his tightly sealed lips.

Class begins. I invite each student to go in and look at the heart, then draw the way it feels. Benito reaches for black charcoal. He outlines the contracted shape of his heart. In its core, he stamps a hard, black, knotted shape.

Then we all move together in Chi Kung. Bodies and minds loosen and relax. We meditate to bring healing energy into our hearts. Once more they draw. Benito is surprised! He reaches for the red and outlines his heart. It's larger now. Colors flit across the page. The black knot has dissolved into open space, sprinkled with fragments of joy. A smile spreads across his face.

I tell them: Some of you may be in prison for perhaps twenty-five years. What do you do to find peace and inner strength? Move with Chi, meditate, and go in. That's where you can cultivate freedom. That's where you can open to space.

Opening to Space: Benito

Transforming Stress

Stress is stuck Chi. Many things can bring stress. Stress is related to the fight-or-flight response, the physiological reaction of the sympathetic nervous system to alarm or danger. Muscular strength is enhanced by adrenaline during a situation that is physically or emotionally alarming. It speeds your heart and dilates your bronchioles to meet increased need for oxygen, surges to skeletal muscles for action, and sharpens your brain's awareness for quick response. It helps bring about optimal reactivity in a challenging situation. But if it is excessive, it can make you shaky, nervous, confused, with senses clouded and reflexes clumsy. This is panic. An ongoing dose of adrenaline results in chronic stress. Chronic anxiety, fear, frustration, irritation, and anger can damage your health.

Chi Awareness and Stress

Chi awareness can help you to manage stress by:

- **Becoming aware of what causes you stress**

  What are your most common experiences of stress in your life? How do you habitually respond to them? What helps or hinders you in effectively dealing with stress? What causes your Chi to feel blocked and stagnant, weak and deficient?

- **Recognizing stress when it happens**

  When you encounter stress, rather than becoming one with it, you have a choice to step back and observe. What is your initial response to stress? Stress can literally pull you off your center. What happens to your balance, breath, heart, skin, muscles, and vision? What happens to your mind?

- **Activating the Witness in response to stress**

  When you encounter stress, engage Tan Tien breathing to calm your body and mind and center your breath. Then activate the Witness, your non-attached observing mind, by bringing your attention above the crown of your head. Feel the wisdom of the Witness flowing to your heart. You now have more of a choice to respond with clearer intention.

- Practicing Chi awareness as a way of life

  Managing stress may also require a change in habits of thinking. It may mean adjusting your priorities: focusing less on cultivating muscular strength and more on cultivating Chi; shifting focus from external demands to inner sensitivities; reducing negative thought patterns and influences and fostering positive ones.

- Engaging practices that support wellness and release chronic stress

  Engage Chi awareness practices, such as Chi hand techniques (page 61), Zhan Zhuang meditation (page 187), the Micro- and Macrocosmic Orbits (page 224 and page 234), or Tiger's Breath Chi Kung (page 264). Receive or do healing energy work or massage. Do hypnotherapy or guided imagery to explore your inner terrain and connect with your inner guides. Do journaling, art, and creative endeavors to release the stuck Chi of stress, to manifest your discoveries, and to arouse curiosity, awe, and joy.

Journaling and Art: Responding to Stress

Arrange drawing/collage materials and sit or stand comfortably in meditation.

Recognizing Your Habitual Responses to Stress

Record in your journal: Recall a specific situation when you felt stress—worried, angry, scared, hurt—in relation to another person. Who was it? What did this person do or say? Notice how your body responds to this memory. What emotions and sensations do you feel and where are they located in your body? Then how did you react?

Now turn to your art supplies. Through collage, colors, textures, shapes, and vibrations, create this interaction.

Activating the Witness

Now close your eyes and re-create the stressful situation in your awareness. Instead of reacting as you did in the past, engage Tan Tien breathing, activate the Witness, and let the wisdom of the Witness pass through your heart. Now how do you choose to react? Record your responses in your journal.

Draw and collage yourself as Witness. What alchemical processes does the Witness apply to your art? Does it use fire to subdue the wood of anger? Does it use metal to replenish the water depleted by fear?

When you journal, record your observations over time concerning your responses to stress. What shifts do you notice in your attitude, relationship, or stressful situation? What is Chi and creative process teaching you?

Meditation: Dissolving Stress in Your Body

Sit or stand in Zhan Zhuang meditation. Naturally and comfortably, engage Tan Tien breathing.

When you are centered and focused, invite your mind and Chi to scan your body for an area of stress or tension. You may find it to be restricted breath, stuck Chi, stagnant blood, constricted muscles, or blocked emotions. Is it in your internal organs, pelvis, back, neck, or head? What shape, color, sound, or temperature do you notice?

Exhaling, let your mind send signals along your nervous system to relax the tension in that area. What changes do you notice? As you inhale, your breath and Chi fill the area; as you exhale, your breath and Chi loosen and break up the tension. As your intention, breath, and Chi fill this area, the tension melts and dissolves.

Now feel cleansing intention and breath, along with Chi, blood, and lymph, flowing like water through this area.

Exhaling, direct the Chi/breath/blood to cleanse and release the dislodged debris outside of your body and give it to the earth. You may feel the release as localized sweating, temperature changes, or air exuding. You may feel it in your feet, palms, organs, fascia, or skin. As the old Chi releases, does your body respond with belching, sweating, laughter, tears, trembling, restlessness, nausea, or dizziness? (Sit down if you need to!)

If the blockage does not release easily, apply Chi hand techniques (for example, use your Chi blaster to break it up, Chi suction to draw it out, Chi brush to sweep it away). You may then want to use your Chi nourisher for support.

Be aware of your heart pumping fresh oxygen-rich blood into arteries, arterioles, and capillaries throughout your entire body. Be aware of the darkened deoxygenated blood returning via the veins back to your heart to be pumped to the lungs where carbon dioxide is released. Feel healthy fresh breath, blood, Chi, and emotions flowing throughout your body.

Journaling and Art: Dissolving Stress

 Record in your journal: What did you discover about your body? In what area were you holding stress? What emotions did you find?

Describe the shape, color, sound, or temperature of stress. Is it a huge boulder, a knotted rope, an ogre, someone you know? Describe its appearance and behavior.

Then express your body's experience of stress through drawing or collage. How do you release stress from your drawing through creativity? Do you tear it? Enclose it? Wash it away with colors? Soothe it with herbs? Bury it under collage?

What Chi hand tools help to dissolve stress? Does your Chi vibrator shake it loose and move it out? Does your Chi blaster break it up? Then does your Chi trowel dig up its roots? Does your Chi nourisher bring healthy fresh energy to this place?

Meditation: Invoking the Healing Presence

Find a quiet nurturing space for meditation. You might want to go to a natural setting where you smell clarifying eucalyptus, hear a stream running over boulders, or see birds flitting through the brush. If you stay indoors you might want to burn cedar or light jasmine incense before you begin. The space surrounding you becomes a place of refuge, a mirror for the sanctuary of the inner body.

Sit or stand in Zhan Zhuang. Naturally and easily, engage Tan Tien breathing. As you feel your feet spreading against the earth, allow yourself to rock gently back and forth and side to side, exploring your balance, allowing your body's undulations to become slower and slower until you find your center.

Close your eyes and bring your attention to the area of your third eye. This inner eye opens, turning its awareness to the inner domain of your body. A *healing presence* appears. What form emerges? Is it a light, sound, emotion, odor? Is it an ancestral spirit, guardian animal, or divine presence?

Send this presence on a journey through your body, directing it to an area of stress or tension. What does it find? How does it react? Feel it use its healing power to transform the blocked energy. How does it work its healing magic? Inhale and feel your breath/blood/Chi penetrate and cleanse the area. Then release the tension on the exhalation and give it to the earth.

Now bring the healing presence behind your third eye. Inhale deeply and on the exhalation send the presence with your breath to the surface of your body just under your skin. Feel it transforming into your protective, healing cushion of guardian Chi, or Wei Chi. Note its color, texture, sound. Feel its protection radiating through the layers of your body into the stillness of your inner core. Feel your body sigh in gratitude. Then rest in this stillness.

Journaling and Art: Healing Presence

Write in your journal: What form did the healing presence take? Where did it find the area of tension? What was the interaction like? How did your body respond? How did the healing presence transform to become the Wei Chi? How did it feel to experience this energy protecting you? How was it to seek the stillness at your core? Could you access this place? Practice this meditation with a sense of patience and permission, for stillness can be as elusive as the sensation at the center of a lightless, soundless, windless cave.

Now from your abundance of art supplies, create the healing presence in your body. Who or what is it? What are its form, color, texture? How does it travel through your body? How does it shift to become the Wei Chi?

In Harmony with Nature

Whenever you do Zhan Zhuang meditation in a comfortable, nurturing, healthy natural setting, you enhance the benefits of the practice. Feeling your feet spreading on the firm earth enhances grounding and centering. Breathing fresh air Chi in rhythm with the breath of nature enhances your exchange of Chi with the environment. Meditation beneath the open sky stimulates your receptivity to heavenly Chi.

Wherever you choose to go in nature, make sure the environment is comfortable, not too warm, cool, windy, or wet. Dress appropriately for the climate. Stand or sit on earth that is level and firm in a place where you feel safe and at home. Bring your journal with you to record your awarenesses.

The following explorations also invite you to connect with the five elements through nature: with metal through the Chi of the fresh natural air you inhale in Tan Tien breathing, with earth as Gaia, with fire as the rising sun at dawn, with wood as the tree, with water as the river.

Meditation: Gaia

 Close your eyes. Be still. Where in nature does your body want to be? At what time of day?

If you can, go there. You may arrive at dawn, noon, dusk, or night. You could commune with deep Yin ocean, warm Yang sun, snow-capped mountain, bubbling volcano, distant galaxy, or the goddess of the moon. Wherever you go, scan with your Chi palm and feel the energy rising from the belly of the earth, gusting off the ocean, shimmering from the heavens. Realize how we are constantly being fed and filled by this energy.

Sit or stand in Zhan Zhuang meditation. Feel your entire body comfortable and aligned. Feel your breath comfortably entering and exiting, each breath long, slow, deep. Your breath is relaxed, your body relaxed, your mind relaxed.

Let your waist area and pelvic basin expand on the inhalation, contract on the exhalation. Allow your breath to enter fully all the corners of your lungs on the inhalation, then exit on the exhalation. You are engaged in Tan Tien breathing.

On the inhalation draw the earth Chi up through the bottoms of your feet, up through your perineum, and into your body. Allow the temperature, energy, and breath of nature to enter and fill your lungs and body with their essence—one breath. On the exhalation send the Chi back through your feet and into the earth. How far down does it go? Listen to your breathing; then listen to nature's breath, her rhythm, her voice. Feel the tug of her energy on your body.

Listen to the breezes among branches and over hillsides. Or to the songs and flight of the birds. Or to the movement and sounds of the insects. Or to the slow movement of creeping lava and the popping and snapping of things burning in its path. Or to the waves breaking on the shore as they push and pull at your body. Feel nature and her whims.

Now listen to the universal ebb and flow within your body. What emotions do you feel? As you observe the energies and sounds around you, realize this rotating world is part of the great spinning Milky Way galaxy. Can you feel the energy in your body cycling in rhythm to the rotating earth and galaxy beyond?

When you are ready, inhale the blessings of the universe. Exhale gratitude.

Journaling and Art: Gaia

Write in your journal: Where in nature did you choose to go and at what time of day? What landscape and climate attracted you? How were the five elements present in this place? What happened to you in this meditation?

Then through art create the feeling of the energy from Gaia ascending into your body. What colors, fragrances, and temperatures do you depict? What elements show up? What forces of nature emerge through creativity?

Meditation: Dawn

NOTE: Never look directly into the sun but keep your eyes averted or your eyelids closed and practice for a short time only.

Kaleo's Journal: Desert Dawn

It's way before dawn, and Elise and I are in Death Valley near Ubehebe Crater. We dance in Tiger's Breath Chi Kung under the vastness and clarity of the night sky. There's such comfort in being with the familiar Dippers and the Pole Star. There's such awe! The spiraling arm of our galaxy lays the swath of the Milky Way. There's such magnitude! We perch on a rather small planet orbiting a mediocre star among the billions of stars in our one galaxy among millions in the known universe!

Moving in Chi Kung feels like spiraling from our inner galaxies within our Tan Tiens, as our palms cast a swath of stars and their constellations across the night sky and our bodies absorb and emit light, sound, and stardust. Our bodies become still, and we stand in Zhan Zhuang meditation under the heavens. We are the stars.

 Now imagine you are joining us (Kaleo and Elise) in meditation. Close your eyes and let your attention turn inward, as you join us in our circle in the desert just before dawn.

Let your body become still. Listen to the desert sounds. Feel the early morning sun slowly beginning to rise, its soft rosy glow lightly touching the vast expanse of desert. The outlines of mountains sharpen. Red-tailed hawk soars above our heads. Coyote watches us curiously at a safe distance through the mesquite.

The rays of sun reach us where we stand with our feet planted on the earth. Our bones lift and reach and our muscles open to receive the warmth. The sun reaches down through the crowns of our heads and our closed eyelids and winds its way through our eye passages. Our brains and endocrine glands nestled deep within their centers awaken and receive nourishment from the sun. Our endocrine system comes into balance.

Feel the ethereal thread that starts in the heavens, enters the crown of your head, and drops through the center of your body and down into Gaia, the earth. This connection with heaven and earth suspends and grounds you.

Inhaling, feel the gentle movement of your body rotating slightly on this axis as the breeze blows. Allow yourself to sway as you keep your connection to center and ground. Exhale and become still. Listen to the footsteps of coyote trotting off into the distance, as you return to the present time and place.

Coyote, Death Valley

Meditation: Tree

Finding the Tree

Go to a wooded setting in nature where you can be alone. Become mindful of all around you. Your senses are aware and you are open. A special tree calls to you, perhaps through its sounds, its scattering of light, or its ancientness. Make sure this tree is in good health. Then stand in front of it and observe. Feel its branches, roots, core. Listen to the sounds it makes as it breathes and moves in the wind. Are its aromas strong or subtle?

Feeling the Tree's Chi

Extend your Chi palms toward the tree and scan its Chi. Feel the Chi radiating from deep within its core. Feel its Wei Chi protecting it just beneath its bark. Scan the membrane of its aura surrounding it. Move in closer and experience its aura exuding and pressing against the aura of your body. Move back and forth until you find a comfortable distance between you and the tree. Your energies will be rubbing against each other, membrane to membrane. Now, facing the tree, sit or stand in Zhan Zhuang meditation.

Breathing with Nature

Inhale and receive the breath from this tree and its environment. Exhale and share your breath with this tree and with other beings of the plant world. You are one with this tree; you are one with all. Understand the interconnectedness. Their oxygen feeds you; your carbon dioxide feeds them; the photosynthesizing green chlorophyll in plant life, in the leaves of the tree facing you, molecularly resembles the red hemoglobin in your blood.

Chi Circuit with the Tree

We are like the tree receiving Chi from the sun, which fills and nourishes its body, and Chi from the earth through its deep roots spreading in the ground. Feel the energy of the tree spreading under your feet. Feel your energy roots twisting into the earth, intertwining with the roots of the tree. On the inhalation draw the energy up through the soft soles of your feet into your legs and up through your body to the crown of your head. Release the energy through your crown into the heavens. The treetop receives this energy, which then descends through its trunk back into its roots. Again inhale the energy from the roots back into your feet. Can you feel the difference in the Chi flowing through you? Allow the Chi to continue to cycle, like a shared Macrocosmic Orbit, between you and the tree.

Becoming the Tree

Do the exercise "Chi Gauge: Harvesting Earth Chi" on page 200. As you engage Tan Tien breathing, inhale and receive the core strength of the tree into your pelvis, chest, and lungs; exhale and feel this strength permeating your heart. Feel wood feeding fire as your heart beats and opens to the Chi of the tree. Now feel Chi extending from your feet as roots reaching down into the ground and spiraling through the moist earth in search of nourishment for your core. How far into the earth do they extend? Feel them growing from the flesh and bones of the ancestors and harvesting ancient wisdom. Now feel the crown of your head open, a treetop stretching skyward, exchanging Chi with the heavens. Feel your arms as branches, the wind passing through them as they reach out and exchange Chi with the environment.

Bringing the Tree's Chi with You

A breeze whispers among tree branches, inviting you to turn around, so that the tree's Chi supports your spine. Inhale and your back opens to receive the core strength of the tree into your shoulder blades, ribs, pelvis, and backbone. Exhale and your spinal cord and its branches of nerves reach down, up, and out to receive sustenance. The tree is a guardian supporting you, shielding you, and embracing you. A voice reaches into your body, through your heart's portal between your shoulder blades. Listen to it echoing through the inner chambers. Hear its tone. Receive the long story of the tree and its abundant messages to enrich your life. The tree's wisdom, support, and Chi accompany you, are part of you, as you move back into the world beyond the woods.

Journaling and Art: Tree

 Write in your journal: With what kind of tree did you encounter? What did you learn from the tree? As you became the tree? How can the tree meditation support you as you move through life?

Then draw, paint, or sculpt yourself as the tree. One student drew bones within branches, a portrait of her face in the belly of the tree, and from its trunk legs extending as large roots into the earth.

Guardian Banyan, O'ahu

Meditation and Journaling: River

 For the following meditations by the river, bring your journal to record your experiences, reflections, and creative ideas. Find a healthy river that makes good river music. Find a spot before it that is close and level, with no barriers between the river and you.

Sit or stand in Zhan Zhuang meditation facing the river. Listen to the river, to its flow. It reminds you that your body is 75 percent water, which comprises your blood, lymph, marrow, and other liquids. Let the fluids in your body rock back and forth, side to side, circle one way then the other, undulations diminishing until you find your center. Find the place of balance over your feet, through your feet. Let the weight of your body fluids sink as you ground in the earth.

Feel your breath comfortably entering and exiting, as your entire waist area and pelvic basin expand on the inhalation, contract on the exhalation. Allow your breath to be full but soft, as it enters into all corners of your lungs, then releases, in Tan Tien breathing.

Let your eyes be in soft focus; at times you may want to close your eyes and just listen. Feel your awareness encompassing both your body and the river's body.

Layers of the River

As you face the river, feel the rhythm, inhale the smells, listen to its sounds. As they call to you, exhale and notice how easy it is to let go and allow your awareness to float on the surface of the water. As your attention floats along the surface, what happens along your skin? Like a heavy leaf, its cup filling with water, your attention sinks into the middle layer of the river. Notice the difference in the rhythm as you sink and travel in this current. What happens inside your layers of fascia and flesh? Then as the leaf descends to the deepest part of the river that flows along the bed, notice the change in the sounds and light. What happens inside your core? What sounds and light reside there?

Write in your journal your experiences of the layers of the river and the layers of your inner being.

Directions of the River

Face the river. As you center your awareness in each of the three Tan Tiens—the mind behind your third eye, the spirit at your heart, the body in your pelvis—notice how each Tan Tien is an eddy with its own spiraling current.

Understand that this river you are facing is ancient. Many tribes and cultures have come and gone during the life of this river. Many events have transpired along its banks and within its currents. The river comes from afar. It brings gifts from many ages, geographies, climates, even creatures and their languages.

- Upriver

When you are ready, face upriver and receive the Chi of the onrushing river, this ancient soul. Upstream, you notice an object floating down the river toward you. Sometimes the object is accompanied by darkness, tempest, or violence, other times transformation and celebration. Sometimes the object bears a sense of loss and weeping, other times laughter and song. Ask the river why it is bringing you this object. Inhale and receive it. Into which Tan Tien does it float? Feel the object with its emotion spiraling in that Tan Tien. Feel its density within you. Accept this gift.

- Downriver

When you are ready, face downriver and feel the cleansing Chi of the departing river. Its rhythmic flow pulls at you. Ask the river what you have to release. What sound do you make as you exhale and let it go? Feel the river pulling it out of you. Feel it leaving. From which Tan Tien does it depart? Watch it. What are its shape, its color, its emotion as it sails off down the river? Watch it being pushed by the waves, dragged by the current, rocked by the wind, swept over waterfalls. Watch as it spirals into the distance and disappears. Exhale and let it go.

- River Before You

When you are ready, face the river straight on as it flows by. Let your hands reach out in front of you, Chi palms facing toward the river. Inhale and feel the Chi of water, its vibrations entering your fingers and palms, toes and feet. As you exhale, let the Chi sink deeper to merge with the rivers of marrow in your bones. Inhale and feel the bones in your arms and legs siphoning this Chi up into your core. As you exhale, let it fill you. Feel your Chi and the Chi of water meeting, dialoguing. Ask the river what you have to share with each other. With gratitude, inhale and exhale your exchange of energy. Feel the liquids in your body in the stillness of meditation cleansing and revitalizing in this river of life.

- Write in Your Journal

  What were your experiences of the directions of the river? What emotions came as you experienced the river coming, leaving, and going by? Where did you feel the emotions in your body? What did you receive, release, and exchange?

Dimensions and the River-flow

- Vision

  Face upriver. As your eyes melt in soft focus, your field of sight expands to include a broader periphery. Now let your depth vision also soften, so you are seeing what is both far and near at once.

- Intuition

  Bring your attention behind you. Feel the soft niche (GV16) between your skull and spine opening. Feel your inner eye opening and your perception expanding to include what is behind you. What do you perceive at your back—with your inner eye, your ears, your skin, your intuitive awareness?

- Time

  Follow a ripple of water as it descends with the river. Realize that this ripple is actually part of the contiguous whole of the river. Realize that each molecule of water is identical to the next and yet each is separate. Realize that there is no real way to separate part from whole, for the instant you decipher a ripple, it disappears back in the body of water. Notice how your perception of time begins to blur, receding into the past and expanding into the future. Feel your awareness shift to encompass the upstream history and the downstream destiny of the river.

- Write in Your Journal

  What were your experiences of the shifting dimensions of space, intuition, and time as your perception of the river shifted? How does your shift in perception affect your awareness of your inner body and the power of Chi?

Voices of the River

Face the river and listen to its many voices.

Listen. Water swirls around rocks, among tree roots, into little pockets of golden leaves, making eddies, riffles, rapids, then leaping away into dark hidden caverns.

Listen. Songs dance with rays of sun on the surface of the river. Sounds splash and dive, laugh and scold.

Listen. Sounds funnel into your ears, explore canal walls, glide down into the cavern of your throat, drop into your chest, pool in the basin of your pelvis.

Words of the river flow into poem or song.

BECOMING STONE
by Elise

How long must I stand here
until I turn to stone

Wheel of life:
no spokes or rim or soft tube
but ring of light
like water in the sun circling me

I become smoother and smoother
until I am rubbed back to nothing
but the river

Becoming Stone, Big Sur

Chi Circuits and Chakras

IX

Chi Circuits

The Microcosmic and Macrocosmic Orbits are ancient Taoist practices dating back thousands of years and shared by many schools of Tai Chi and Chi Kung. These Chi circuits harvest the Chi from the heavens, environment, and earth. They circulate the Chi through the body in a way that is focused and fundamental to all other Chi pathways. They balance the seven chakras, or wheels of energy, in the body for greater emotional, spiritual, physical, and energetic openness and protection.

Zhan Zhuang standing meditation is an excellent posture for circulating Chi in the Micro- and Macrocosmic Orbits. You can also practice the Orbits in sitting or lying meditation.

Elise's Journal: June 1995, Mother's Passage

Mother's breath comes as a struggle now. Cancer controls her body. Her keen hazel gaze turns inward. Her hand is cool but grips mine firmly. She speaks little but her hearing is sharp.

We bring music into her room. My brother plays his golden flute, while the rest of us sing the hymns she has chosen for her funeral. Her expression, strained with pain, transforms into a radiant smile. Her breath calms.

My mother's body is my body. Her dying is my dying.

Mom's Christianity has supported her through her years, the tough times, the dreams come true. Now is the test, not of faith but of continuity. How will the prayers and beliefs translate into the reality of after-death? Death is a mystery we all share, its passage a tunnel through unknown landscapes. My spirituality is eclectic, but differences seem irrelevant now. I reassure her: "Jesus will be there to lead you to God." Who am I to say so? Yet I feel her embrace the support I offer. I hope it will help her journey. Whatever issues we have struggled with as mother and daughter fade to wisps. In the end, love is all that matters. It stays behind, it guides forward, it endures.

Edith, Maui, 1991

Two days and nights I sleep next to her on one side, my dad on her other. Reminds me of being a kid, awakening from a nightmare and crawling in next to her where the monster couldn't find me. But now she is the one facing strange landscapes and overwhelming adventures.

The third night seems very long. I stand beside her many hours, holding her hand. I wonder how long my stamina can last.

I shift to stand in meditation. I feel my body centering, grounding. My feet open to the support of earth, my crown to the support of the heavens. The earth's Chi flows up through the soles of my feet, up my legs, up my spine, and out through the crown of my head to an apex a few inches above. The energy crests, mingling with heavenly Chi, then travels back down through my crown, down the front of my head and torso, down my legs, out through the soles of my feet, and back into the earth a few feet below. The circuit of energy between heaven and earth through my body along the pathway of the Macrocosmic Orbit restores my strength. I feel my breathing relaxing and deepening as it fills and empties from my pelvic Tan Tien. I feel my mind alert but calm. I feel my heart open, as the energy travels through my arms, connecting me through my hands to my mother.

During the night I feel divine presence in the room. The ambience is electric, but mom's breathing seems peaceful. Just before dawn, dad slips away to another room to get some sleep. After he leaves, mom turns onto her side and her breath struggles again. I begin to massage her back. Her breath becomes my breath. Outside, a mockingbird begins its medley as the world prepares to emerge from night. The sound of her breath releases, and she lets go.

Great awe fills the room. I stay with her, with the trembling inside my body and around it, alongside her body's stillness. When I touch the crown of her head, the portal to heavenly Chi, I sense her spirit departing toward a light far beyond the rising sun.

You left me still in my skin

but you still visit
when the silver drop
descends the silken thread

then disappears

Microcosmic Orbit

The energy of the Microcosmic Orbit flows up the body's back (Governing Vessel/Yang) and down the front (Conception Vessel/Yin). The Governing Vessel begins at the coccyx and travels up the midline of the back over the crown of the head to the roof of the mouth. Here it bridges to the Conception Vessel, which travels along the midline of the front to the base of the torso at the perineum, where it bridges to the Governing Vessel. The two bridges between the Conception and Governing Vessels (perineum/coccyx and tongue/roof of mouth) also communicate with the two pumps (sacrum and sphenoid bones) for the cerebrospinal fluid, which bathes the spinal cord and brain.

Microcosmic Orbit Pathway

The landmarks along the path of the Microcosmic Orbit correspond to the acu-points along the Conception and Governing Vessels. Direct the Microcosmic Orbit in its circuit as follows:

Microcosmic Orbit Pathway

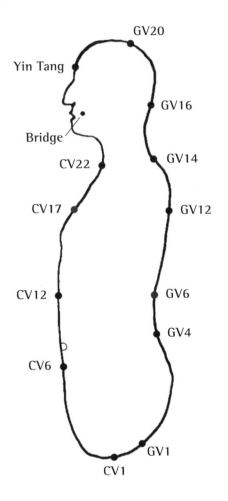

1 Begin two finger widths below your navel at the Sea of Chi (CV6), portal to the pelvic Tan Tien, then proceed

2 to the center of the perineum (CV1/Meeting of Yin), bridging to the tip of the coccyx (GV1/Long Strong) at the base of your torso

3 to the center of your lower back behind your navel at your Ming Men (GV4/Gate of Life)

4 to the center of your middle back behind your solar plexus (GV6/Spinal Center)

5 to the center of your upper back between your shoulder blades behind your heart (GV12/Body Pillar)

6 to the base of your neck at C7 (GV14/Big Hammer)

7 to the top of your neck at the hollow under the occipital ridge (GV16/Wind Mansion)

8 to the crown of your head (GV20/One Hundred Meeting)

9 to the third eye (Yin Tang)

10 to the bridge of your tongue at the roof of your mouth

11 to the sternal notch at the base of your throat (CV22/Celestial Chimney)

12 to the center of your sternum beside your heart (CV17/Chest Center)

13 to your solar plexus (CV12/Central Duct)

14 then to the Sea of Chi (CV6).

Microcosmic Orbit and the Chakras

The chakras are seven wheels of energy and spiritual power in the core of the body, located at the: (1) root of the spine, (2) hara in the lower abdomen, (3) solar plexus, (4) heart, (5) throat, (6) third eye, and (7) crown.

The seven chakras fall under the influence of a predominant element: root/earth; hara/water; solar plexus/wood; heart and throat/fire; third eye and crown/metal.

Chakra Influences

	Element	Sphere	Quality
1 Root	earth	earth/body bridge	rootedness, groundedness, security, pleasure, movement, nurturance, balance, acceptance of embodied self
2 Hara	water	pelvic Tan Tien	genetic and ancestral wisdom, gestation, birth, creativity and the stamina to bring it forward and grow toward one's potential
3 Solar Plexus	wood	upper/lower body bridge	acceptance and valuing of self and others, self-esteem, individuality, power balanced with flexibility in decision making and asserting oneself in the world
4 Heart	fire	heart Tan Tien	freedom and joy in connectedness and intimacy with self, others, and the world
5 Throat	fire	body/head bridge	speaking and requesting, receiving and giving, manifesting and sharing the heart's truth
6 Third Eye	metal	mind Tan Tien	mental vision, logic, insight, and clarity balanced with intuition, dreams, and imagination
7 Crown	metal	body/heaven bridge	openness and receptivity to divine awareness and influence

The even numbered chakras (hara, heart, third eye) are also associated with the Tan Tiens (energy fields) of the pelvis, heart, and mind. The odd numbered chakras are associated with bridges between spheres of influence: The root bridges earth and the body; the solar plexus bridges lower and upper body; the throat bridges body and head; the crown bridges body and heaven.

The Conception and Governing Vessel acu-point landmarks along the path of the Microcosmic Orbit correspond to the front and back portals of the seven chakras. As the Chi flows smoothly and intentionally through the Microcosmic Orbit, it helps bring energetic, alchemical, physical, mental, emotional, and spiritual harmony through its influence on the chakras. It balances Yin and Yang: front and back, inner experience and relationship to the outer world, and root and crown, so that one is grounded, as well as open to divine guidance.

Chi Awareness: Microcosmic Orbit and the Chakras

Stand in Zhan Zhuang or sit in meditation. If you desire, holding the master points for balancing the Governing Vessel (Small Intestine 3/Back Ravine, page 138) and Conception Vessel (Lung 7/Broken Sequence, page 115) before you begin helps stimulate the flow of Chi in the Microcosmic Orbit.

Find your center, your place of balance. Feel your feet grounding in the earth, your perineum open to the earth, your crown open to the heavens. Feel your entire body comfortable and aligned.

Engage Tan Tien breathing. Let your waist area and pelvic basin expand on the inhalation and contract on the exhalation, as your breath softly but fully enters and exits your lungs.

1 Close your eyes and focus on your pelvic Tan Tien (CV6). Invite your Chi to gather in this place of creation and gestation. How does it feel as the energy collects? Feel awe for the energy growing and glowing, for this pulsing, spiraling galaxy within.

2   On an exhalation, allow the soft glow of your breath to release and descend from your pelvic Tan Tien to the perineum at the floor of your pelvis (CV1). Breathe and feel this Chi spiral and pool in this sacred basin, chalice of mystery. Receive nurturance in this realm of earth, this place of survival, comfort, grounding. Explore this place that bridges Yin and Yang, Conception and Governing Vessels. Breathe and feel the point (GV1) of the triangular shaped coccyx.

3   Inhale and your breath washes up your sacrum to the center of your lower back between your kidneys. You are opposite your navel, in the Ming Men, the Gate of Life (GV4). Soak in this realm of water, this place of endurance and energy, ancestral wisdom and origins.

4   Inhale and invite your breath to spiral to the center of your middle back behind your solar plexus (GV6). Explore this realm of wood: place of flexibility, the ability to choose and act among options.

5   Inhale and your breath rises to the center of your upper back between your shoulder blades just behind your heart (GV12). Discover awe in this realm of fire, this place of freedom, of opening your wings to soar.

6   Inhale and your breath lifts to the base of your neck at C7 (GV14). Relish this place of reaching out and touching; of expressing, sharing, and manifesting your heart's truth; of bridging the intention of your mind and the joy of your heart through action.

7   Inhale and your breath floats to the top of your neck beneath the occiput in the soft niche (GV16) at the medulla oblongata, your primal brain. Cherish this realm of metal, this place of dreams and imagination.

8   Inhale and your breath ascends to the crown of your head (GV20). You may feel it shoot out of your crown to merge with heavenly Chi and crest like a fountain to cascade back down and enter the crown again. Receive the divine inspiration and cosmic awareness awaiting you at this gateway.

9   When you are ready, on an exhalation, let your breath glide down your frontal bone to the third eye (Yin Tang). Awaken to this place of logic, vision, and clarity.

10 Exhale and your breath slips to the roof of your mouth to meet the tip of your tongue. You may feel your tongue tingling with the current of Chi as it bridges the Governing and Conception Vessels.

11 Exhale and your breath rolls down your tongue and into the base of your throat at the sternal notch (CV22). Breathe and savor the freshness of breath. Feel your breath vibrating in your throat. Receive the power of voice, of requesting, receiving, and expressing your heart's truth.

12 Exhale and your breath releases down into the center of your chest in the area of your heart, protected by your sternum bone (CV17). Enjoy this place of love, joy, and intimacy with yourself, your environment, and others.

13 Exhale and your breath travels down to your solar plexus (CV12). Feel the power and strength of your respiratory diaphragm. Thrive in this place of self-esteem, self-confidence, and self-worth.

14 Exhale and your breath descends into your pelvic Tan Tien (CV6). Feel your inhalation expanding, your exhalation contracting. Feel your feet sinking into the earth and receive the support and nurturance of Gaia, the mother. Allow awe and gratitude to gather with breath and Chi in this place of origins, gestation, birth, and potential for growth.

15 You may direct the circulation of energy along this path one time slowly or several times quickly. When you are finished, gather the Chi in the pelvic Tan Tien for safe and efficient storage: men by placing the right hand over the left over the navel, women by placing the left hand over the right over the navel. Feel the spiraling of Yin and Yang, the alchemical balance of the elements, the bridge between you, heaven, and earth. Feel the universe within.

Journaling: Microcosmic Orbit

What was your experience of the orbit of Chi? How would you describe in words, colors, textures, sounds your sensation of it? How wide was its pathway? How deep?

At what points and chakras did you feel the Chi most strongly? At what points and chakras did you feel disconnected, uncertain, or vulnerable?

Microcosmic Orbit and Chakra Balance

Kaleo's Journal: Gayle's Voice

Gayle glared at her mask mold on the table. The empty white shell stared back at her. She felt irritated: somehow cut off, disconnected from her body, from her heart. Frustration welled within her. There was no flow of creativity. Just angry silence.

Her voice strained with frustration: "It's the lips of my mask. They're pinched, sealed tight. They want to open and breathe!"

I knew Gayle's history: Thirty years ago, for a few years as a child, her father sexually molested her. To protect her mother and younger siblings, she stored the ugly secret behind her tightly locked throat.

After years of psychotherapy, Gayle had come to understand that a way to healing was to release the stuck energy (Chi) through talking honestly with her therapist, sometimes weeping, sometimes raging, always letting her heart's truth flow freely in that safe setting.

Now her process was inviting her to take another step through art on her journey of healing. Her body knew what it wanted. At first, she hesitated. Then, with a sharp blade, she sliced open and pried apart the lips of her mask. She trembled. Her hand faltered. Tears fell. She cut deeper, wider.

When the mask, under pressure and slightly moistened by her tears, came apart at the seams, she dropped the knife and ran sobbing from the room.

Alone, she sat in meditation. Tan Tien breathing calmed her.

Her heart and throat understood the importance of completing her mask process. When she returned to the room, she angrily tore the mask mold completely apart. Fragments of its shell lay before her. She released a sigh. Her breathing flowed more smoothly. Suddenly, she knew what to do. Excitedly, she cut numerous circles from the gauze fragments, then painted them in hues of lavender, soft blue, iridescent green, and glitter. Then with loving care, she used needle and thread to string a *lei* of flowers.

Her mask transformed into a *lei aloha* (garland of love). She wore it encircling her neck as she further empowered herself through sharing her story with the group.

After experiencing the Microcosmic Orbit a few times, you will become familiar with its pathway. You will also cultivate a more intimate awareness of the chakras, as you spend time with them and discover their personalities, needs, desires, strengths, and vulnerabilities.

Sometimes you will find that a certain chakra needs cleansing or nourishing or special attention. After teaching long and intensive workshops, Kaleo often finds his root chakra guiding him to the garden to weed, dig his hands into the moist earth, and soak up the fragrances and energies of the plants.

Remember that you are like an antenna that transmits as well as receives energy waves. For example, after doing massage or Reiki with a client experiencing emotional distress, you may have absorbed toxic energy. You may feel related symptoms of being exhausted, fatigued, stagnant, or overwhelmed. Engage the following guided imagery to discover which chakra is most strongly affected and what kind of attention it needs.

Chi Awareness: Microcosmic Orbit and Tending the Chakra

In a quiet, private place, stand, sit, or lie in meditation. Engage Tan Tien breathing. Let your waist area and entire pelvic basin expand on the inhalation and contract on the exhalation, as your breath softly but fully enters and exits your lungs. Feel each breath long, slow, deep, and relaxed.

Then direct the Chi in its pathway along the Microcosmic Orbit. Feel your awareness, breath, and Chi flowing together and exploring the chakras. Some will feel strong and confident, some vulnerable and weak, some excessive, some diminished. Notice how the Chi moves through the region of each chakra.

Be still and listen. Which chakra calls out to you? How does it signal: through image, congestion, or emotion? What kind of attention does it need?

Realize each chakra itself is a portal to another realm. Does your root need greater stability through grounding in the earth? Is your hara ready for creative productivity? Does your solar plexus motivate you with confidence? Does your heart long for intimacy with another? Does your throat feel a balance between giving and receiving? Does your third eye seek more time in the world of the subconscious through dreamwork and guided imagery? Does your crown invite you more deeply into your practice of meditation?

What kind of attention is it requesting? How can the other chakras help? Does your heart (fire) need more fuel (wood) from your solar plexus and more mental clarity (third eye/metal)? Does your spiritual awareness (crown/metal) ask for compassion (heart/fire) or grounding (root/earth)?

Allow the Chi to continue circling in the Microcosmic Orbit, exploring, cleansing, nourishing, and balancing this chakra. Synchronize your Tan Tien breathing with the Microcosmic Orbit. With each inhalation the breath travels up the spine (Governing Vessel) and into the crown. With each exhalation the breath flows down the front (Conception Vessel) into the perineum. How does the chakra respond?

When the circling of Chi feels complete for now, harvest and store the Chi in your pelvic Tan Tien, men by placing the right hand over the left over the navel, women by placing the left hand over the right over the navel. Let your Chi palms enjoy the feeling of fullness and ripeness of stored Chi.

Chi Scanning, Journaling, and Art: Tending the Chakra

As your Chi flowed in the Microcosmic Orbit, in which chakras did you notice stuckness or congestion? In which did you notice openness or responsiveness? Which chakra called to you for attention? What did the Chi circling through the area near this chakra feel like? Did it get stuck, rush through, skip over, become weak? How did it respond to the attention brought to it through the running of the Microcosmic Orbit?

Now bring your attention to this chakra. For example, perhaps, like Gayle, you felt that the Chi was not flowing smoothly through your throat area. Have you needed to clamp your jaws tight to silence your voice? Do you reach out to others, taking care of their needs, yet neglecting your own? Do you avoid asking for and receiving what you need?

Touch the front and back of your throat, neck, and shoulders (or whatever chakra asked for attention). Are their textures and temperatures different? How do the muscle layers beneath feel? Are they pliable or tense?

Use your Chi palms to scan your throat, sides of neck, and C7 area. Notice if the front portal of the chakra at the throat has different energy than the back portal at C7. What Chi hand techniques does your throat area need? Does it ask for your Chi blaster to break up congested Chi? Or your Chi pump to boost depleted Chi?

Now, do a drawing, painting, or sculpture of your throat (or whatever chakra was asking for attention). Let your Chi palms reach out and choose colors and textures, then channel them into the shape and image of the chakra. Does it want the moodiness of phthalos, the heat of reds, the brilliant golden light of the sun? Does it want the structure of wire, the embrace of flowers, the seclusion of burial in earth? Does it need the fragrance of lavender or rose petals? Does it want its back and front portals to open, so that the fragrance wafts through?

As you create, feel the response of the chakra in your body. How does your inner chakra respond to its mirror in art?

Then when you feel ready, scan your art with your Chi palm. Is there an area that attracts your palm? An area that repels it? An area that seeks attention? What vibrations do you feel? Listen quietly. What emotions, images, or messages come up for you?

Listen to your body. Does it want to rip, cut, caress, add layers? Notice how your body contracts with alarm, quivers with excitement, or sighs with satisfaction as you make changes to your art work. Notice how your chakra shifts. Notice how your awareness shifts.

Macrocosmic Orbit

The Macrocosmic Orbit includes the Microcosmic Orbit, with its influence on the chakras, plus the pathways of Chi through arms and legs. The balancing of root and crown, of the body as a bridge between earth and heaven, is strengthened by the Macrocosmic Orbit.

Chi Awareness: Macrocosmic Orbit Practice

 Stand in Zhan Zhuang or sit in meditation on a chair. If you desire, hold the master points for the Governing and Conception Vessels (Small Intestine 3 and Lung 7) to help stimulate the flow of Chi in the Microcosmic Orbit.

Find your center, your place of balance. Feel your feet grounding in the earth, your perineum open to the earth, your crown open to the heavens. Feel your entire body comfortable and aligned.

Engage Tan Tien breathing. Let your waist area and entire pelvic basin expand on the inhalation and contract on the exhalation, as your breath softly but fully enters and exits your lungs.

1 Inhaling, feel your Chi collecting in your pelvic Tan Tien then spreading along its walls and floor of your pelvis. Observe the Chi in the perineum dividing into two channels and traveling down into each sitting bone. Exhaling, release the Chi down the back of each leg and foot (Yang meridians) and into the earth.

2 Let the Chi sink. Note how far down it travels into the earth. Inhaling, invite the Chi to ascend from the earth through the Bubbling Well (Kidney 1) in the center of each forefoot, up the inside of each leg (Yin meridians), to merge and enter the base of the torso where the Conception Vessel bridges to the Governing Vessel.

3 From there the Chi travels up the path of the back (Governing Vessel) to the base of the neck at C7, the seventh cervical vertebra (GV14).

4 Exhale as the Chi divides into two channels to travel over the shoulders and down into the armpits (axillae), then down along the inner aspect of each arm (Yin meridians), along the palm of each hand (Pericardium 8/ Labor Palace), and out the fingertips.

5 Inhale and fresh Chi enters your fingertips and travels up along the back of each arm (Yang meridians), along each shoulder, to converge again at the base of the neck (C7).

6 From there the Chi continues in the Microcosmic Orbit up the back of the head into the crown. You may feel it shoot out of your crown to merge with heavenly Chi and crest like a fountain to cascade back down and enter the crown again. Exhale and the Chi descends the front of the head to glide into the bridge (tongue/roof of mouth), where it enters the Conception Vessel and flows down the front of the torso, back into the pelvic Tan Tien.

7 You may direct the circulation of energy along this path one time slowly or several times quickly. Feel the Orbits flowing with Chi. Feel your Chi palms (P8) vibrating with Chi after your practice. Now gather the Chi in the Tan Tien of the pelvis for safe and efficient storage: men by placing your right hand over your left over your navel, women by placing your left hand over your right over your navel. Feel the microcosm within your body spiraling in harmony with the macrocosm beyond your body.

Integrating the Orbits

Chi awareness involves not only specific exercises but permeates your existence. There are many ways to incorporate the Orbits and their influence on the chakras into other areas of your life.

When walking in the woods, doing Tai Chi or Chi Kung, doing massage or Reiki, dancing hula, or doing other creative activities, engaging Tan Tien breathing and activating the Orbits help you connect more strongly with the surrounding energies. Your senses and intuition awaken and feel alive. You listen more deeply to the messages of the wind, animals, plants, and people.

To prepare for guided imagery, you may activate the Microcosmic Orbit to heighten your receptivity to the realms of the subconscious. As the portals to the chakras open, enter into the inner landscapes and welcome the emergence of your inner guides.

As you make art, activating the Orbits and chakras invigorates your muse, stimulates the flow of creative juices, and supports your process of creative gestation and embodiment. Your senses awaken to spreading colors and sculpting the forms of your heart's truth.

In doing bodywork or healing energy work, the Orbits activate the power of the chakras. You ground and center in the earth, so that your root and hara are strong and full of Chi. The compassion in your heart, the ancestral wisdom in your DNA, and the inspiration of the divine channel through your body and out your hands in Chi transmission. The Orbits inspire creativity in your touch. They recharge you after doing healing work.

When your chakras are open and in balance, their physical, energetic, mental, emotional, and spiritual receptivity and power are more available for your use. When you harvest Chi from heaven, earth, and environment, your resources are great.

Root Chakra: Bridge to Earth Chi

Chi Awareness: Root Chakra

Begin by standing in Zhan Zhuang. You may also do this practice sitting on a chair if desired. You may want to be in a place where the support of the earth feels tangible. One of our favorite places is the crater's edge of Kīlauea Volcano's newly formed land, dipping into the ocean off the Big Island of Hawai'i.

Let your body rock back and forth, side to side, circle one way then the other, undulations diminishing until you find your center, your place of balance. Feel your feet grounded on earth, your perineum open to earth, your crown open to the heavens. Your entire body relaxes in comfortable alignment.

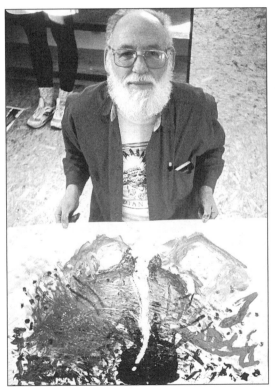

Funneling Earth Chi: James

Engage Tan Tien breathing. Let your waist area and entire pelvic basin expand on the inhalation and contract on the exhalation, as your breath softly but fully enters and exits your lungs.

As your breath presses down into the bottom of your pelvis like the waves of a sea pressing into their vessel of earth, inhale the aroma of ocean. Exhale into the mystery and stillness of the depths. As your breath spreads into the floor of the basin, your perineum softens and opens. Inhale the fragrance of moist earth. Feel the power beneath earth's crust as her Chi ascends to join the Chi gathered in your pelvis.

As earth Chi enters, notice any sensations or emotions—of comfort, nourishment, support, grounding, pleasure. Notice the gentle rocking rhythm, as the Chi touches the base of your spine. Then rest.

Hara Chakra: Residing in the Pelvic Tan Tien

The pelvis is like a chalice. It is a vessel of ancestral sources, wisdom, and power. It is the container of sexuality, of processes of elimination, of the main energy field, the pelvic Tan Tien. It is where creativity enters the body, waste is released, and energy is stored. It is a crucible hinged by ligaments and cartilage and protected by fascia and muscles.

The Micro- and Macrocosmic Orbits help us to harvest Chi from heaven, earth, and environment to store in the pelvic Tan Tien for our use. They remind us of the intimate relationship between ourselves and the universe. Zhan Zhuang helps us cultivate and connect with the quiet power of the Tan Tien. Chi Kung movement, such as Tiger's Breath, helps us channel the Chi stored in the Tan Tien throughout the body. It also helps the pelvis become a more pliable vessel by loosening the soft tissues, lubricating the hip and sacroiliac joints, and softening the groins, so that the lower back and legs have more freedom of movement.

There is a better balance of firmness and receptivity when the principle of flexibility is incorporated. If something is too brittle, it is more likely to shatter; if it is pliable, it can absorb shock. All the stored tension, which feels like protection, can actually bring weakness instead of strength. But if flexibility is combined with strength, if creativity is combined with intelligence, if nurturing is combined with passion, Yin and Yang again may support each other.

Tan Tien breathing helps us access and stimulate the pelvic Tan Tien. It accesses ancestral wisdom. It brings Chi from the creative and abundant womb of the universe into the realm of personal creative and abundant potential in the pelvic Tan Tien. It guides us to understand, develop, and use Chi through the conscious direction of the breath. It helps us to focus Chi within our bodies and to direct it beyond our bodies purposefully.

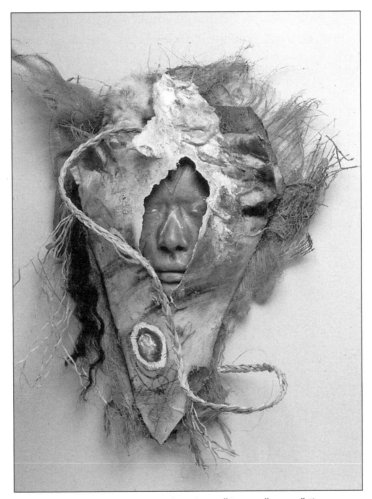

Emergence by Kaleo (mask, 18″h x 12″w x 6″d)

Chi Awareness: Hara Chakra

Stand in Zhan Zhuang. Engage Tan Tien breathing. Let your waist area and entire pelvic basin expand on the inhalation and contract on the exhalation. Your pelvis is a basin filled with a calm clear sea. Its sides stay steady, to keep the liquid from spilling. Is your pelvis even, not tilted left or right, forward or back?

Direct the Chi to flow in the Microcosmic then Macrocosmic Orbits. When you are ready, harvest and store the Chi in your pelvic Tan Tien. Notice the sensations stirring in this center. What do you feel? Is creativity incubating? What do you see, hear, or smell? Notice the sensations radiating from this center of creativity as a sphere, vertically (up to your solar plexus and down to your perineum) and horizontally (to the sides of your torso, your navel in front, and your Ming Men in back).

Then move from the center of this sphere. As it turns like a gyroscope, does it inspire you to move in free-flowing, creative Chi Kung or to dance with Chi awareness?

Feel your pelvic Tan Tien shifting your weight and turning your torso. Let its power guide your arms and legs in movement.

Your pelvis opens and closes. It breathes, receiving the Chi of the universe and allowing the Chi to settle and absorb into its walls.

Sense the weight of your viscera embraced by your pelvic structure. Feel your organs moving, gliding, opening, and closing within this vessel.

Become aware of the liquid and its currents, of the fertile deep dark ocean that the Taoists say resides within the pelvis. Let it inspire you in movement. And when you are finished, rest.

Guided Imagery: Encountering Your Muse

 Sit or lie in meditation. You may want to be in a place of comfort and beauty, a place where you feel creative intimacy and adventure.

Engage Tan Tien breathing. Feel your waist and pelvic basin expanding and contracting, all their visceral contents of intestines and reproductive organs moving. Now use your fingerpads to gently probe your navel. Explore its rim and edges, and feel the landscape and its underlying textures. Notice how the navel connects you to different organs in your body. Explore its center, and feel the beam of Chi connecting to your Ming Men. Notice how the walls of the navel open and close as you inhale and exhale. This is Conception Vessel 8/ Spirit Gate, the portal through which you first received nurturance in your mother's womb. What emotions surface as you hover at this threshold? What was your experience before you were born?

Now you are nurturing yourself. On the next inhalation, feel how your navel opens to receive. On the next exhalation, feel how it contracts and draws in, inviting your breath through its gateway, into another space, another time, another state of awareness.

You find yourself entering a long tunnel. Breathing gently, listen to the echo of your breath as it takes you deeper into relaxation. As you move through the tunnel, touch its walls. How do they feel? Notice how the light changes as you enter more deeply. You are safe and comfortable. Your breath relaxes your body and mind, and you allow yourself to journey further into the tunnel.

Notice the fine membrane at the tunnel's end, its light, its color. You feel so relaxed that it is easy to follow your breath through this thin barrier. You find yourself on the other side, standing on a ledge, peering into the sea of Chi in your pelvic Tan Tien, the ocean in the basin of your pelvis. What is the sound of your breath stirring the ocean?

As you dive into the sea of the Tan Tien, waves radiate and lap at the rim of your pelvis. You find yourself breathing as easily and naturally as a fish under water. As you journey into the depths of the ocean, feel the different layers of water, their temperatures and currents, the diminishing light. As you descend deeper into the depths, the floor of the ocean gives way to an opening leading to a cave. This is the domain of your creative energy. What is the air in this cavern like? Reach out and touch the walls. What evidence of life do you discover?

Your pupils dilate to accommodate the darkness, and you notice a form resting in the far corner of the cave. At first all you can see is a glow around an obscure shape. What color is the aura? As your night vision grows clearer, you see that the form begins to move and its face turns and stares at you. This is the face of your muse. Whose face emerges from the shadows? Your muse invites you to come closer. Can you allow yourself to let go? What does it feel like to give up control, to release fear and embrace trust, as you meet your muse?

She whispers to you: her name, her song, her invocation.

Your muse guides you back to the interior of the cave. You follow. Look around. What colors and shapes do you see? Are there images or glyphs carved on the walls? Are there ritual tools or vessels for creativity? Reach out and touch. What textures and sensations do you feel? What emotions run through you as you experience this mysterious place? What creative possibilities lurk in the shadows? Explore this deep interior of your being.

Your muse leads you deeper into the interior. When it is time, she gives you her blessing and urges you to enter a large tunnel. Then she takes her leave and disappears back into the remote recesses of her dwelling place. Inhale and embrace yourself with your breath. Exhale and say the invocation of your muse.

You find yourself in a chamber, dark and rich with smells and textures. Memories begin to surface. However, you notice a light in the distance. As you move toward the light, you can hear the pounding of blood. It invites you on. You approach the light. You feel mist. You hear waves pounding against a shore, flowing in, flowing out. Soon you smell fresh air. A thin membrane separates you from the light. You exhale and push through the membrane. You exit the tunnel and enter awareness of yourself sitting or lying in meditation.

Art and Writing: Your Muse

Write your muse's name, her song, her invocation.

Then draw, paint, or sculpt your muse. What form does she take? What is her facial expression? How does she move? How is she dressed? What is her skin like? What is the sound of her voice? What tools of creativity does she carry? What about her stimulates your creative juices to flow?

She may inspire you to create the tunnel of the umbilical cord with its dark walls and delicate membrane and threshold to the sea. Or she may urge you to mold yourself as fetus in your mother's womb.

Then place your muse's incarnation and invocation at the entrance to your cavern of creativity. Honor her each time you begin to create.

Jennie's Journal: Conception

After a long hiatus, this piece marked a reengagement with my creative process. This event was prompted by my massage with Kaleo. During that session, I felt my spine, ribcage, pelvis, and muscles existed as tectonic plates, and it seemed that much of my core creativity was trapped in these places of tension and discomfort.

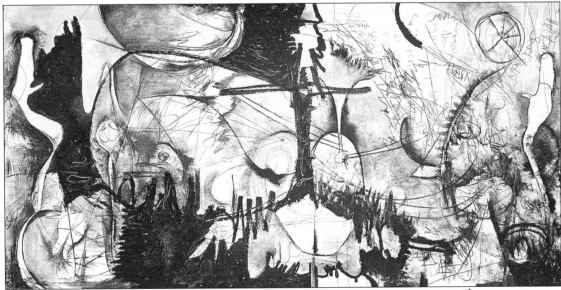

My Own Secret Shaking by Jennie (oil painting, 72″w x 36″h)

When I returned home, I began with the intention to invite these tectonic plates, or two halves of myself (right and left, male and female), to unite. I wanted to mark and motion myself back together again, drawing on the essence of life and the creative force. During the process, the piece became a multi-layered document to my experience as woman, body, artist.

About three months after this piece, my partner and I became pregnant. I now see this piece as a birth piece—evoking the artist and teacher in me, the primal mother, who creates, nurtures, and births new life through the womb.

Solar Plexus Chakra: Cultivating Acceptance

Chi Awareness: Solar Plexus Chakra

Stand in Zhan Zhuang or sit in meditation. You may want to be in a place of comfort, strength, and beauty, a place where you feel empowered. Engage Tan Tien breathing.

Then bring your awareness to your breath filling the circumference of your body at your solar plexus. Touch your solar plexus and notice the arching doorway formed by the ribs. Feel the entire area expanding on the inhalation, contracting on the exhalation. As the breath enters and leaves this area, be aware of any imbalance, discomfort, tension. Notice any asymmetry in how your breath fills and empties from front, back, sides. You may want to use your Chi palms to scan your solar plexus area. What do they find?

If you notice discomfort or tension in the front of your solar plexus, ask yourself: Do I value who I am and what I do? Do I feel strong and secure in my identity? Or do I merge too much with the expectations of others and forget myself?

If you notice discomfort or tightness in your back behind your solar plexus, ask yourself: Am I overly rigid in my opinions? Am I inflexible in my judgments of others? Have I made the boundaries of my identity so strict that I cannot grow and change?

If you notice discomfort in your left side, ask yourself: Do I worry too much about things I cannot change?

If you notice discomfort in your right side, ask yourself: Am I stuck in relationship to my purpose on earth, my work in the world?

Allow your breath to continue to enter and exit your middle torso, bringing it with caring intention and loving acceptance into any area of imbalance or tension. Let the inhalation explore the tension, the exhalation soothe it. Inhale acceptance, exhale surrender. Keep breathing this way and observe how your emotions shift. Observe how the sensations in your middle torso change.

Power Shield: Billy

Apply Chi hand techniques to your solar plexus area. What does it want? Your Chi suction to extract excess Chi? Your Chi nourisher to feed healthy Chi? Your Chi drill to probe and fathom deeper levels of understanding? Does it need the help of the element water (hara), to nourish and support wood (solar plexus) in its growth? Does wood grow into a source of protection or power?

When you feel your entire middle torso area relaxed and at ease, let your breath descend to your pelvic Tan Tien. Then rest.

Heart Chakra: Tending the Spirit

Kaleo's Chant

". . . Ē ka Dan Zhong, me ka Shen Zhu, ke aupuni o ke aloha mau loa, e kahe mālie ke ao ola . . . ." Heart Center, region of everlasting love, may the sacred light flow gently in, bringing healing . . . .

The Shen, the spirit of the heart, is sovereign, presiding over the rest of the spirits of the body. It requires peace to feel welcome in its home. This practice will help you tend to the needs of the Shen to bring gentle, supportive stillness to the heart.

Chi Awareness: Heart Chakra

Stand in Zhan Zhuang or sit in meditation. You may want to be in a place of comfort, beauty, and joy, a place where you feel harmonious intimacy with your environment, yourself, and others.

Circulate the Chi in the Orbits. As the Orbits spin, use your Chi palms to scan the area of your heart. Do you find a heart open with compassion and hope or cautious and closed shut? What emotions need to be cleansed in order for the heart to be at peace? Do you find rage from an unhealthy relationship? Do you find isolation from disappointment in intimacy?

What does your heart need for balance? Does it need the clarity of the mind or the centeredness of the root? Does it need the work of your Chi suction to drain excess or Chi pump to invigorate? Apply Chi hand techniques as desired to the area of your heart. If your heart desires comforting touch, place your Chi palm over the middle of your sternum (CV17). Listen. How does your heart respond?

When your heart feels comfortable and relaxed, inhale and feel the refreshing air Chi entering your nostrils. Observe how its temperature warms as it circulates over blood vessels in the walls, gliding smoothly into your throat and chest. What are the colors and textures of your breath descending into the space of your heart? Feel the breath expanding, filling your ribcage, pressing gently into the inner lining of your ribs and sternum. Then feel the breath release.

Listen to the sound of your breath in the rivers of blood entering the chambers of your heart. Each breath brings calm. Each breath ushers in quiet joy. Feel the realm of the heart gently pulsing in harmony. You are cultivating a harmonious abode for the Shen. What image appears? A meditation cave? A kiva? A warm campfire? A grove of favorite trees? An intimate gathering of loving family or friends? What kind of environment supports your heart's peace?

As your heart rests in the embrace of loving and protective support, allow your arms to relax at your sides. Enjoy this realm of intimate stillness.

Twins: Katie and Terri

Throat Chakra: Heartsong

Chi Awareness: Throat Chakra

In a comfortable place with pleasing sounds, stand in Zhan Zhuang or sit in meditation. Engage Tan Tien breathing. Find the rhythm of your breath and your center of balance and close your eyes.

Bring your attention to your shoulders. Let your scapulae descend toward the earth. Feel the base of your neck at C7 open and relaxed. Notice how, as the base of your neck relaxes, your clavicles relax. Feel the seven cervical vertebrae of the neck, with the disks like porous sponges between them, stacking over your shoulders, clavicles, and ribcage. Invite your breath into the cavern of your throat and feel its vibrations rippling the tunnel walls. The breath spreads up your neck, lifting the base of your skull off the top of your neck. Let your head float, then gently rock back and forth, side to side, circle one way then the other, undulations diminishing until you find that place where your head and the bridge of your neck are relaxed and balanced over your shoulders.

As your head, neck, and shoulders open and relax, your arms also open and relax, ready to reach out, to do your bidding, to share your heart's desire through the expression of your handiwork or the connection of touch.

Now notice the area at the base of your throat above the sternal notch. As your entire body relaxes and your attention comes to focus in this area, do you find it tender, vulnerable, pulsing, like a songbird chick ready to loose its first song?

What is the sound of your throat opening? What is your heart's true song? Go ahead. Sing it out. And when you are finished, rest.

Releasing Voice: Aurélia

Kaleo's Journal: Aurélia's Voice

Smearing, kneading, pushing, and pulling with massage oil, charcoal, and pastels, Aurélia struggled with her drawing. As she massaged it with the inquisitive and intuitive hearts of her palms (P8/Labor Palace), she felt her throat respond to her touch. She heard its plea and understood. As she tore open the throat of her drawing and listened to the ripping of paper, a guttural sound sprung from her throat. A voice choked back from her difficult childhood left her body. Once it released, she excitedly finished her drawing. She empowered her voice, giving it a new place in the world through creativity.

Mind Chakra: Beam of Light

Chi Awareness: Mind Chakra

Stand in Zhan Zhuang or sit in meditation. Engage Tan Tien breathing and feel yourself grounding. Feel your body aligned and relaxed, your head and seven cervical vertebrae stacked and centered over your shoulders and ribcage. Let your head gently rock back and forth, side to side, circle one way then the other, undulations diminishing until you find that place where you feel your vertebrae and head are comfortably balanced and stable over your shoulders.

Inhale, and direct your attention, breath, and Chi to flow as one in the Orbits. As the Chi flows along the back of your neck, feel the base of your skull lifting off the atlas at the top of your neck. Notice both your head and body becoming lighter and more at ease. On the next inhalation, as the soft niche between the top of your spine and the base of your skull (GV16) opens, fresh Chi streams in. Observe the size and shape of the opening. What are the temperature and color of the stream filling your inner cranium?

This Chi bathes your medulla oblongata and embraces your brain and its center (pituitary, hypothalamus, and pineal glands). On the next inhalation, the Chi expands into the walls of your inner temples and the floor of your cranial vault (sphenoid bone). It fills the deep sockets of your eyes, cleansing and relaxing them. As your eyeballs sink in relaxation, your third eye awakens. On the next inhalation, fresh Chi enters into the lens of your third eye as a beam of indigo light. Feel it explore this area, bringing harmonizing energy into the realm of logic and analytical thought.

The light expands to fill your entire cranium and Tan Tien of the mind. Feel the embrace and support. Somewhere in that space between logical mind and imagination, a portal opens to integration. What is the shape of the portal? What is the sound of it opening? Feel the current moving through and connecting the two dimensions. Feel your entire head light and open, yet grounded and connected, to your spine, your body, the earth beneath your feet. And when you are finished, rest.

Mind Chakra: Carolyn

Crown Chakra: Bridge to Heavenly Chi

Chi Awareness: Crown Chakra

In a comfortable place, on a warm evening under the stars, stand and ground in Zhan Zhuang or sit in meditation. Engage Tan Tien breathing. Find the rhythm of your breath and your center of balance and close your eyes. Let your breath open and relax the joints of your body. Now with your breath, circulate the Chi through the Orbits.

There are many plates of bone in the skull joined by sutures. With your fingertips explore the midline of the top of your head until you find the small linear crevice. Rest the heels of your palms on the left and right temples of your skull and place your fingerpads along this crevice, the sagittal suture. On the next inhalation, ever so gently, squeeze and lift the sides of your cranium with your palms, hold for a few seconds, then, ever so gently, release them. You may want to repeat this action. Now, with your palms still on your left and right temples and your fingerpads along the sagittal suture, listen. Feel the rhythmic pulse deep within your cranium. Feel cranial plates quietly shifting. Enjoy this moment of intimacy with this deep pulse. What is its sound? What is its timing?

When you are ready, scan with your Chi palm for heat rising from your crown chakra. When you sense this current, using your Chi sword about an inch above your crown, spiral counterclockwise. Feel the energetic opening of your crown chakra.

Feel the crown like a small mouth, open to the heavens. Feel your Chi rise through the opening like a fountain cresting, mingling with heavenly Chi. Aim for the brightest light among the stars. Feel the vastness and the intelligence of the universe. Listen. Can you hear its vibration? What is the sound of the pulse of the universe? What is the timing?

The Chi descends back through the opening at your crown to continue its pathway in the Orbits. Each circuit graces you with heavenly Chi. Feel the Chi within you enlarging, the aura around you expanding, your Chi reaching out into the universe. And when you are finished, rest.

Crown Chakra: Gaelyn

The Ethereal Thread and the Chakras

The ethereal thread is an energetic current passing through the axis of the body and connecting you to the energy of heaven and earth. On its way through your body, it passes through the seven chakras.

Chi Awareness: Journey of the Ethereal Thread

 Stand and ground in Zhan Zhuang or sit in meditation, as your perineum and crown remain soft and open. Engage Tan Tien breathing and close your eyes.

Soften your pelvis over your relaxed legs and let your sacrum hang. Notice its rhythmic swivel. Stack your vertebrae up your back, as your ribcage centers over your pelvis. Now let your chest and shoulders soften, relax, and widen, so that your arms hang naturally from their open shoulder joints. Your body weight hangs from your stacked bones. Feel the top of your neck lift off the atlas, so that your head becomes buoyant and your neck long and open. All the muscles in your face relax.

Inhale and feel your third eye opening. Look inward and up toward the heavens with your inner eye to observe an ethereal thread. See how it descends from the zenith of the heavens into your crown, which bridges your body and heaven. What are the color and size of this ethereal thread? What is its texture? How does the thread change as it moves through your crown?

Observe the thread passing through the center of your cranium and into the realm of the third eye, the *Tan Tien of the mind,* world of the snow-capped mountains. At the center of this world, the thread enters a clear mountain lake and passes through the depths and out the basin of the lake.

Observe the thread bridging your head and body at your throat. Feel your throat tingling and pulsing. What happens to the thread as it descends the throat? Does it tremble and hum with the inspiration of voice?

Feel the thread descending into the chest, into the *Tan Tien of the heart,* where it encounters a huge volcanic crater bubbling with molten lava. Observe the thread passing through the lava and out the bottom of the crater.

Follow the thread down through the center of your torso. Observe it bridging your upper and lower body at your solar plexus. What happens to the thread as it passes through the solar plexus? Does it quiver with recognition of the significance of its journey? Is it steady and confident as it bridges what is above and what is below?

The thread descends on down into the hara, the *Tan Tien of the pelvis,* where it encounters a great sea. It enters the ocean and travels down through the layers. What do you find in the depths? What mysteries swim in the dark currents?

Follow the thread bridging your body and earth as it passes through the soft perineum and descends into the center of the earth.

Inhale into your pelvic Tan Tien. Feel the ethereal thread trembling, as your breath expands outward from your core and ripples through the layers of organs, bones, muscles, and skin into the energy aura that surrounds your body. Exhale and feel your physical and energetic bodies nurturing and supporting each other.

Art and Journaling: Journey of the Ethereal Thread

Write in your journal: Which bridge seemed most significant to you: crown, throat, solar plexus, root? Which Tan Tien will you draw first: mind, heart, pelvis? What pulled you into it? Which Tan Tien feels strongest in you? Which is asking for cultivation?

Using large sheets of paper (three for the Tan Tiens or seven for the chakras) and an abundance of drawing/collage supplies, create the ethereal thread and its passage through your body. How does it traverse the chakras? What symbolizes the ethereal thread? What connects the sheets of paper? Hemp, cordage, wire, silken thread?

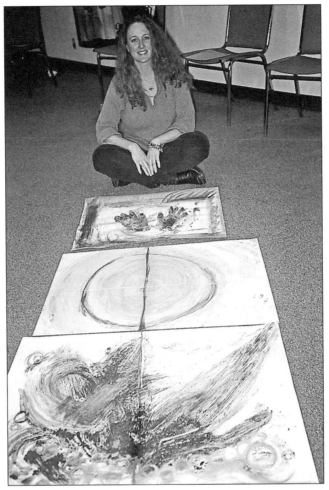

Ethereal Thread: Julie

Chi Awareness: The Guardians of the Three Tan Tiens

The Tan Tiens of the mind, heart, and pelvis are powerful sources of deep wisdom. They have different terrains as well as different guardians. Which Tan Tien will you explore today?

Stand in Zhan Zhuang or sit in meditation. Engage Tan Tien breathing and close your eyes. Let your breath open and relax your body's core. Then bring your attention to the crown of your head.

Observe the ethereal thread passing from the heavens into your crown. The thread descends into the realm of your third eye and the Tan Tien of your mind. Enter into the landscape of the clear mountain lake in the world of snow-capped mountains. Follow the thread as it descends through your throat and into the Tan Tien of your heart. Enter into the landscape of the lake of lava in the volcanic crater. Follow the thread as it descends through your solar plexus and into the realm of your hara and the Tan Tien of your pelvis. Enter into the landscape of the great sea in the basin of the pelvis. Follow the thread as it shimmers down through your root, out through your soft perineum, and into the earth.

Which of the three landscapes, mind, heart, or pelvis, seems most inviting today? Return to this domain and explore the landscape. What do you find there? Travel to the center of the terrain and look into the lake, lava, or sea. Your reflection lies in the depths of the liquid. It transforms into the face of the *guardian*. Who is the guardian rising from the depths of the Tan Tien to meet you? What secrets does it guard? What treasures does it protect?

Listen to a question emerging from your core. Offer it to the guardian. How does the guardian reply? What secret does it share with you? What lesson does it impart? The guardian offers you a flask. What is the taste of pristine lake water, or warm liquid from the crater, or the salt of the sea?

Thank the guardian and inhale softly. Exhale and the wind of your breath ripples the surface of liquid. Watch the face of the guardian disappearing into the depths.

Journaling and Art: The Guardians of the Three Tan Tiens

To which Tan Tien did you travel today? What was enticing about this region? Who was the guardian you encountered? What were your question and its answer? How did you feel after drinking the liquid from the flask? What significance do these events hold for you? Draw the guardian of the Tan Tien, the landscape, the flask.

Each time you travel to a different Tan Tien and encounter its guardian, embody it in art.

When you have traveled to all three regions, met all three guardians, and given them creative expression, bring your art pieces together. What does their collective message say to you?

Guardian: Elma

Chi Awareness: The Drop and the Ethereal Thread

Stand in Zhan Zhuang or sit in meditation. Engage Tan Tien breathing and close your eyes. Your crown and perineum remain soft and open.

Your sacrum sits softly in your pelvis. Your vertebrae stack one above the other up your back. Your chest is soft and relaxed and your shoulders are wide. Your arms hang with open joints. Your face is relaxed. Your head is relaxed, softly floating atop your spine.

From the zenith of the heavens, the ethereal thread descends through the core of your body and down into the earth. Far above you a droplet of moisture has condensed on the thread and is gliding down toward your crown. It squeezes through the opening in your crown and travels down the thread through the Tan Tien of your mind, the bridge of your throat, the Tan Tien of your heart, the bridge of your solar plexus, the Tan Tien of your pelvis, the root of your body. The droplet squeezes through the center of your soft perineum and descends the thread. As it enters the earth, the ethereal thread shimmers and disappears. Enter the emptiness at your core.

This is Wu Chi.

Tiger's Breath Chi Kung

Foundations of Tiger's Breath Chi Kung

Kaleo's Journal: Tiger Stalking

Broad green leaves shade the thick moist earth of rainforest. Fragrance of ʻawapuhi blossoms permeates the air. White tiger's feet prowl, explore, and melt into the softness of earth. Soles of feet open and draw in the richness of earth's Chi. Bones, muscles, and tissues understand. Tiger trusts his body and its ancient wisdom of instincts. His mood is self-contained, solitary.

Guttural breath emerges from deep in the cavern of his belly, his Tan Tien. Tiger stripes move like waves across undulating muscles, which ripple and sometimes shudder as Chi flows through meridians.

Chakras pulse and breathe, opening into tunnels to other realms: of spirit, of emotions, of distant eras. They've done this before in another time and place.

Crown pulses and opens to receive the divine essence, the intelligence, and the Chi of the heavens.

Background

Chi Kung penetrates deeply into the layers of the body, beneath the skin, fascia, and muscles, into the inner pulse of organs, the surge of Chi in meridians, and the tracks of the ancestors in the twisting paths of DNA. Chi Kung's roots go back 5,000 years. Its quest continues to beckon, promising glimpses into deep mysteries, discoveries of profound value, and personal revelations embedded in universal truths.

The ancient principles and practices of Chi Kung persist through eons of secrecy. They endure the scrutiny of contemporary science. They straddle the chasm between science and spirituality, bowing respectfully to both, yet not dependent on any test or school, any dogma or belief, for their durability.

Chi Kung is like its spiritual source, the Tao. It is not any one thing. It cannot be pinned down. It changes. It *is* change. Yet you can count on it. It has continuity. It endures—as long as anyone is around to keep its wisdom alive. And even if not, the entire universe is an expression of Chi Kung, the work of Chi.

Tiger's Breath is just one of thousands of Chi Kung practices. It is a form we developed over many years as an integration: of many levels of traditional wisdom; of body, mind, and spirit; of physical exercise, energetic balancing, meditative awareness, and body prayer. It combines influences of our extensive study with many qualified teachers and personal practice in Chi Kung, as well as Tai Chi, Traditional Chinese Medicine, acupressure, massage, hatha yoga, meditation, hypnotherapy, and breathwork. Together we bring fifty years of combined practice to our sharing of Tiger's Breath. The entire form takes about fifteen minutes to perform and is too long and its movements too intricate to portray adequately in the context of this book. However, the Tiger's Breath opening sequence presented in this chapter has a beneficial and comprehensive influence in and of itself.

We combine Chi Kung with creative process for greater self-awareness and integration. Our practices with Chi evolve from our love of Chi Kung and related disciplines; our practices in creativity evolve from our love of art, poetry, prose, and the inner journey. When we acquired our foundations and degrees in our creative practices (Kaleo in painting, drawing, and lithography and Elise in literature and writing), we, as students, were highly encouraged to discover and express our *inner artists*. We have found that, in harvesting, combining, and integrating the wisdom of the two realms, practices with Chi become more creative and practices with creativity become infused with greater vital energy. Their dance feels as essential to us as the dance of Yin and Yang.

Practice

We feel that whatever practice you do should be engaged with integrity, with the wisdom of the teachers, of the ancestors, and of your own devoted practice. We encourage you on your journey of awareness and expression of your inner artist and your resources of Chi to discover and manifest your uniqueness.

When you practice Tiger's Breath Chi Kung, you may want to consider the five element influences. You may want to practice where there is abundant fresh air to strengthen your lungs (metal) or release old stuck grief. You may want to practice in the presence of a freely flowing river to boost your stamina or nourish your water element. You may want to practice in a woods to let the trees absorb stress and stimulate motivation. You may want to practice with a circle of friends to feed your fire element's need for intimacy and connectedness with others. You may want to practice in cloth shoes on firm earth for centering and grounding in the earth element.

We are nature. In Tiger's Breath Chi Kung we breathe and move in rhythm with nature. We are mind. In Tiger's Breath Chi Kung we open to wonder at the intelligence of the universe beyond (macrocosm) and the universe within (microcosm). We are Chi. Tiger's Breath Chi Kung will help you to feel the cleansing, harvesting, moving, transmitting powers of Chi.

As you engage Tiger's Breath Chi Kung, respect its ancestral wisdom. If you feel inspired, study acupressure and Traditional Chinese Medicine to deepen your understanding. Then explore and discover your core, your inner core of Chi, and let it dance with your inner artist through the integration of Chi and creativity.

In all of us our ancestors, spirit guides, and teachers are alive. Every day, in all kinds of situations, we share their wisdom with others. Some day we all become the ancestors, living on through influencing those who follow.

Kaleo's Journal: September 2006, Becoming the Ancestor

Just before my father died a few months ago, he joined us—his four children and our spouses—as we held hands and encircled his hospital bed. He inherited his mother's Chinese superstitions, and death and its silence always frightened him; however, the sacred silence in his hospital room tingled with respect, honor, and love.

"Ē kō mākou makua i loko o ka lani . . . . " Our *'ohana* (family) prayed together in accordance with our different spiritual beliefs. I can still see Dad's face glowing with pride and love as he looked at all of us. He understood that he and my mother achieved what they had devoted their entire lives to—a close family. As the primary caregiver of my mother during the many years she suffered with Alzheimer's until she died, he modeled fierce devotion, reminding us of what it means to be family.

As we gathered around him, my father saw himself, his parents, his grandparents, and all the ancestors in us. As his children, we are their blood, marrow, bones, DNA. We are their spirit, their shadow, their wisdom.

In the last years of his life, Dad understood the power of his ancestors as he practiced Chi Kung with Elise and me. He marveled at his legacy when he saw the books we wrote. Through the flesh and bones of his descendants and through our creative journeys, he lives on.

Kaleo's mother sings and plays *'ukulele* as father dances *hula*

We all come from various histories and cultures. We express different personalities, struggles, vulnerabilities, and gifts. Every painting, poem, dance, or Chi Kung form is unique with its own physicality, personality, and Chi. Each reveals the evolution of the practitioner's body and soul.

Tiger's Breath Chi Kung Opening Sequence

1   Opening to Heaven and Earth (Chi Breathing)

Stand in Zhan Zhuang with your feet together. Let your palms face the sides of your legs and your fingertips extend downward toward the earth. Balance on the nine points of the bottom of each foot: the pads of the five toes, the two balls, the mid outer arch, and the center of the heel. Place the tip of your tongue on the roof of your mouth behind your upper teeth to bridge the Governing and Conception Vessels.

Engage Tan Tien breathing. Quiet the three Tan Tiens of your mind, heart, and pelvis. Feel the pulsing of your seven chakras. Feel the Micro-Macrocosmic Orbits stirring. Feel your entire body opening to the heavens and the earth. You are the universe.

2   Tiger's Eye Sweeping (Chi Suction, Scanner, Brush)

2a   Step out with your left foot to the side, so that you are standing with feet parallel and hips' distance apart. Bring your hands out in front of you and to the sides. As you continue Tan Tien breathing, feel your joints open and breathing. Your feet (K1) and perineum (CV1) absorb Chi from the earth. Your crown (GV20) absorbs Chi from the heavens. Feel the core of your body full of Chi. Feel the Chi around your body, its texture, its density, its temperature. Feel your Chi palms (P8) and axillae (H1) absorbing environmental Chi. You are nature.

2b   Then bring your palms in medially to feed your pelvic Tan Tien. With fingertips pointing toward each other and slightly curved in toward your midline, scan your Chi aura. Feel its bounce. Inhaling, sweep your palms up the front of your torso.

2c   Exhaling, sweep your palms around your neck and scan and brush your Chi aura.

2d   Inhaling, bring your palms to the back of your skull, scanning and brushing the Chi aura as you go. Your elbows are separated and your fingers point beneath the occipital ridge (GV16).

2e Then, as your elbows come together without touching, sweep your palms over your crown.

2f Exhaling, sweep your palms down in front of your face, elbows together but not touching. As your palms reach your throat, your elbows begin to spread apart.

2g With your fingers pointing toward each other but not touching, scan and brush down the Chi aura at the front of your torso.

2h Quietly exhale the inner sound of metal (*hsss*) as you move down.

2i Release waste Chi into the earth.

3 Pulsing Tiger (Chi Pump)

3a Breathe and harvest fresh earth Chi with your palms, feet, and perineum into your Tan Tien. With your fingertips send the Chi into your coccyx and sacrum to stimulate the Microcosmic Orbit (Governing Vessel).

3b With fingertips pointing toward each other and slightly curved in toward your midline, inhale and bring earth Chi up to your heart area. Breathe and with your palms pulse Chi into your lungs and heart.

4 Tiger's Eye Washing and Feeding Crown to Perineum (Chi Nourisher)

4a Exhale as your palms sweep around and feed Chi into your throat, then chin, jaw, and ears.

4b Separate your elbows and point your fingers into the soft niche beneath the occipital ridge (GV16).

4c Inhaling, bring your elbows together but not touching; then with your palms pull the membrane of Chi over your crown chakra.

4d Exhaling, sweep your palms down in front of your face, washing and feeding your third eye chakra. As your palms reach the bridge, feel your tongue's tip against the roof of your mouth bridging the Microcosmic Orbit.

4e As your palms face your throat chakra, your elbows begin to spread apart, and you wash and feed down your front, fingers pointing toward each other but not touching. Feel your palms and fingers vibrating with Chi and stimulating the Microcosmic Orbit (Conception Vessel).

4f Quietly exhale the inner sound of metal (*hsss*) as you sweep your palms down your throat, heart, solar plexus, hara, and root chakras to your perineum.

4g Release waste Chi into the earth.

5 Tiger's Mouth

5a Breathe and harvest fresh earth Chi through your palms, feet, and perineum. Then inhale and bring the Chi around each side to your lower back.

5b Make a triangle with your thumbs and index fingers (not touching). The triangle encloses your Ming Men (GV4), and your right and left tiger's mouths (LI4) cleanse and feed the right and left kidneys. Breathe.

5c Inhale and drag your tiger's mouths along your waist (Belt Vessel) out to your sides.

5d Quietly exhale the inner sound of water (*chru*) as you shoot your hands forward with elbows flexed, palms open and facing up, with your fingers pointing forward and open like a fan. Feel stagnant and negative Chi shooting out of your arms through your fingertips and falling at a distance to the earth.

6   Greeting the Sun (Chi Brush, Siphon, Nourisher)

6a   Inhaling, flex your knees and lengthen your lower back and begin to bend forward at your hips.

6b   Quietly exhale the inner sound of wood (*shhh*) as your palms brush Chi down your outer and back legs (Yang) and out your feet and toes, releasing waste Chi.

6c   Then with knees flexed in a half-squat, lengthen your lower back, raise your arms (palms facing each other) to stretch out and up alongside your ears, and greet the sun. Breathe. Feel Chi washing down from the heavens into your crown and fingertips and down your arms, into your torso. Feel earth Chi ascending through your feet, up your legs, and into your torso. As you continue Tan Tien breathing, feel heavenly and earth Chi mingling in your Tan Tien.

6d Then medially rotate your upper arm (humerus) bones so the backs of your hands turn to face each other.

6e Inhale and fold your torso over your knees as you draw your hands back toward you until they come down alongside your inner feet and point to earth.

6f As you continue inhaling, bring fresh earth Chi into your feet and up your inner legs (Yin), while you roll your spine up over your flexed knees.

6g   Come back to standing position. Breathe. Your palms now feed your pelvic Tan Tien.

7   Sweeping Yin and Yang, Left Side (Chi Brush, Knife)

7a   Inhaling, brush your right palm up the right side of your torso (ascending colon) along the nipple line. Then brush out across your upper chest to your left shoulder's hollow (as your left palm turns to face up).

7b   Quietly exhale the inner sound of fire (*haaa*) as you brush your right palm down your inner left arm (Yin) and cleanse waste Chi out your fingertips.

7c Draw the waste Chi out and use your Chi knife to cut the connection.

7d As your left palm turns to face down, inhale and with your right palm bring fresh restorative Chi up your outer left arm (Yang), shoulder, and neck.

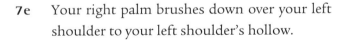

7e Your right palm brushes down over your left shoulder to your left shoulder's hollow.

7f Exhale and continue brushing down the left side of your torso along the nipple line, over your lower abdomen (descending colon), and back to the right side of your body.

8 Sweeping Yin and Yang, Right Side (Chi Brush, Knife)

8a Inhaling, brush your left palm up the right side of your torso (ascending colon) along the nipple line to your right shoulder's hollow (as your right palm turns to face up).

8b Quietly exhale the inner sound of fire (*haaa*) as you brush your left palm down your inner right arm (Yin) and cleanse waste Chi out your fingertips.

8c Draw the waste Chi out and use your Chi knife to cut the connection.

8d As your right palm turns to face down, inhale and with your left palm bring fresh Chi up your outer right arm (Yang), shoulder, and neck.

8e Brush across your upper chest to your left shoulder's hollow.

8f   Exhale as your left palm brushes Chi down the left side of your torso along the nipple line over your lower abdomen (descending colon).

9   Releasing Chi into Earth

Quietly exhaling the inner sound of earth (*hooo*), release waste Chi from your fingertips into the earth.

10   Harvesting Earth, Environmental, Heavenly Chi (Chi Siphon, Brush, Nourisher, Suction)

10a   Continuing Tan Tien breathing, gather fresh earth Chi into your palms. Inhale and sweep your arms out to your sides and rotate them so that your palms face up. Continue sweeping up, as your fingers reach out to scoop environmental Chi.

10b Keep sweeping your palms up to the point above your head where you can feel the Chi ball between your palms. Breathe and harvest heavenly Chi.

10c Then direct the heavenly Chi with your fingertips into your crown.

10d As you quietly exhale the sound of triple warmer fire (*eeee*), your palms wash Chi from your crown down the chakras all the way to your feet.

10e Bring your hands out in front of you and to the sides. As you inhale, open all the joints of your body and suction fresh Chi into your joints, bones, flesh, orifices, and internal organs. As you exhale, let the Chi permeate deeper into your cells.

10f Breathe and feed your pelvic Tan Tien with your Chi palms.

11 Storing Chi (Chi Nourisher)

11a **(Women)** Store Chi in the pelvic Tan Tien by placing your *left* hand over your *right* over your navel.

11a **(Men)** Store Chi in the pelvic Tan Tien by placing your *right* hand over your *left* over your navel.

11b Extend your arms down and out until your palms face the sides of your legs. Bring your left foot in next to your right foot. Close with a personal chant, prayer, or invocation of your muse.

To view a video of this Tiger's Breath introductory sequence, visit www.kaleoching.com.

Benefits of Tiger's Breath Chi Kung

Kaleo finds that doing the Tiger's Breath opening sequence between massage clients helps him to cleanse any deleterious Chi he may have absorbed, to replenish expended Chi, and to stretch his muscles and open his joints. We (Kaleo and Elise) also do it in the morning as prayer to set our intentions for the day. We do it during times of stress to center and ground, to calm the mind, and to gain clarity. We do it prior to creative process to invoke the muse and ancestral guides.

Tiger's Breath Chi Kung opening sequence employs *Tan Tien breathing* and all its benefits. It uses *Chi hand techniques* to balance the flow of Chi in the body, nourish and cleanse the *five element organs and their twelve meridians,* and activate the *Eight Extraordinary Vessels.* Stimulating the Governing Vessel and the Conception Vessel moves Chi in the midline of the torso and head along the *Microcosmic Orbit.* Stimulating the Yin and Yang Bridge Vessels, the Yin and Yang Regulator Vessels, and the twelve organ meridians moves Chi in the arms and legs (*Macrocosmic Orbit*) and in the sagittal planes of the body. Stimulating the Belt Vessel moves the Chi in the circumference of the body, balancing upper and lower parts. Stimulating the Penetrating Vessel moves Chi in the core of the body and balances the *chakras.*

Specifically, the movements of Tiger's Breath Chi Kung opening sequence benefit your Chi body in the following ways:

1   **Opening to Heaven and Earth (Chi Breathing)**

   · Integrates the Tan Tiens of the body (pelvis), mind (third eye), and spirit (heart)

   · Bridges the Governing and Conception Vessels (Microcosmic Orbit) at the mouth/tongue and perineum/sacrum

   · Builds Wei Chi

2 **Tiger's Eye Sweeping (Chi Suction, Scanner, Brush)**

- Activates the feet (Kidney 1), perineum (Conception Vessel 1), Penetrating Vessel, axillae (Heart 1), Chi palms (Pericardium 8), and crown (Governing Vessel 20) for Chi absorption

- Feeds the Belt and Penetrating Vessels

- Scans and brushes the aura of Chi around your body

- Benefits the metal element by releasing stuck emotions (grief) and Chi from the lungs (*hsss*)

3 **Pulsing Tiger (Chi Pump)**

- Stimulates the Microcosmic Orbit (Governing Vessel)

- Nourishes the thymus gland, heart, and lungs

4 **Tiger's Eye Washing and Feeding Crown to Perineum (Chi Nourisher)**

- Feeds fresh Chi into and releases stagnant Chi from your throat (thyroid and parathyroid glands), chin and jaw (parotid and salivary glands), ears (acu-points), and brain (pituitary, hypothalamus, and pineal glands)

- Activates the dream center (GV16) at the medulla oblongata

- Balances crown, third eye, throat, heart, solar plexus, hara, and root chakras

- Stimulates the Microcosmic Orbit (Conception Vessel)

- Descends and cleanses stomach meridian

- Supports the cerebrospinal fluid pumps (sacrum and sphenoid) and craniosacral rhythm and the opening/closing of pelvic joints and cranial sutures

- Benefits the metal element by releasing stuck emotions (grief) and Chi from the lungs (*hsss*)

5 **Tiger's Mouth**

· Activates Belt Vessel (enhances Wei Chi and immune system, balances upper and lower body, activates the pelvic Tan Tien)

· Nourishes Ming Men (Governing Vessel 4) and kidneys

· Cleanses and releases stuck Chi from the Belt Vessel

· Benefits the water element by releasing stuck emotions (fear) and Chi from the kidneys (*chru*)

6 **Greeting the Sun (Chi Brush, Siphon, Nourisher)**

· Stimulates the Yang leg and arm meridians (Stomach/Large Intestine, Gall Bladder/Triple Warmer, and Bladder/Small Intestine) and Yang Bridge and Regulator Vessels

· Stimulates the Yin leg and arm meridians (Spleen/Lung, Liver/Pericardium, and Kidney/Heart) and Yin Bridge and Regulator Vessels

· Cleanses and feeds the Yang and Yin leg meridians

· Stimulates the Macrocosmic Orbit leg pathways

· Strengthens abdomen, legs, and back

· Channels nourishment from the heavens into the eyes (do not look directly at the sun!), brain and nervous system, and endocrine glands (pituitary, hypothalamus, and pineal)

· Nourishes crown, third eye, throat, heart, and solar plexus chakras with heavenly Chi

· Nourishes root and hara chakras with earth Chi

· Benefits the wood element by releasing stuck emotions (anger) and Chi from the liver (*shhh*)

7 **Sweeping Yin and Yang, Left Side (Chi Brush, Knife) and . . .**

8   Sweeping Yin and Yang, Right Side (Chi Brush, Knife)

·   Cleanses and feeds the Yin (Lung, Pericardium, Heart) and Yang (Large Intestine, Triple Warmer, Small Intestine) meridians of the arms

·   Stimulates the Macrocosmic Orbit arm pathways

·   Regulates the large intestine by following its pathway through the abdomen, up the right (ascending colon), across (transverse colon), and down the left (descending colon and rectum); supports its function of letting go of what is no longer needed

·   Benefits the fire element by releasing stuck emotions (withdrawal) and Chi from the heart (*haaa*)

9   Releasing Chi into Earth

·   Releases Chi stuck on bones and between muscle layers into the earth

·   Benefits the earth element by releasing stuck emotions (worry) and Chi from the spleen (*hooo*)

10   Harvesting Earth, Environmental, Heavenly Chi (Chi Siphon, Brush, Nourisher, Suction)

·   Cleanses and nourishes Penetrating Vessel, ethereal thread, and chakras

·   Feeds body with Chi of earth, environment, and heaven

·   Benefits the endocrine system by cleansing the triple warmer (*eeee*)

11   Storing Chi (Chi Nourisher)

·   Stores Chi in the pelvic Tan Tien and nourishes internal organs and reproductive system

·   Connects the outer galaxy (macrocosm) with the inner galaxy (microcosm), the Divine without and the Divine within

·   Cultivates gratitude and supports transition from Chi Kung practice to daily life

Tiger's Breath Chi Kung and Creativity: Origins

Chi is with you prior to your conception, in the sexual energy exchanged between your parents and in the pre-heaven essence, or ancestral Chi, that mingles in their union. Chi supports your creation and your development. The "big bang" origin of the universe in which we live is an expression of Chi, and your conception was a little bang of creative Chi.

The Eight Extraordinary Vessels form at the very beginning of life. The Penetrating Vessel is primordial in its influence on the core of the body; the Governing and Conception Vessels, dividing the body vertically, manifest in the splitting of the fertilized egg into two cells; the Belt Vessel, transecting the body horizontally, manifests in the splitting into four.

Tiger's Breath Chi Kung: Before Consciousness

Perform the opening sequence of Tiger's Breath Chi Kung. Feel the glow and strength of your Chi pulsing in, through, and around you. Then come to stand in Zhan Zhuang. Feel the weight of your body sinking as you ground into the earth. Feel the ethereal silken thread passing from heaven to earth through your body at the core as the spiritual dimension of the Penetrating Vessel.

Breathe naturally and observe how the thread quivers. Exhale and see how it disappears. As it does so, feel yourself traveling back through time, through the years, through your adolescence, early childhood, back to your very first memory. How old are you? Where are you? What is happening? What are your sensations, your emotions?

Breathe gently. On the next exhalation, feel how you surrender and sink deeper within your body. Allow yourself to travel back further, before your first memory into earliest infancy. Then before that, into the womb, way back into the earliest phases of your life. You are a collection of cells, without recognizable form, yet everything is there within you, part of you, everything necessary to the maturation of you as an adult human being.

What forms you as this young embryo? Feel your precious cells. Feel your DNA inscribing your being with ancestral messages. Feel your instincts bathing in the fluids of your cells. Feel your Chi pulsing in its primordial pathways. Even now, so early, feel its vibration, its color, its texture, as it performs its first tasks in the wee sphere of your new life.

Breathe softly and feel how you are supported within and around. A cord feeds you. A fluid sac holds and protects you. A being you have yet to know as mother carries you and feeds you, not only physically, but energetically, emotionally, spiritually. And beyond her, the earth and the vast universe also hold you, feed you, support your becoming. For you, there is not yet any doing. Only waiting.

Art and Journaling: Embryo

 From your art supplies create your experience of yourself as embryo. Will you use paper and drawing media? Or will you sculpt the minute world of your being and the vast world beyond, which awaits your entry? Before you begin, let your adult consciousness merge with its embryonic origins once more. Then create from your instincts, your DNA, your primordial Chi.

When you have finished, write in your journal. What was it like to be in the world before consciousness? How did you create this world? Did you begin with yourself as embryo? Or with your surroundings?

Now through art create your experience of yourself as a parent or creator. You may want to sculpt a cast of your body. Then collage pictures, photos, mementos of your children or of your artistic creations onto it.

Tiger's Breath Chi Kung: Meridians and Vessels

Tiger's Breath Chi Kung stimulates the twelve "ordinary" meridians of Chi with their pathways near the surface of the body. It also stimulates the Eight Extraordinary Vessels with their more mysterious pathways of Chi deep in the interior. Although the ordinary meridians are easily accessed via acu-points on the surface, their influence permeates the core of the body as they connect with their corresponding organs. Although the sphere of influence of the Extraordinary Vessels is strongest in the core of the body, they can be accessed at the surface through acu-points they share with the ordinary meridians (except the Governing and Conception Vessels, which have their own acu-points along the body's midline). In Traditional Chinese Medicine, everything is always interrelated, a balance of Yin and Yang spiraling.

Tiger's Breath Chi Kung: Rivers and Reservoirs

Begin by standing in Zhan Zhuang to balance, ground, and open to the heavens, environment, and earth. Feel how Tan Tien breathing invigorates and nourishes you. Feel your inhalation expanding your Tan Tien, dropping into your pelvic bowl, and filling the lobes of your lungs. Feel your exhalation releasing. Your muscles and connective tissues sink in relaxation. Your bones are strong and supported by the earth.

Breathing softly, feel the presence of earth. It has its own breath, its own Chi. As you inhale, feel the breath traveling from the earth up your inner feet and legs, into your perineum and sacrum, up your spine, to the crown of your head. As you exhale, feel the breath traveling down your face, along the bridge of your tongue, and into the front of your torso, then down the backs of your legs, and into the earth. Inhale and notice your relationship with the earth as it sends the Chi back up your inner legs. Exhale and let earth Chi gather in your pelvis. Inhale as the Chi ascends your back to the base of your neck. Exhale and the Chi flows over your shoulders, into your armpits, down your inner arms, then out your hands. Inhale and feel the tingling of your fingers, hands, and forearms as the environmental Chi returns up your outer arms to the base of your neck, then up the back of your neck and head, and into your crown.

Notice your relationship with heavenly Chi as it sends Chi into your crown and brain. Exhale as the Chi glides down your face and the front of your torso to gather in your pelvic Tan Tien.

Notice how easily this cycle repeats itself. As you breathe, allow your whole body to absorb the Chi of the earth, the environment, and the heavens. Let the macrocosm feed you as microcosm. You and the universe are one in the mingling of Chi.

You have just run the Micro- and Macrocosmic Orbits. As you practice Tiger's Breath Chi Kung, be aware of these Orbits flowing in their circuits. Feel the rivers of meridians running along the surface of the body with their tributaries branching through the core. Be aware of the reservoirs of Extraordinary Vessels providing storage and supply of Chi for the organs and meridians. Feel your entire body as a network of Chi rivers, tributaries, and reservoirs. Be aware of the fluid channels of Chi traveling through your movements. And as you move in Chi Kung, touch the Chi in the air. Feel its temperature, humidity, texture. Let your arms slice through, your body press into, your fingers and palms carve and hold this Chi that surrounds you.

Then as you finish your Tiger's Breath form, come to stand in meditation. Close your eyes. Be aware of your body as landscape. The pathways of Chi are your natural resources. They feed and nourish you. Your Chi Kung practice nourishes them. Your outer environment, combined with your patterns of eating, sleeping, breathing, and processing emotions and information, uses and replenishes your resources of Chi. Be aware just now of all the things that support your inner landscape and bring it greater health and vitality: your Chi Kung practice, creativity, healthy eating and sleeping habits, rejuvenating activities, people, and environments. Notice how your Chi responds. Do you feel its rivers laughing, its reservoirs sparkling? Allow your awareness to bask in the nurturing aura of all these things that support you.

Your Chi palms are pulsing and warm. See them emitting Chi. Feel the Chi flowing out of your palms and fingers, glowing around your body, urging you to move into writing and painting with this Chi.

Art and Journaling: Rivers and Reservoirs of Chi

In your journal or from your art supplies, create and describe the rivers and reservoirs of Chi in your body, the Chi around your body and exuding from your hands, the Chi in the environment around you. Describe and create how moving in Tiger's Breath Chi Kung accesses, stirs, and motivates the channels of Chi within you.

How do journaling and drawing deepen your awareness of the interactions among your body's tissues, organs, meridians, and vessels?

What were all the positive influences, and how do the healthy habits, environments, activities, and people manifest in this wild inner world?

Tiger's Breath Chi Kung: Internal Organs and Five Elements

Begin by standing in Zhan Zhuang to balance, ground, and open you to the heavens, environment, and earth. Feel how Tan Tien breathing invigorates and nourishes you, as your inhalation expands your Tan Tien, drops into your pelvic basin, and fills your lungs. As your exhalation releases, feel your muscles and connective tissues sink in relaxation. Feel your bones strong and supported by the earth.

Begin to move in Tiger's Breath Chi Kung. As you inhale, feel the breath (metal element) in your lungs. Notice the tingling in your skin and its pores as they breathe in rhythm with the filling and emptying of your lungs. As you fill your lungs from bottom to top, do you notice the white or silver color of fog or mist entering? Feel Chi permeating the organ of your skin. As you move in Tiger's Breath, notice how your Chi palms move stagnant Chi out of your lungs and large intestine then harvest fresh Chi into these organs. Notice, as these organs flush toxins and receive fresh blood, nutrients, and Chi, how they begin to feel and function better. When you exhale, quietly let the inner sound (*hsss*) and excessive emotion of metal (stuck grief) and its old color exit. Then inhale and bring in the color of the pristine white of divine inspiration. Notice how, as your lungs breathe more easily, your entire body responds. Now let the expansion and contraction of your lungs, large intestine, and skin and the flow of Chi throughout your body move you in Tiger's Breath Chi Kung.

As you continue to move in Tiger's Breath, notice, as your body moves, how the interconnective tissues pull, stretch, and massage your kidneys (water element). Notice your brain and nervous system, your bones and marrow, their impulses and movements flowing in synchronicity. As you continue Tiger's Breath, do you notice the blue or black color of water settling, moving, flowing through your body? Water conducts electricity. Feel Chi being conducted through your body's liquids and the marrow of your bones. Notice how your Chi palms move stagnant Chi out of your kidneys, bladder, and reproductive organs, then harvest fresh Chi into these organs. Notice, as these organs flush toxins and receive fresh blood, nutrients, and Chi, how they begin to feel and function better. When you exhale, quietly let the inner sound (*chru*) and excessive emotion of water (unnecessary fear) and its old color exit. Then inhale and bring in the sparkling blue or rich black of endurance, courage, and stamina. Notice how, as your kidneys breathe more easily, your energy increases. Now let the expansion and contraction of your kidneys, bladder, bones, and all the rivers and oceans of fluids throughout your body move you in Tiger's Breath Chi Kung.

As you continue to move in Tiger's Breath, notice, as your body moves, how the interconnective tissues pull, stretch, and massage your liver (wood element). Notice your tendons, ligaments, and joints, supple and synchronized in flowing movement. As you continue Tiger's Breath, do you notice the green color of wood spurting, growing, spiraling, climbing? Feel the suppleness of Chi penetrating your body's joints. Notice how your Chi palms move stagnant Chi out of your liver and gall bladder then harvest fresh Chi into these organs. Notice, as these organs flush toxins and receive fresh blood, nutrients, and Chi, how they begin to feel and function better. When you exhale, quietly let the inner sound (*shhh*) and excessive emotion of wood (undue anger, stress, frustration, or resentment) and its old color exit. Then inhale and bring in the rich green of strong motivation, growth, decisiveness, and manifestation. Notice how, as your liver breathes more easily, your body relaxes and releases stress. Now let the expansion and contraction of your liver, gall bladder, and all the joints throughout your body move you in Tiger's Breath Chi Kung.

As you continue to move in Tiger's Breath, notice, as your body moves, how the interconnective tissues pull, stretch, and massage your pericardium and heart (fire element). Notice your blood and cardiovascular system pulsing in synchronized movement. As you continue Tiger's Breath, do you notice the red color of fire surging, purging, and invigorating all the cells throughout your body? Feel the warmth of Chi being transported through your body's circulatory system. Notice how your Chi palms move stagnant Chi out of your heart, pericardium, small intestine, and triple warmer (endocrine system) then harvest fresh Chi into these organs and glands. Notice, as these organs and glands flush toxins and receive fresh blood, nutrients, and Chi, how they begin to feel and function better. When you exhale, quietly let the inner sound (*haaa*) and excessive emotion of fire (withdrawal or alienation) and its old color exit. Then inhale and bring in the vibrant red of connectedness, intimacy, and love. Notice how, as your heart and pericardium breathe more easily, your circulation improves. Now let the expansion and contraction of your heart, pericardium, and entire circulatory system move you in Tiger's Breath Chi Kung.

As you continue to move in Tiger's Breath, notice, as your body moves, how the interconnective tissues pull, stretch, and massage your spleen (earth element). Notice your muscles and flesh, how they undulate in flowing movement. As you continue Tiger's Breath, do you notice the yellow color of earth shifting and settling throughout your body? Feel the Chi surging through open, warm, lengthened, flexible muscles. Notice how your Chi palms move stagnant Chi out of your spleen and stomach then harvest fresh Chi into these organs. Notice, as these organs flush toxins and receive fresh blood, nutrients, and Chi, how they begin to feel and function better. When you exhale, quietly let the inner sound (*hooo*) and excessive emotion of earth (chronic worry or anxiety) and its old color exit. Then inhale and bring in the golden yellow of calm, peace, centeredness, and groundedness. Notice how, as your spleen breathes more easily, your digestion improves. Now let the expansion and contraction of your spleen, stomach, entire digestive tract with all its sphincters, and the relaxed muscles of your body move you in Tiger's Breath Chi Kung.

When you have finished, as you harvest Chi from earth, environment, and heaven into your crown and direct it down your midline, feel the vibration of the triple warmer and release its inner sound (*eeee*). Then draw Chi into your body and store it in your pelvic Tan Tien. Then rest.

Art and Journaling: Five Element Landscape

 In your journal or from your art supplies, create the interior landscape of organs, tissues, emotions, colors, sounds, and symbols.

How do the five elements show up in your inner landscape? Is there the pure white of divine light? The sapphire blue of fresh water? The verdant green of a well nourished spring forest? The warm red touch of fire? The rich golden yellow of fertile earth? How are the organs and elements in your body interrelated and dependent on one another?

As you do Tiger's Breath Chi Kung, how does moving from your internal organs, these sources of energy and life, deepen your awareness of your Chi and its movement through your body?

Charlie Lucke

Tiger's Breath

Tiger's Breath Chi Kung: Animal Awareness

The white tiger inspires Kaleo as he moves in Tiger's Breath Chi Kung. What animal instincts and sensitivities have you felt stirring in you as you sink deeply in Zhan Zhuang or move fluidly in Chi Kung? Does dragon, monkey, snake, or horse come to you from the Chinese Zodiac? Does bear come from the dark cave or wolf from the remote tundra? Does eagle lift you in flight? Does dolphin undulate your spine and guide you deep into the sea of creative mysteries? Invite your Chi Kung totem animal to emerge!

Tiger's Breath Chi Kung: Animal Movement

Prepare to do Tiger's Breath Chi Kung. As you calm your mind, your breath, and your body, allow your attention to sink deeply into your pelvic Tan Tien and engage Tan Tien breathing.

Inhale and feel how your pelvic bowl and all the tissues supporting it receive your breath and relax. Your Tan Tien breathing is efficient, relaxing, nourishing. Feel how each inhalation fills and feeds the walls of your pelvis. Feel how each exhalation frees you from any aimless thought or habitual tension. As you inhale deeply, you notice the smell of an animal's nest or den. You feel safe and comfortable and accept its invitation. Enter the den. Notice a slight movement. An animal stirs. Listen as it awakens and travels around its den. Feel its warm breath feeding the muscles and tissues of your pelvis. Feel your breath becoming animal breath.

As your breath moves in and out and your tissues expand and contract, listen. Your animal is making its sound. Is it a low growl, or a contented purr, or a patient hum? What animal's voice echos in your belly? What animal's voice resonates with your breath?

What animal's skin, muscles, bones, and organs tingle and quiver within you? What animal readies itself to move you in Chi Kung? You feel its presence, its alertness, its poise, its instinctive bodily awareness eager to guide you in the familiar sequence.

As the animal within you moves you in Tiger's Breath, you reach a point, perhaps between an inhalation and exhalation, where you feel an opening in your awareness. Step through that opening and the breath of your animal releases. What is its sound?

Who are you? Eagle soaring over mountains? Panther stalking in the jungle? Wolf sauntering over snow-covered fields? Otter twirling in the surf? Dragon snaking among stars? Free of thought, one with movement, you become Chi Kung. Stretch and glide, flex and spiral, in rhythm with animal instincts.

Within the dance lies a message for you. What is it?

Then when you are ready, let animal awareness guide you to your art supplies.

Art and Journaling: Animal Chi Kung

How does your animal express itself through art? Does it smear color on paper with paws, or trace lines with claws, or sprinkle the aromas of its favorite herbs? Does it dash glitter like the stars of the night sky? Or draw the trees that hide its movements? Does it burrow into the art as into the den where it sleeps? Does it rub its fur and scales against the art piece to make the shapes of you and it together moving in Chi Kung? Does it mold a mask of your face behind which you and your animal become one?

Then, when your animal comes to rest, write in your journal: Who is your Chi Kung animal and what have you learned from it? What does it experience through you? What lessons do you have to share with each other?

After, allow your animal to return to its den within your body. Where does it reside? In your pelvis, your heart, your mind? In your shoulder's hollow (Lung 1) or your large intestine or along your spine? Feel it resting quietly, satisfied about this encounter with you of exploring and creating through ancient movement.

Then when you are ready, return to your daily world. You can always sense this animal's presence. Just as Chi itself, your animal is always there with you, for you.

XI
Conclusion

As you continue combining your awareness of Chi with your own explorations in creativity, notice your joy of discovery as you apply your expanding wisdom to other areas of your life. Feel your deepening understanding enhancing such endeavors as massage, yoga, martial arts, gardening, dancing, working on the computer, or hiking up a mountain. Notice how your relationships with yourself, your partner, family, colleagues, and friends benefit, shift, deepen.

In exploring the processes in this book, you have learned many techniques in Chi awareness. You have experienced how Tan Tien breathing massages your internal organs, builds Chi, and strengthens your immune system. You have used your Chi palms for deeper understanding of yourself, others, and your creative explorations. You have experienced the alchemical transformations of the five elements energetically and creatively. You have explored the surrender of lying meditation, the focus of sitting meditation, the strength of standing meditation. You have felt the power of Chi circling in the Orbits and harmonizing the chakras. You have gained flexibility, strength, and balance through moving in Tiger's Breath Chi Kung. You have nourished your body and spirit through the connection between your Chi and the Chi of the heavens, earth, and environment. You have entered the stillness and inner peace at your core.

Some practices have invited you to focus your mind and train your body as you explore. But always the invitation is there to create. You are unique. Only you feel what your body feels. Only you have your emotions just as you have them. Only you experience your epiphanies as you do. Only you create as you do.

XII

Breath of the Universe

In a serene place in nature, stand or sit easily and naturally in Zhan Zhuang. As your eyes gently close, receive the comfort of this haven. Feel the temperature around you. Let your feet spread over the soft, welcoming earth beneath you. Let your spirit enter into the spaciousness of your inner being. You are in harmony with the heavens and earth.

Inhaling, welcome breath into your nostrils. Taste breath gliding down into the cavern of your throat. Feel it descending through your torso, slipping into the anticipating walls of your pelvic vessel, and filling your Tan Tien with precious Chi. Observe breath glowing into your supple lungs and pressing gently into the chamber of your ribs, ascending into your skull and spreading into the inner lining of your cranium. Then exhaling, feel breath releasing, cleansing, soothing the interior of your body.

Inhaling, enjoy the continuous wave of breath ebbing and flowing. All your cells breathe and absorb Chi. Let breath sway you, so you rock back and forth, side to side, circling one way then the other, undulations diminishing until you find the vessels of your pelvis, ribcage, and skull comfortably balanced and aligned over your feet. Then on the next exhalation, let go. As your muscles and flesh sigh in relaxation, feel your bones strong and supported by Gaia, the earth.

Savor your breath. Feel rich blood circulating through your body. Feel rivers and reservoirs abundant with Chi. Your flesh, organs, and bones are alive, breathing, generating warmth. Your nervous system tingles with signals. Your chakras are open and aware as they scan the field of energy around you. They notice its climate, texture, ambience. What do they feel? A warm glow? A cool current? Divine presence?

Inhale and your awareness turns to the spaciousness of your core. Breathe softly, mindfully. Do you smell a fragrance of familiar herbs or flowers, hear the harmony of inner sounds, see colors of energy glowing in your core?

Let your consciousness interact with the energy fields inside you, around you, and beyond you. Let your awareness dance between your inner and outer worlds. Where do they meet? Do they meet at the aura of Chi around your body? How far out does your aura extend? Or do they meet at the surface of your skin? Or at the energy membrane of the Wei Chi beneath your skin, or between your muscles, or deep inside your bones? How far inside you does the energy around you touch?

You are alive! Feel the force of gravity pull you, the Chi of the planets tug you. Let the hidden constellations of stars twirl you. Listen. Your muse is inviting you to explore, discover, and express. Feel creativity pulsing and urging muscles, sinews, and bones to stretch and flex, to spiral and release. Maybe it jiggles you so you bounce, or nudges you so you sway, or tickles you into laughter, or empowers you to shout. Maybe it sits on its haunches and howls at the moon or prowls like a cat through the jungle. Does it want to lean into the Chi of a tree, or bubble like the Chi of a brook, or play with the Chi of the breeze spiraling around you? Does it want to snuggle down among the wildflowers?

Trust. Dance with the heavens and earth. Listen and respond to your own creative source of Chi. Create your own personal, unique choreography—a moving mythology from your body and soul.

You are the beat of your heart. You are alchemy embodied. You are rivers and reservoirs of Chi. You are the breath of the Universe. You are Chi and creativity.

Appendix: Materials, Herbs, and Spices for Art

A bounty of art supplies is like a huge buffet. Feast in all the colors, aromas, textures, temperatures, densities, shapes, and images. Respond to them as they inspire joy, abundance, and creative freedom. The following are some supplies, including art materials, plus herbs and spices for use in art, that you might want to include in your buffet.

Art Materials

Drawing and Painting Surfaces
Large white drawing paper (36" x 48"), charcoal or pastel drawing paper, stretched canvas, canvas panel, board, fabric

Drawing Media
Colored pencils, markers, inks, water soluble pencils and crayons, oil pastels, oil bars, charcoal and graphite sticks, chalk pastels with workable fixatives or permanent finishes; protective gloves to use when working with any toxic media; massage or baby oil, turpenoid for smearing and blending oil pastels and oil bars or cleaning

Collage Media
Magazines, photos, old ticket stubs, announcements, letters, journal excerpts, decorative or handmade papers, imitation gold and silver leaf

Acrylic Paints

Reds: cadmium light, cadmium medium, alizarin crimson, pink; blues: cobalt, ultramarine, cerulean, turquoise, phthalo; yellows: cadmium medium, hansa light, Naples, ochre; greens: permanent light, cadmium medium, chromium oxide, hooker's, phthalo; purples: dioxazine purple, violet, magenta; browns: burnt sienna, raw umber, red oxide; iridescents: sapphire blue, emerald green, pearl white, dragon red, violet, silver, gold, bronze; titanium white and Mar's black

Glitter

Bright red, fuchsia, orange-red, violet, apricot, ocean blue, prussian blue, meadow green, chartreuse, champagne, black, crystal, gold, bronze, silver, colored sand, sand, dirt

Metallic Powdered Pigments

Bronze, gold, silver, olive, green, white, blue

Adhesive Materials

Acrylic gel, acrylic gloss or matte medium, modeling paste, glue guns with glue sticks, masking tape, painter's tape

Molding and Sculpting Materials

Plaster gauze rolls (4″ wide), papier-mâché, cardboard, newspaper, air-dry clay, sculpture wire, balsa wood

Tools

Brushes (variety of sizes and textures), water and mixing bowls, scissors, utility knives, awl, wire cutters, tweezers, stapler, palette, palette knives, needle and thread (different colors), scrapers, wire, clay tools, gloves, safety glasses, blow-dryer

Embellishments

A wide assortment of crystals, stones, minerals, beads, shells, natural materials, fibers, fabric, sisal, raffia, bones, furs, feathers, wigs, colored foil

Herbs and Spices for Art

We include many herbs and spices among the art supplies we provide. At times we harvest fresh lavender, horehound, mullein, or comfrey from our garden to bring to our classes. The following catalogue of herbs and spices is intended to arouse your muse, not as instruction in medicinal remedies. Their selected functions are intended for you to apply symbolically to your creative process.

Western Herbs for Art

Bathe or weave lavender into your canvas to bring calm and comfort and to treat its skin. Make a salve with comfrey, calendula, or Hawaiian sea salt and paint it onto the wounds of your art piece. Use aloe vera to heal the emotional as well as physical skin of your art. Add thyme or borage blossoms for courage in making changes in your life. Use yarrow stems for divination in your drawing of ancestral influences.

Aloe Vera
> Heals skin lesions, burns

Anise
> Relieves digestive problems, cramps, coughs by loosening phlegm; since the Middle Ages nursing mothers have used it for lactation

Black Cohosh
> Stimulates menstruation; relieves cramps; facilitates labor and delivery

Borage
> From Celtic word for courage; alleviates melancholy; soothes the heart; may tonify the adrenal glands

Burdock
> Tonic for lungs and liver; purifies blood; for endurance and strength

Calendula
> Soothes and softens skin; antiseptic; heals burns and wounds

Chamomile
Soothes; reduces tension; helps insomnia, neuralgia, skin problems; relieves menstrual cramps; calms nerves and stomach

Cinnamon
Antiseptic; stimulant; relieves nausea, diarrhea; clears the brain

Comfrey
For irritated skin, burns, sores, aching joints; helps mend broken bones

Corn
"Giver of Life"; used by many Native American tribes in art and ceremony

Dandelion
Builds and strengthens the blood; treats anemia; good for liver diseases

Eucalyptus
Cleanses the lungs and lymph system

Fenugreek
Expectorant for coughs and colds; relieves sore throat, skin irritations, diabetes (lowers blood sugar)

Flax
Laxative; used as poultice for inflammations; helps pulmonary infections

Garlic
Antibiotic; helps prevent heart disease and cancer; used for tuberculosis, dysentery, typhoid; lowers blood pressure

Ginger
For colds, coughs, sore throats, flu, digestive problems; has heating and drying properties; stimulates circulation; a bath in ginger water soothes

Hawaiian Sea Salt
Cleanses and draws out infections; colon cleanser; preservative

Hops
For flavoring and preserving (beer); aids digestion; stimulates the appetite

Horehound

For coughs and sore throats; diaphoretic (breaks fever); aids digestion

Kelp

Source of iodine; good for the endocrine system; cooling and nourishing

Lavender

For nervous tension and depression; uplifting, purifying, soothing qualities; good on insect bites; for indigestion and headaches

Lemon Grass

Antiseptic; revitalizing; for circulation, digestion, acne, oily skin

Mint

Cool, stimulating, refreshing, uplifting scent and taste; for indigestion, flatulence, colds, flus; name comes from Minthe, a nymph changed by Persephone into a plant to protect her from Hades, god of the underworld

Mullein

Flowers and leaves relieve respiratory congestion and ear infections; protected Ulysses against enchantress Circe; in India, used as protection against evil spirits; seeds are poisonous and should never be used

Mustard Seed

Strong preservative; used as poultice to draw blood to lungs or arthritic, rheumatoid area; induces vomiting; in Christianity, a symbol of faith

Nettle

Rich in iron, treats anemia; relieves hay fever, inflammation from allergies, chest and nasal congestion; increases milk supply in lactating mothers; for vaginal yeast infections and excessive menstrual flow

Oregano

Greek name meaning "Joy of the Mountains"; attracts bees and butterflies; for colds, headaches, coughs, irritability, exhaustion, menstrual pains

Peppermint

For indigestion, heartburn, gas, nausea, vomiting; stimulates gastric lining; good for nervous system

Rose

Cleanses blood and tones capillaries; aids circulation (add to massage oil); connected to the heart, as a symbol of love

Rosemary

For memory and fidelity (may be found at weddings or funerals); dried stems stripped of leaves can be used as "smudging" (purifying with smoke) sticks for cleansing

Sage

Estrogenic (for menstrual irregularities and menopausal symptoms); aids digestion; relieves colds; tonifies nervous system; used for "smudging" in Native American ceremony

Sesame

Relieves constipation, hemorrhoids, genito-urinary infections

Star Anise

Warms; aids digestion; stimulates appetite; alleviates coughs

Thyme

From *thymon* (Greek for courage); for bravery and vigor; thymol oil extraction is used as an antiseptic, for preserving biological specimens, and in embalming

Yarrow

Named *Achillea millefolium* from association with Achilles at the battle of Troy, who used yarrow to stop blood flow and heal warriors; Chinese used stems for the I Ching, Celts for divination

Chinese Herbs for Art

These herbs can be used in the alchemy of your creative process to express the shifting and balancing of the five elements.

Bai He (Lily Flower)

Benefits lungs (metal); relieves coughs, sore throat; calms the spirit

Bai Mu Er (Wood Ear, Black Fungus)

Nourishes lungs (metal) and stomach (earth)

Bai Shao (Peony)
Tonifies blood (fire); regulates menses; nourishes, regulates liver (wood)

Bei Chi (Astragalus)
Major Chi tonic; strengthens the Wei Chi (guardian Chi); benefits lungs (metal), spleen (earth)

Bei Sha Shen (Sand Root, Ginseng for lungs)
Benefits lungs (metal); alleviates coughs, constipation, and fevers; nourishes stomach (earth)

Dang Gui (Chinese Angelica Root)
Benefits heart (fire), liver (wood), spleen (earth); moistens intestines and frees the bowels; tonifies, invigorates, moves blood; regulates menses

Dang Shen (Codonopsis)
Poor man's ginseng; tonifies spleen (earth); relieves fatigue, diarrhea; tonifies lungs (metal)

Deng Xin Cao (Juncus)
Clears heat out of the heart and small intestine channels (fire); for insomnia and restless sleep

Du Zhong (Eucommia Bark)
Tonifies liver (wood), kidneys (water); strengthens and nurtures bones, sinews, cartilage

Fu Ling (China Root)
Benefits lungs (metal), heart (fire), spleen (earth); clears excess moisture; diuretic; calms the spirit; for digestive problems; strengthens spleen

Gou Gi Zi (Wolfberry)
Tonifies liver (wood), kidneys (water); aid for impotence, back pain; benefits the eyes

Gou Ji (Dog Spine)
Tonifies liver (wood), kidneys (water); strengthens sinews, bones, spine, lower back, extremities

Gu Zhi (Cinnamon Twig)
Regulates Chi; brings warmth and disperses cold; improves circulation

Hai Long (Pipe Fish)
Tonifies kidneys (water); for debility in the elderly and impotence; disperses stagnant blood

Hai Ma (Sea Horse)
Benefits liver (wood), kidneys (water); invigorates blood

Hong Hua (Safflower)
Invigorates and moves blood

Hong Zao (Chinese Date)
Tonifies spleen (earth); alleviates diarrhea, fatigue, shortness of breath; benefits heart (fire); nourishes blood (anemia); calms the spirit (anxiety)

Ji Xue Teng (Chicken Blood Bark)
Benefits heart (fire), liver (wood), spleen (earth); tonifies and moves blood; for irregular or painful menstruation, vertigo, weak extremities in elderly

Ou Jie (Lotus Root)
Stops bleeding; clears heat in lungs (metal) and stomach (earth)

Sheng Jiang (Ginger Root)
Soothes stomach (earth); warming; relieves nausea and vomiting

Tu Fu Ling (Smilax)
Benefits liver (wood), stomach (earth); for joint pain, hot skin lesions

Xuan Shen (Scrophularia)
Benefits kidneys (water), lungs (metal), stomach (earth); reduces fevers, cools, nourishes Yin (sore throat, constipation, swollen red eyes)

Zhu Ru (Bamboo Shavings)
Benefits gall bladder (wood), lungs (metal), stomach (earth); clears heat and congestion in lung

Zhu Ye (Bamboo Leaf)
Benefits stomach (earth), heart, small intestine (fire); clears heat (mouth sores, painful gums); relieves irritability

Glossary

The following definitions are not comprehensive but illuminate usage in this book.

abdominal breathing
Chi breathing in which the soft belly expands on the inhalation and contracts on exhalation

acrylic medium
gel, gloss, or matte; in art, fast-drying clear, transparent to translucent substance that acts as glue, or when tinted, as the base for paint

acu-point
acupressure/acupuncture point along the meridians of Chi near the surface of the body

acupressure
energy work using gentle touch applied to acu-points

'āina **(Hawaiian)**
land, earth

akua **(Hawaiian)**
spirit, god, supernatural being

aloha **(Hawaiian)**
in the presence of divine breath, to share breath, compassion, love, kindness, mercy

ancestor

one's predecessor genetically, ethnically, geographically, or spiritually

aura

energy generated by and enveloping the body of a person, being, or object

chakra

from Sanskrit, one of (usually) seven wheels of energy in the human body, each with its own intelligence, emotional influence, and spiritual power; located at: base of the spine, lower abdomen, solar plexus, heart area, throat, third eye, and crown

Chi 氣 (Chinese)

bioelectric current of energy, vital life force

Chi Kung (Chinese)

also spelled "Chi Gung," "Qigong," "Chi Gong"; means "energy work"; affects the physical, emotional, spiritual, and energetic bodies; a healing arts practice for cultivating, directing, storing, and transmitting Chi

Chi Nei Tsang (Chinese)

Chi Kung internal organ massage

Chi palm

energetic power of the palm of your hand; usually the non-dominant Chi palm is best for scanning (Yin) and the dominant Chi palm is best for transmitting (Yang) Chi; although the entire palm is sensitive to Chi, an especially powerful concentration of Chi may be felt in the heart of the palm at the Pericardium 8 (Labor Palace) acu-point

coronal plane

divides the body into front and back

craniosacral rhythm

gentle deep pumping of cerebrospinal fluid by the sphenoid bone in the cranium and the sacrum bone in the pelvis

DNA

deoxyribonucleic acid, blueprint of genetic information

ethereal thread
energetic current passing through the axis of the body and connecting it to the energy of heaven and of earth

Extraordinary Vessels
deep reservoirs for the rivers (meridians) of energy in the body; eight "strange flows" of energy occurring in four Yin/Yang pairs: Conception and Governing Vessels, Yin and Yang Bridge Vessels, Yin and Yang Regulator Vessels, and Penetrating and Belt Vessels

five elements
in Traditional Chinese Medicine, metal, water, wood, fire, and earth, the five alchemical influences on the body's organs, meridians, systems, and processes

guided imagery
a technique combining principles of hypnotherapy and shamanic journeying to access wisdom, images, and messages from subconscious realms

Hun (Chinese)
ethereal soul, the spirit of the liver

Ke Akua **(Hawaiian)**
God, Divinity, Universal Spirit

lei **(Hawaiian)**
garland, wreath, necklace; typically of flowers, leaves, seeds, shells, or feathers

lomilomi **(Hawaiian)**
deep kneading massage, infused with the power of nature, *pule,* and *aloha,* that affects physical, emotional, and spiritual levels of the recipient's being

Macrocosmic Orbit
in Chi Kung a circuit of energy that follows the path of the Microcosmic Orbit and includes paths along the legs and arms

mahalo **(Hawaiian)**
expression of gratitude

median plane
divides the body along the midline

meridian
in Traditional Chinese Medicine, twelve rivers of energy that travel in the body and are connected to the five element organs in six Yin/Yang pairs: Lung/Large Intestine/metal, Kidney/Bladder/water, Liver/Gall Bladder/wood, Heart/Small Intestine/fire, Pericardium/Triple Warmer/fire, Spleen/Stomach/ earth; can be accessed via acu-points

Microcosmic Orbit
in Chi Kung a circuit of energy that follows the path along the midline of the body of the Conception and Governing Vessels; starts at the pelvic Tan Tien and travels down the front of the torso, up the back of the torso and head, and back down the front to return to the Tan Tien

Ming Men (Chinese)
Governing Vessel 4, Gate of Life, located between lumbar vertebrae 2 and 3, source of Yang and fire for the body in general and for the kidneys in particular

occiput
base of the back of the skull

perineum
center of the body at the base of the torso between the anus and genitals

Po (Chinese)
corporeal soul, the spirit of the lungs

pule (Hawaiian)
prayer

Quan Yin (Chinese)
goddess of compassion

reverse breathing
Chi breathing in which the abdomen and pelvic basin contract from all sides on the inhalation and expand on the exhalation

sagittal plane
divides the body parallel to the midline

Shen (Chinese)
mind-spirit, the sovereign spirit of the heart

Sifu (Chinese)
teacher

spirit guide
in general, any helper from the spirit world; or more specifically, one's primary helper from the spirit world, who manifests one's deepest resources of inner wisdom and compassion; although its form may change over time, its essence remains constant

Tai Chi (Chinese)
internal martial art form that cultivates and directs the flow of Chi

Tan Tien (Chinese)
"field of elixir"; reservoir of Chi; may refer to one of three Tan Tiens: mind (upper), heart (middle), pelvis (lower); when not specified, refers to the pelvic Tan Tien, just below and inside the body from the navel

Tan Tien breathing
Chi breathing following the same principles and rhythm as abdominal breathing but the entire waist and the basin of the pelvis, as well as the abdomen, expand on the inhalation and contract on the exhalation

totem animal
also animal ally or power animal; embodies the power of the whole animal species; acts as a personal helper and guide and embodies qualities important to the individual with whom it connects

transverse plane
divides the body horizontally

Wei Chi (Chinese)
protective Chi circulating just beneath the surface of the skin, protecting the body against invasion from deleterious external influences

Witness
archetype of the non-attached observing mind

Wu Chi (Chinese)
in Chi Kung, stillness, emptiness, state of Yin and Yang merged into one

Yang (Chinese)
along with Yin, one of a pair of complementary and interdependent opposites; Yang qualities are active, masculine, light, challenging, empty, positive, solar, ascending, expanding, etc.

Yi (Chinese)
intention, the spirit of the spleen

Yin (Chinese)
along with Yang, one of a pair of complementary and interdependent opposites; Yin qualities are still, feminine, dark, surrendering, solid, negative, lunar, descending, contracting, etc.

Zhan Zhuang (Chinese)
Chi Kung standing meditation posture, meaning to stand like a tree, a staff, or a stake

Zhi (Chinese)
the will, the spirit of the kidneys

Selected Bibliography

Allen, Pat B. *Art Is a Way of Knowing: A Guide to Self-knowledge and Spiritual Fulfillment Through Creativity.* Boston: Shambhala Publications, Inc., 1995.

Andrews, Ted. *Animal Speak: The Spiritual and Magical Powers of Creatures Great and Small.* St. Paul, MN: Llewellyn Publications, 1995.

Audette, Anna Held. *The Blank Canvas: Inviting the Muse.* Boston: Shambhala Publications, Inc., 1993.

Austen, Hallie Iglehart. *The Heart of the Goddess: Art, Myth and Meditations of the World's Sacred Feminine.* Berkeley, CA: Wingbow Press, 1991.

Beinfeld, Harriet, and Korngold, Efrem. *Between Heaven and Earth: A Guide to Chinese Medicine.* New York: The Ballantine Publishing Group, 1991.

Bensky, Dan, and Gamble, Andrew, compilation and translation. *Chinese Herbal Medicine Materia Medica.* Seattle, WA: Eastland Press, 1993.

Biel, Andrew. *Trail Guide to the Body.* Boulder, CO: Andrew Biel, 1997.

Boyne, Gil. *Transforming Therapy: A New Approach to Hypnotherapy.* Glendale, CA: Westwood Publishing Co., Inc., 1989.

Bremness, Lesley. *The Complete Book of Herbs.* New York: Viking Studio Books, 1988.

Brennan, Barbara Ann. *Hands of Light: A Guide to Healing Through the Human Energy Field.* New York: Bantam Books, 1987.

Brown, Joseph Epes. *Animals of the Soul.* Rockport, MA: Element, Inc., 1992.

Bruyere, Rosalyn L. *Wheels of Light: Chakras, Auras and the Healing Energy of the Body.* New York: Fireside, 1994.

Bugeja, Michael J. *The Art and Craft of Poetry*. Cincinnati, OH: Writer's Digest Books, 1994.

Calais-Germain, Blandine. *Anatomy of Movement*. Seattle, WA: Eastland Press, 1993.

Carter, Joseph J. *Touching Spirit*. Berkeley, CA: Joseph Carter, 2000.

Cassou, Michell, and Cubley, Stewart. *Life, Paint and Passion: Reclaiming the Magic of Spontaneous Expression*. New York: G.P. Putnam's Sons, 1995.

Cheng, Man-ch'ing. *T'ai Chi Ch'uan: A Simplified Method of Calisthenics for Health and Self Defense*. Berkeley, CA: North Atlantic Books, 1981.

Chia, Mantak. *Awaken Healing Energy Through the Tao*. New York: Aurora Press, 1983.

Chia, Mantak. *Iron Shirt Chi Kung I*. Huntington, NY: Healing Tao Books, 1986.

Chia, Mantak. *Taoist Ways to Transform Stress into Vitality: The Inner Smile, Six Healing Sounds*. Huntington, NY: Healing Tao Books, 1985.

Chia, Mantak and Maneewan. *Awaken Healing Light of the Tao*. Huntington, NY: Healing Tao Books, 1993.

Chia, Mantak and Maneewan. *Fusion of the Five Elements I*. Huntington, NY: Healing Tao Books, 1989.

Chuen, Lam Kam. *The Way of Energy: Mastering the Chinese Art of Internal Strength with Chi Kung Exercise*. New York: Gaia Books Limited, 1991.

Churchill, Randal. *Become the Dream: The Transforming Power of Hypnotic Dreamwork*. Santa Rosa, CA: Transforming Press, 1997.

Churchill, Randal. *Regression Hypnotherapy: Transcripts of Transformation, Vol. I*. Santa Rosa, CA: Transforming Press, 2002.

Cirlot, J. E. *A Dictionary of Symbols*. New York: Philosophical Library, 1971.

Cohen, Kenneth S. *The Way of Qigong: The Art and Science of Chinese Energy Healing*. New York: Ballantine Books, 1997.

Cooper, J. C. *Symbolic and Mythological Animals*. London: The Aquarian Press, 1992.

de Mello, Anthony. *Wellsprings: A Book of Spiritual Exercises*. New York: Doubleday and Co., 1986.

Diaz, Adriana. *Freeing the Creative Spirit: Drawing on the Power of Art to Tap the Magic and Wisdom Within*. New York: HarperCollins Publishers, 1992.

Eden, Donna, with Feinstein, David. *Energy Medicine*. New York: Jeremy P. Tarcher/Putnam, 1998.

Edinger, Edward. *Anatomy of the Psyche*. La Salle, IL: Open Court, 1985.

Ellis, Andrew, Wiseman, Nigel, and Boss, Ken. *Fundamentals of Chinese Acupuncture*. Brookline, MA: Paradigm Publications, 1991.

Ellis, Andrew, Wiseman, Nigel, and Boss, Ken. *Grasping the Wind*. Brookline, MA: Paradigm Publications, 1989.

Fox, Matthew. *Original Blessing*. Santa Fe, NM: Bear and Company, 1983.

Fox, Matthew. *The Reinvention of Work*. San Francisco: HarperCollins Publishers, 1994.

Frantzis, B. Kumar. *Opening the Energy Gates of Your Body*. Berkeley, CA: North Atlantic Books, 1993.

Gach, Michael Reed. *Acupressure's Potent Points: A Guide to Self-Care for Common Ailments*. New York: Bantam Books, 1990.

Gach, Michael Reed. *Basic Acupressure: The Extraordinary Channels and Points*. Berkeley, CA: Acupressure Institute, 1999.

Gach, Michael Reed. *Intermediate and Advanced Acupressure Course Booklet*. Berkeley, CA: Acupressure Institute, 2002.

Gach, Michael Reed, and Henning, Beth Ann. *Acupressure for Emotional Healing*. New York: Bantam Books, 2004.

Galante, Lawrence. *Tai Chi: The Supreme Ultimate*. York Beach, ME: Samuel Weiser, Inc., 1981.

Ganim, Barbara. *Art and Healing: Using Expresssive Art to Heal Your Body, Mind, and Spirit*. New York: Three Rivers Press, 1999.

Goldberg, Natalie. *Wild Mind*. New York: Bantam Books, 1990.

Goldberg, Natalie. *Writing Down the Bones*. Boston: Shambhala Publications, Inc., 1986.

Guenon, Rene. *The Great Triad*. Cambridge, UK: Quinta Essentia, 1991.

Gunther, Bernard. *Energy Ecstasy and Your Seven Vital Chakras*. North Hollywood, CA: Newcastle Publishing Company, Inc., 1983.

Haas, Elson M. *Staying Healthy with the Seasons*. Berkeley, CA: Celestial Arts, 1981.

Hammond, D. Corydon, Ph.D., editor. *Handbook of Hypnotic Suggestions and Metaphors*. New York: W. W. Norton and Co., Inc., 1990.

Harner, Michael. *The Way of the Shaman: A Guide to Power and Healing.* New York: Bantam Books, 1980.

Hausman, Gerald. *Turtle Island Alphabet.* New York: St. Martin's Press, 1992.

Holmes, Peter. *The Energetics of Western Herbs.* Boulder, CO: Snow Lotus Press, Inc., 1997.

Horwitz, Tem, and Kimmelman, Susan, with Lui, H. H. *T'ai Chi Ch'uan: The Technique of Power.* Chicago: Chicago Review Press, 1976.

Hua-yang, Liu, translated by Wong, Eva. *Cultivating the Energy of Life.* Boston: Shambhala Publications, Inc., 1998.

Hunter, Marlene. *Creative Scripts for Hypnotherapy.* New York: Brunner-Routledge, 1994.

Jahnke, Roger. *The Healing Promise of Qi.* Chicago: Contemporary Books, 2002.

Jou, Tsung Hwa. *The Tao of Meditation, Way to Enlightenment.* Warwick, NY: Tai Chi Foundation, 1983.

Jou, Tsung Hwa. *The Tao of Tai-Chi Chuan, Way to Rejuvenation.* Warwick, NY: Tai Chi Foundation, 1981.

Kaptchuk, Ted J. *The Web That Has No Weaver.* New York: Congdon and Weed, 1983.

Kit, Wong Kiew. *The Art of Chi Kung: Making the Most of Your Vital Energy.* Rockport, MA: Element, Inc., 1993.

Kowit, Steve. *In the Palm of Your Hand.* Gardiner, ME: Tilbury House, 1995.

Krishna, Gopi. *Kundalini.* Boston: Shambhala Publications, Inc., 1971.

Larre, Claude, and Rochat de la Vallee, Elisabeth; transcribed and edited by Hill, Sarah. *The Eight Extraordinary Meridians.* Cambridge, England: Monkey Press, 1997.

Larre, Claude, and Rochat de la Vallee, Elisabeth; translated by Stang, Sarah. *Rooted in Spirit.* Barrytown, NY: Station Hill Press, 1995.

Larre, Claude, Rochat de la Vallee, Elisabeth, and Schatz, Jean; translated by Stang, Sarah. *Survey of Traditional Chinese Medicine.* Columbia, MD: Traditional Acupuncture Institute, 1986.

Lewis, Dennis. *The Tao of Natural Breathing.* San Francisco: Mountain Wind Publishing, 1997.

Liu, Da. *T'ai Chi Ch'uan: A Choreography of Body and Mind.* New York: Harper & Row, Publishers, 1972.

Lo, Ben, Inn, Martin, Amacker, Robert, and Foe, Susan. *The Essence of T'ai Chi Ch'uan: The Literary Tradition.* Berkeley, CA: North Atlantic Books, 1985.

London, Peter. *No More Secondhand Art: Awakening the Artist Within.* Boston: Shambhala Publications, Inc., 1989.

Lozoff, Bo. *It's a Meaningful Life.* New York: Penguin Putnam Inc., 2000.

Maciocia, Giovani. *The Foundations of Chinese Medicine.* Edinburgh: Churchill Livingstone, 1989.

Maciocia, Giovani. *The Practice of Chinese Medicine.* Edinburgh: Churchill Livingstone, 1994.

MacRitchie, James. *Chi Kung: Energy for Life.* London: Thorsons, 2002.

MacRitchie, James. *The Chi Kung Way.* London: Thorsons, 1997.

Mariel, Elaine N. *Essentials of Human Anatomy and Physiology, 5th ed.* Menlo Park, CA: Benjamin/Cummings Publishing Company, Inc., 1997.

Marin, Gilles. *Five Elements, Six Conditions: A Taoist Approach to Emotional Healing, Psychology, and Internal Alchemy.* Berkeley, CA: North Atlantic Books, 2006.

Marin, Gilles, with Chase, Michele. *Healing from Within with Chi Nei Tsang: Applied Chi Kung in Internal Organs Treatment.* Berkeley, CA: North Atlantic Books, 1999.

Matsumoto, Kiiko, and Birch, Stephen. *Extraordinary Vessels.* Brookline, MA: Paradigm Publications, 1986.

McGill, Ormond. *Grieve No More, Beloved: The Book of Delight.* St Clears, UK: The Anglo American Book Company Ltd., 1995.

McGill, Ormond. *Seeing the Unseen: A Past Life Revealed Through Hypnotic Regression.* Williston, VT: Crown House Publishing Ltd., 1997.

Metzger, Deena. *Writing for Your Life: A Guide and Companion to the Inner Worlds.* San Francisco: HarperCollins Publishers, 1992.

Mindell, Earl. *Earl Mindell's Herb Bible.* New York: Simon and Schuster, 1992.

Mitchell, Stephen. *Tao Te Ching.* New York: Harper and Row, 1988.

Mole, Peter. *Acupuncture: Energy Balancing for Body, Mind and Spirit.* Rockport, MA: Element Books, Inc., 1992.

Mookerjee, Ajit. *Kundalini: The Arousal of the Inner Energy.* New York: Destiny Books, 1983.

Mutke, Peter H. C. *Hypnosis: The Mind/Body Connection*. Glendale, CA: Westwood Publishing Co., 1987.

Nelson, Richard. *The Island Within*. San Francisco: North Point Press, 1989.

Nelson, Richard. *Make Prayers to the Raven*. Chicago: University of Chicago Press, 1983.

Ni, Maoshing. *The Yellow Emperor's Classic of Medicine: A New Translation of the* Neijing Suwen *with Commentary*. Boston: Shambhala Publications, Inc., 1995.

Ody, Penelope. *The Complete Medicinal Herbal*. New York: Dorling Kindersley, Inc., 1993.

Oliver, Mary. *A Poetry Handbook*. San Diego, CA: Harcourt Brace and Company, 1994.

Packard, William. *The Art of Poetry Writing*. New York: St. Martin's Press, 1992.

Palmer, Martin, O'Brien, Joanne, and Ho, Kwok Man. *The Fortune Teller's I Ching*. New York: Ballantine Books, 1986.

Rainer, Tristine. *The New Diary*. Los Angeles: Jeremy P. Tarcher, Inc., 1978.

Reid, Daniel. *Chinese Herbal Medicine*. Boston: Shambhala Publications, Inc., 1993.

Reid, Daniel. *The Complete Book of Chinese Health and Healing*. Boston: Shambhala Publications, Inc., 1994.

Reid, Daniel. *A Complete Guide to Chi-Gung*. Boston: Shambhala Publications, Inc., 1998.

Rezendes, Paul. *Tracking and the Art of Seeing: How to Read Animal Tracks and Sign*. Charlotte, VT: Camden House Publishing, Inc., 1992.

Samuels, Michael, and Lane, Mary Rockwood. *Creative Healing: How to Heal Yourself by Tapping Your Hidden Creativity*. San Francisco: HarperCollins Publishers, 1998.

Schipper, Kristofer. *Taoist Body*. Berkeley, CA: University of California Press, 1982.

Smith, Huston. *The World's Religions*. New York: HarperCollins Publishers, 1991.

Tansley, David V. *Subtle Body: Essence and Shadow*. New York: Thames and Hudson, Inc., 1988.

Teeguarden, Iona Marsaa. *Acupressure Way of Health: Jin Shin Do*. New York: Japan Publications, Inc., 1978.

Tilford, Gregory L. *Edible and Medicinal Plants of the West*. Missoula, MT: Mountain Press, 1997.

Veith, Ilza, translation and introduction. *The Yellow Emperor's Classic of Internal Medicine*. Berkeley, CA: University of California Press, 1966.

Wang, Simon, and Liu, Julius L. *Qi Gong for Health and Longevity*. Tustin, CA: The East Health Development Group, 1995.

Wauters, Ambika. *The Book of Chakras: Discover the Hidden Forces Within You*. New York: Barron's Educational Series, Inc., 2002.

Weiss, Gaea and Shandor. *Growing and Using the Healing Herbs*. New York: Wings Books, 1992.

Wong, Eva. *The Shambhala Guide to Taoism*. Boston: Shambhala Publications, Inc., 1997.

Worsley, J. R. *Traditional Chinese Acupuncture, Vol. One: Meridians and Points, 2nd ed*. Rockport, MA: Element Books, Inc., 1993.

Yang, Jwing-Ming. *Chi Kung: Health and Martial Arts*. Boston: Yang's Martial Arts Academy, 1985.

Yang, Jwing-Ming. *The Root of Chinese Qigong: Secrets for Health, Longevity, and Enlightenment*. Roslindale, MA: YMAA Publication Center, 1989.

Yang, Jwing-Ming. *Yang Style T'ai Chi Ch'uan*. Hollywood, CA: Unique Publications, Inc., 1982.

Yang, Jwing-Ming, and Bolt, Jeffery. *Northern Shaolin Sword*. Boston: Yang's Martial Arts Academy, 1985.

Ziyin, Shen, and Zelin, Chen. *The Basis of Traditional Chinese Medicine*. Boston: Shambhala Publications, Inc., 1996.

About the Authors

ELISE DIRLAM CHING, RN; M.A. Transpersonal Psychology; M.A. English; CAMT (Certified Acupressure Massage Therapist); CHT (Certified Hypnotherapist); Chi Kung teacher. Elise is a published and award-winning poet and has been a Registered Nurse at the San Francisco County Jail for the past twenty-four years.

KALEO CHING, M.A. Art; Certified Lithographer, Tamarind Institute; CAMT; CHT; Chi Kung teacher. Kaleo is an exhibiting and award-winning artist and teaches Chi Kung and bodywork classes at the Acupressure Institute in Berkeley, California. His private bodywork practice integrates acupressure, Hawaiian lomilomi massage, Chi Nei Tsang, and hypnotherapy.

Elise and Kaleo co-teach maskmaking, art, and Chi Kung classes for the John F. Kennedy University Arts and Consciousness Department and other institutions in the San Francisco Bay Area and beyond. They also coauthored *Faces of Your Soul: Rituals in Art, Maskmaking, and Guided Imagery with Ancestors, Spirit Guides, and Totem Animals* (North Atlantic Books, 2006).

To view a video of Tiger's Breath Chi Kung introductory sequence, a gallery of masks with poetry, color photos of student artwork, and a calendar of classes, visit **www.kaleoching.com**.